KU-257-603

# Techniques and Problems of Assessment

A practical handbook for teachers

Edited by

## H. G. Macintosh

*Secretary, Southern Regional Examinations Board for the Certificate of Secondary Education*

Edward Arnold

© Edward Arnold (Publishers) Ltd. 1974

First published 1974
by Edward Arnold (Publishers) Ltd.,
25 Hill Street, London W1X 8LL

ISBN: 0 7131 1816 4

All Rights Reserved. No part of this publication may be
reproduced, stored in a retrieval system, or transmitted
in any form or by any means, electronic, mechanical, photocopying,
recording or otherwise, without the prior permission
of Edward Arnold (Publishers) Ltd.

Set in 10 on 11 Plantin and
printed in Great Britain by
Fletcher & Son Ltd,
Norwich

# Preface

Any book which is concerned as this one is with an area of professional activity—assessment*—that lays great stress upon the clear definition and concise statement of objectives, should make plain at the outset its own objectives. These are three in number.

(1) To provide practical advice with a minimum of technical jargon for teachers and those training to be teachers, about the nature, construction and use of certain techniques of assessment, all of which are currently employed in the assessment of pupils in secondary schools.

(2) To discuss in practical terms with a minimum of technical jargon for teachers and those training to be teachers, a number of major current problems associated with assessment with particular reference to the secondary level of education.

If these first two objectives are achieved then it is hoped that a third more long term objective will be realized also, namely:

(3) To encourage the teaching profession to discuss more knowledgably, to read more widely, to enquire more deeply and above all to participate more actively in assessment in all its practical aspects and by so doing to improve their quality as teachers.

The key words or phrases in these objectives are 'practical', 'with a minimum of technical jargon', 'teachers and those training to be teachers' and 'secondary level'. This book will have failed in its intention if its contents do not give practical help to teachers who as a profession have become increasingly involved in recent years in the assessment of their own pupils in relation to both internal and external examinations. While much of what is said in the chapters that follow is applicable to assessment at all levels the illustrations and references will all be to the secondary level at which the book is pointed.

The contents, as the title suggests, are divided into two major sections,

---

* The word 'assessment' as used here and throughout the book has come to replace 'test' and 'examination' as providing a more appropriate description of the range of techniques now being tried out within the examining system at the secondary level.

Techniques and Problems. This division is inevitably artificial since the practical use of any technique of assessment creates as well as helps to solve problems and no discussion upon problems of assessment can be divorced from the techniques which are employed. There will, therefore, be constant cross-reference between the chapters whose sequence is designed to permit a logical development of the subject for the reader.

In addition a brief general introduction and the last three chapters are used to knit the book together; the introduction by discussing the definition of objectives which must be the starting point for all well-planned assessment and the last three chapters by considering central issues which necessitate the drawing together of information and ideas which have appeared throughout the book. The first of these three 'The Preparation of School-based Assessment' requires careful thought to be given to all the techniques and problems that have been discussed earlier in the book, not in isolation but in relation to the objectives of the particular curriculum being assessed. The second 'Measuring Attainment for Curriculum Evaluation' underlines as a central issue a point which it is hoped that the individual chapters will have brought out in a more piecemeal fashion namely that assessment is an integral and natural component of the total educational process and not something alien and external to it. The final chapter on 'The Value for the Teacher of Research into Assessment' shows that research into problems and techniques of assessment contrary to the beliefs of most teachers can be of practical value. For this to be achieved in practice, however, close co-operation between teachers and researchers is essential and this means, on the one hand, that researchers must present their proposals and evidence in a language that teachers can understand, and on the other that teachers must recognize that assessment is a demanding professional activity whose mastery is worthy of their best endeavours.

Inevitably, a book of this size cannot hope to describe or discuss in detail topics to which several chapters could be devoted and upon which complete books have indeed been written. Its intention is to identify the central issues and to suggest lines of thought which individuals can follow up for themselves. For those who wish to do this, further reading is essential and an extensive reading list is given at the end of the book divided into general and chapter subject headings. Certain of the chapters have also made specific reference to further reading within their text. These references will be given at the end of those chapters and should be used to reinforce the reading list.

# Acknowledgments

The Editor would like to acknowledge his great indebtedness to the contributors, without whom this book would have remained an idea, to those who kindly agree to reproduce material—individual acknowledgments are given in the text—to his colleagues at the Southern Regional Examinations Board, D. E. Hale and K. Kenyon for much valuable help in the preparatory stages and to Mrs M. Emery and Miss J. Street for deciphering and typing portions of the manuscript.

H.G.M.

# Contents

# Contributors

| | |
|---|---|
| B. Argent BSc (Hons) | City & Guilds of London Institute, Examination Techniques and Development Unit |
| M. T. Deere BSc(Eng) ACGI C(Eng) FIMecE | Senior Lecturer, Department of Education, University of Technology, Loughborough |
| J. F. Eggleston BSc FIBiol | Professor, School of Education, University of Nottingham |
| G. M. Forrest MEd | Director of Research, Joint Matriculation Board |
| D. E. Hale MA (Ed) | Deputy Secretary, Southern Regional Examinations Board for the Certificate of Secondary Education |
| H. G. Macintosh MA | Secretary, Southern Regional Examinations Board for the Certificate of Secondary Education |
| J. C. Mathews BSc FRIC | Senior Lecturer in Curriculum Development, Department of Educational Research, University of Lancaster |
| R. B. Morrison BSc PhD AKC | Director, Educational Measurement Research Unit, School of Education, University of Reading |
| D. L. Nuttall PhD | Principal Research Officer, National Foundation for Educational Research |
| B. Park MA(Oxon) MA (Leeds) | Deputy Secretary, Yorkshire Regional Examinations Board for the Certificate of Secondary Education |

*Contributors*

| | |
|---|---|
| T. J. Rogers | Formerly Secretary, North Western Examinations Board for the Certificate of Secondary Education |
| W. Sheridan BSc (Econ) Dip Psych | Lecturer, School of Education, University of Reading |
| R. J. Whittaker BA | Senior Assistant Secretary, Joint Matriculation Board |
| R. Wood PhD | Senior Research Officer, University of London School Examinations Department |

The views expressed in the book are those of the contributors themselves and do not necessarily reflect those of the organizations for whom they work.

# General Introduction

**Defining objectives**

The first requirement for any assessment is that it must be carefully planned. This means that those concerned with its development must themselves be clearly aware of what they want to do and why and must be prepared to tell this to others. The basic components of any assessment are four in number.

(A) The objectives of the course proposed for assessment.

(B) The skills to be developed in the course and the content to be covered—the syllabus.

(C) The techniques of assessment to be used.

(D) The weighting of the various parts of the assessment.

These components are set out in their relative order of importance and the starting point must be the objectives. After considering the problems of defining objectives in this Introduction, the remainder of the book will be concerned primarily with the third component—the techniques and their associated problems. One chapter will, however, as already indicated, look at all four components in relation to the development of school-based assessment. The apparent neglect of skills, content and weighting is not because they are unimportant but because they are matters which must be left to those who are actually developing the courses. Decisions taken here must stem from a consideration of objectives, of course content and skills; when these have been established and clearly stated they will in their turn determine the nature and weighting of the assessment to be adopted. Thus assessment must come at the end and not at the beginning. If this does happen, then appropriate decisions can be taken upon the techniques of assessment to be used and the most useful help and advice can be obtained because the right questions will have been asked. 'Good' assessment (and this book will be concerned amongst other things with discussing what is meant by 'good' in this connection) is a direct reflection of the extent to which planning has been properly carried out and intentions clearly stated. It is to the first stage of this planning that the remainder of this Introduction will be directed.

The defining of objectives explicitly is not something which comes easily to teachers, although they inevitably define them implicitly through the learning experiences they provide for their pupils and the questions they ask them in tests of all kinds. The two key questions which need considering are 'Why define objectives?' and 'How to define objectives?'.

## Why define objectives?

The short answer to this question is that if people do not know where they are going or what they are doing, they will be unable to find out whether they have arrived or what they have achieved. In education, as in any other field of activity, people can learn a great deal from their mistakes. In order, however, to do this it is first of all necessary to identify the mistakes or the unsatisfactory features, whether they be in curricula or teaching methods or materials, and then correct or improve them. This means that evaluation must take place and, therefore, that comparisons must be made. At some stage in every aspect of educational activity someone has to stand back and ask questions such as 'What are we doing?', 'How successful are we being?', and 'In what ways can we do better?'. This can only be done if two things have happened.

(1) That statements of what is being undertaken and of the objectives which it is hoped to achieve are in existence.

(2) That these statements have been set down in writing so that others can read and discuss them.

It is not sufficient for evaluation purposes for individuals to say that they know what they are doing. They must be in a position to ensure that other people know as well.

Here it is worth while pausing and trying to clarify the terminology used. In talking about the problem of defining objectives, a large number of words or terms are used, all too often indiscriminately, as for example, aims, objectives, operational objectives, behavioural objectives. This can only cause confusion and unless people know what they mean when they use particular words they can hardly be expected to think more clearly about what they are doing. It is not suggested that the definitions made here are any better than others that could be made but they may help. Most people, when asked to justify a course of action or solve a problem, approach the matter, initially, in general rather than in specific terms and their first thoughts are, therefore, put forward in a rather general way. They then go on to work out, in detail, appropriate strategies or reasons. So it is with teachers. When asked to consider the reasons for teaching a particular course or, put in another way, to justify its value, their initial response tends to be given in general terms. It seems reasonable to call these responses 'statements of aims'. If they are then asked to devise or discuss appropriate teaching strategies for realizing these aims and for demonstrating this realization to other people, then the responses, if they are to be worth anything, must become more definite and concrete. It seems reasonable to call these responses 'statements of objectives'. Objectives thus apply both to teaching and to assessment and it is for this reason that the word objectives is used in this Introduction. The great problem in the past has been that the external examination system has made it difficult to ensure that teaching objectives and assessment objectives coincide. The current extension of teacher involvement makes a greater degree of coincidence possible, although complete agreement is unlikely to be achieved in practice. Apart from any limitations that may exist in the techniques currently available and in people's mastery of them, practical considerations such as time and cost must be taken into account and realistic tasks provided for those being assessed.

Despite these problems, however, substantial agreement between the objectives of teaching and assessment can and ought to be achieved. But this will only be done if the clarity of the communication about what is happening and what is required is substantially improved. The statements of objectives for both teaching and assessment must, therefore, be made in a form which makes them susceptible to observation, description, and assessment. The frequent use of the words 'behavioural' and 'operational' in relation to objectives underlines this point. Students must be doing something which can be observed and described if courses of study and their own achievements are to be evaluated.

It is comparatively easy to talk about and stress the need for defining objectives but it is far less easy actually to undertake it and this leads to a consideration of the question of how to define objectives.

## How to define objectives?

Many teachers, both experienced and inexperienced, find it difficult and distasteful to define objectives in relation to courses of study and assessment. They convey the impression that definition will in some way degrade and make impersonal something that ought essentially to be a personal and a subjective matter. It is often asserted that the important objectives are intangible and hence impossible to state in terms which can be measured. The claim is made that students develop certain attitudes, values or skills that are not immediately apparent and may not indeed reveal themselves until later in life, long after they have left school or college. Teachers putting forward this point of view will often end up by saying that to them these are the only objectives that matter and that they cannot anticipate in what form they will show themselves in their pupils. Nobody would deny that there are many intangible long-term outcomes of instruction, both good and bad, but to claim that these are the only ones that are important is to adopt the untenable position of being unable to prove that one has ever taught anything. If any real attempt is to be made to evaluate courses and curricula and to bring together the objectives of courses of study and their assessment in a meaningful way then it is necessary to state the outcomes of such courses. This means that objectives need to be put down in a form which can be communicated to others and observed by others.

The statement of objectives is not an esoteric airy fairy operation in which rarified researchers engage; on the contrary it is, and indeed it must be, an intensely practical and realistic operation which can only be properly undertaken by practising teachers. Individual teachers, or better still groups of teachers (since it is through the rubbing together of ideas in discussion that points of view are best clarified), ought first of all to decide what they consider to be important in their particular courses of study for their particular students at their particular schools. Most teachers tend to answer the question of what they consider to be important in terms of content rather than in relation to skills or in terms of what their students can or cannot do at the end of the course. Nevertheless these same teachers will very often make demands upon their students in relation to these last two points by means of the questions they set or the problems they pose in the classroom. The danger of stating one's objectives in terms of content only is that the coverage of that content becomes all important. Unless content is used for some purpose, instead of as an end in itself, it becomes meaningless. It is, however, equally undesirable to state objectives purely in terms of skills and the degree to which they have been mastered.

Statements of skills can be as woolly and lacking in rigour as statements of content. 'To develop critical thinking', for example, is not a particularly helpful objective unless we know in what area it is to be undertaken (content) and unless we define what we mean by critical thinking. We must have evidence before we can accept that critical thinking is taking, or has taken place, and this we cannot obtain until we know what we are talking about. Thus not only must the content be provided but the skills themselves must be further defined in relation to the students for whom the course is intended.

What is wanted, therefore, is a statement of objectives which combines a judicious blend of content and skills. In order that any such statement can be communicated to others (and it is worth stressing that assessment is in essence a communication problem) then it is not enough to specify independently the content to be covered or the skills that students are expected to acquire. It is necessary to relate the skills to specific content. The use of grids to present statements of objectives, because they are convenient visually and valuable for the purpose of constructing assessment can be unfortunate in this respect since they do not sufficiently emphasize the essential interrelationship between content and skills. The skills appear listed along one co-ordinate and the content along another and the impression is all too easily given that they are separate instead of interlocking dimensions.

The problem of how specific a statement of objectives ought to be is often of concern to teachers. No universal answer can be given to this question except to say that the statement must be sufficiently specific to communicate its message plainly. It must be related to the learning experiences being provided for the pupils and the nature of the objectives themselves. Since there is a tendency for too many statements of objectives to be lacking in clarity it is desirable initially to be more, rather than less, specific. Such an approach will serve to discourage woolly thinking.

It is possible that the word 'specific', as used in the last paragraph, does not properly convey the essence of the problem and in the next paragraph the phrase 'fineness of structure' has been used instead. The two taken together may, perhaps, provide a clearer picture of what is required.

## Fine structure

By way of illustration of possible degrees of fineness one can take the following general objective 'Understanding of relationships'. This is an assessable objective, but not in the form in which it has been presented since it fails to provide a great deal of relevant information. It therefore needs to be re-stated as, for example, 'Understanding of the ideas of proportional representation' or 'Understanding of relationships involving more than two variables'. We can now begin to set questions upon it but it would be helpful, indeed essential, to have further information. In what medium, for example, do we wish this ability to be demonstrated, i.e. by the use of graphs or verbally or what content do we wish to use for the demonstration? By the time all these points have been spelt out the structure has become very fine indeed and the requirements have been narrowed sharply in relation to the questions we intend to ask. Objective and structured questions in particular demand a fine structure in order to realize their full potential. When using more open-ended questions the structure needs to be less fine although this should not encourage looseness of wording and vagueness in presentation. Moreover, one should always bear in mind that the fineness of structure required will vary from subject to subject and from level of student to level of student. The basic criteria for the acceptability of any objective ought always to be 'Is its message clear and does it serve the purpose for which it was intended?'. This clarity and this purpose must in its turn be carried over into the assessment used.

In practical terms a possible way of achieving this clarity would be to answer the following three questions.

(1) What do we want to do?
(2) How can we achieve what we want to do?
(3) How can we assess whether we have achieved what we want to do?

On occasions the first question might read 'What are we doing and why?' although this might lead to despair or complacency according to the answer given.

This underlines the point made earlier that assessment should be placed at the end and not at the beginning. When the third question has been answered, a rough and ready, but practical statement of objectives ought to have been achieved. Such a statement which is better developed in consultation and discussion with colleagues rather than in isolation, can be further discussed and refined if it is intended to use it as the basis for formal assessment, whether external or school-based. The range of approaches to the assessment used must be as varied as possible, including for example, both internal and external, continuous and terminal assessment, and this range will be fully explored in subsequent chapters.

## Taxonomies

In this country teachers are more familiar with statements of objectives based upon content than with statements based upon skills and the emphasis needs shifting. But enough has been said to suggest that to neglect content, provided it is a vehicle and not an end in itself, would be to provide an unbalanced statement of the objectives of any course of study. In the production of statements of objectives many have found that the use of a taxonomy is helpful since this demands a more systematic approach to the classification of educational objectives than most teachers have previously experienced. A number of published taxonomies have been produced recently (the word taxonomy is one which is more frequently used in the biological sciences meaning a hierarchical or orderly arrangement). The first and best known of these were prepared by Benjamin Bloom and his associates. The original publication in 1956 dealt with the 'cognitive domain' and this is the one which primarily concerns us here. This taxonomy grouped cognitive objectives into six major classes. In ascending order of complexity these are:

(1) Knowledge.
(2) Comprehension.
(3) Application.
(4) Analysis.
(5) Synthesis.
(6) Evaluation.

Each class of objectives is itself broken down into sub-categories, although these are inevitably a little artificial. A somewhat simpler taxonomy has been suggested by R. L. Ebel as follows.

(1) Understanding of terminology (or vocabulary).
(2) Understanding of fact and principle (or generalization).
(3) Ability to explain or illustrate (understanding of relationships).
(4) Ability to calculate (numerical problems).
(5) Ability to predict (what is likely to happen under specified conditions).
(6) Ability to recommend appropriate action (in some specific practical problem situation).
(7) Ability to make an evaluative judgment.

Two points need to be made upon the taxonomies referred to here. First, they require amplification on lines suggested early in this Introduction in relation to the subjects with which those developing particular statements of objectives are concerned. Second, taxonomies do not provide all the answers. They provide a stimulus to thought about educational problems and objectives and are a source of ideas for teachers both in teaching and assessment. They encourage the use of critical faculties. They are, however, artificial and Bloom in particular is almost certainly too detailed for every-day use. They can perhaps best be described as essential pieces of starting equipment. Just as the journey to the moon had to start with a lot of equip-ment which was subsequently jettisoned, so particular taxonomies in their formal written form should be thrown overboard after their principles have been grasped. This *caveat* should be borne in mind when studying any suggested table of objectives based upon a taxonomy whatever the subject concerned.

A consideration of the suggestions made in this Introduction will, it is hoped, have made it easier for teachers to set about defining their objectives. Ways of assessing these same objectives and some of the problems associ-ated with that assessment will be considered in the chapters that follow.

# Techniques
# of Assessment

# 1 Open-Ended Questions

## W. Sheridan

The essay is the typical open-ended question: one in which neither the content nor the style of answer is made explicit to the examinee. In principle at least, examinees have a great deal of freedom to answer such questions in their own way. Any consideration of open-ended questions, however, needs to be set within the general framework of techniques of assessment, discussion of which has become the concern of many teachers in recent years.

Much of this discussion has centred round two interrelated problems; those of content sampling and of question style. The essence of the first problem lies in the relationship between the content of the assessment, the knowledge and skills being assessed and the knowledge and skills taught and learned during the courses which precede the assessment. In practice, any formal assessment procedure will be concerned with only a sample of the course content unless assessment is to be totally continuous with teaching. Many considerations—time and cost among them—make this impracticable. Ultimately, therefore, there is a selection from the work of the course used in the assessment. If any assessment is to be a valid analogue of this work then there has to be some way of ensuring that its constituent parts do in fact test that knowledge and those skills which the course was designed to impart. In other words, the assessment must be based on the aims of the course and not upon what is easiest to test within it.

This problem of content sampling is a major one since there is an implicit inference that the results of one assessment can be regarded as being applicable to other assessments which, had they been set, might have used a different sample of questions. The evidence to support such inferences may well come, however, from current developments in assessment which are making use of the concept of hierarchical arrangement of cognitive skills.[1] We may thus be enabled to make judgments about the course as a whole from the answers given to a sample of questions.

Formal assessment procedures based on open-ended questions can be seen to lie about mid-way along a continuum of procedures which differ from each other by the extent to which the questions asked explicitly sample more or less of the course. This continuum ranges from the thesis or project report, at one extreme, where apparently only one question is being asked, to the objectively marked test where a relatively large number of questions are asked. An examination paper which asks candidates to answer all fifty questions, explicitly samples more of the possible topics of the course than the typical open-ended examination where candidates have to answer at the most four or five questions. In order to use the answers given to such open-ended questions so as to make inferences about answers to other questions and combinations of questions, it is essential that all the questions asked should implicitly sample a wide range of knowledge and skills. This requirement suggests that each open-ended question should be designed in such a way that it forces candidates to process a great deal of information in producing an answer. For many people, open-ended questions are particularly valuable in assessment because candidates have to choose from a range of knowledge, that which bears on the subject of the question. It is this essential requirement, that candidates have to be selective in the information which they use, that is seen as the distinctive quality of open-ended questions. Another way of looking at the process of answering open-ended questions is to suggest that candidates have to sample the content of the course, to recognize the relevant sections of the course, and to order these sections to meet constraints imposed by the specific question asked. This is in contrast to objectively marked questions where most of the sampling and a great deal of the ordering has already been done by the examiner.

Writing open-ended questions which do produce this ideal response from candidates is one of the most difficult tasks for the examiner who is always between two extremes. On the one hand there is Scylla, the question which results in a simple regurgitation of facts in a pre-prepared answer requiring only a good memory and journalistic fluency—the stand and deliver question. Examiners tend to lean towards this type of question in order to be fair to all candidates. On the other side is Charybdis—clever, elegant questions but so elliptic that candidates fail to see their point. An external examiner is at a disadvantage here compared with the internal teacher–examiner who is able to use a word or phrase from the course which has special significance for his pupils and this tells them what he is aiming at in the particular question. Many teachers feel that the end product of trying to avoid these two lures is an external examination paper which is so bland that it fails almost completely to reflect the pattern, style and emphasis of their teaching. Examination papers that are deadly dull affairs, unrelated to the kind of activity and excitement even of the teaching and learning that has gone before, can have a bad backwash effect on teaching which may become orientated towards just passing the examination. Teachers may feel there is no point in doing anything else as candidates do not have a chance to display any substantial part of their quality and only dull prepared reinterment of disinterred bones is required.

One of the most useful recent developments in external examinations has been the use of external moderation of internally set examinations. (See Chapter 14.) This can permit the use of examination questions which reflect the specific teaching and learning that has gone on without reducing the national currency of the examination. Under this system open-ended questions can be set which are less bland and more testing of the full range of cognitive skills because each question can be more informative to those answering them.

One facet of the open-ended question is the lack of information which is explicitly given to the candidates. They are not told how to answer them, nor are they told what aspects are regarded as important. To use an extreme example, the question 'Prove as best you can that $2 + 2 = 4$' explicitly tells the candidate very little. To answer this question in a satisfactory way it is necessary either to guess what the examiner had in mind, which would be a matter of chance, or to use other sources of information as to what content and style of answer are required. This lack of information is again in marked contrast to objectively marked questions where both the content to be used and the style of response are made quite explicit.

It has been suggested that open-ended questions should be written so as to give more explicit information about the content regarded as important by the examiner. We find if this is done, that instead of the usual ten to twenty word question, for example 'Give an account of the manufacturing industries in the north west of England' that additional information is given to the candidates, i.e. '. . . under the following headings (a) changes in the textile industry (b) new and expanding industries on Merseyside'. In many ways the longer version of the question, which has now become structured, is the better one. (For a more detailed discussion of the structured question see Chapter 2). There are so many possible answers to the shorter version that the candidate would be faced with an impossible task of selection. The longer version makes explicit the lines upon which the answer should be developed. Although this kind of suggestion for improvement of open-ended questions has been made quite frequently, there appears to be little or no published research on the effect of writing questions in this form. One obvious effect is that marking will be easier because of the explicit content asked for. On the other hand, because of the specific content mentioned, a candidate who knows about other manufacturing industries but who does not know about either textiles or Merseyside would find the longer version unanswerable. Examiners who write questions of this longer type have, therefore, to be sure that the content mentioned is generally regarded as more important than that omitted.

The way in which open-ended questions depend so much for their successful answering on candidates' memory for factual information is a major problem. It can be a matter of luck whether the relevant information is available to them and it can be argued that this extreme dependency on memory acts as an impediment to the thought processes which ought to be being examined. There has been an increase recently in the number of examinations where candidates are provided with reference material or notes and books which are available for consultation during the examination. The intention is that more searching questions can thus be written aimed at the candidates' ability to use, rather than remember, factual knowledge. It appears that examiners who have made use of this technique believe that it leads to a more effective examination, partly because this is the way candidates work throughout their course and also partly, perhaps, because the examination is more like a real-life work setting. There are problems involved in this modification of the usual procedure, and it is sad but true that relatively little research has been done in trying to solve them when compared with work on other forms of question. Perhaps the major problem is the matter of how much reference material should be provided and in what form. There is the danger that a candidate could be swamped by a great mass of material. There is also the very practical problem of the availability of sufficient copies of the reference material for all candidates.

Neither of these problems is in principal insoluble for at a simple level these are being continually solved throughout the teaching of the course. But the examination setting is obviously different. Much criticism of examinations has indeed been based on the fact that they are special occasions and become what has been called 'big bangs'. Basic to the criticism implied in this description is the problem of time limits. Critics of all examinations point out that a candidate has some thirty-five minutes to answer each question on the examination paper, an unrealistic time limit for anything like a complete answer to many questions. It may be indeed that complete answers are far better achieved by a different assessment procedure than an examination question paper, perhaps the project report or special study. The examination paper involving an essay response is particularly a test of the candidates' ability to be both selective and fluent in the handling of ideas when working under constraints, notably that of time. This kind of ability is by no means an unworthy one for schools to aim at developing.

The selectivity that candidates are expected to display in an examination leads to what is recognizably the most serious difficulty with open-ended questions, namely unreliability of marking. Reliability can be discussed and measured in a number of ways, but it is really concerned with the extent to which an examination is fair to all candidates. To put it in another way, it is the extent to which an examination can be depended upon to lead to the same decision about candidates if the whole assessment procedure were repeated under similar conditions on another occasion. With all assessments there is some unreliability stemming from the candidates themselves who for many reasons would produce different answers if re-examined. But with the open-ended question, the candidates are at the mercy of their memories because no content is provided for them to consider. It seems that open-ended questions are intrinsically more unreliable than most other forms of question and it is difficult to see how this unreliability can be reduced without removing from the candidate the onus to be selective, the real justification for their use. There is a very marked absence of development work into ways of retaining the valuable qualities of open-ended questions and at the same time reducing the sources of unreliability.

There is a great deal of research which demonstrates the unreliability of the marking of these questions.[2] Most of it has been concerned to demonstrate marker rather than candidate unreliability. This stems from the fact that the answers to open-ended questions are never simply right or wrong. The answers are not specified as they are in multiple-choice items where candidates choose one of a number of alternatives as the right answer. Every answer to an open-ended question is different. On the other hand, the process by which candidates produce answers is often clear to the marker. In multiple-choice questions, conversely the processes used by the candidates may be different but the answers given can only be one of the four or five alternatives offered. By restricting the range of possible answers and by agreeing that only one shall be deemed right, marker unreliability has thus been cut to that bare minimum which could result from clerical errors, rather than errors of judgment. In marking open-ended questions, however, the marker is making judgments over every answer and attempts to reduce marker unreliability have usually involved techniques for controlling the possible drift of standards of judgment.

One technique for controlling this source of unreliability is to produce an analytic marking scheme. This scheme states what must appear in a good answer and what marks shall be awarded for each fact or idea. It aims at making the marking as objective as possible by removing most of the points upon which an examiner has to exercise judgment. Such marking schemes can become very complicated in order to obtain objectivity. So much so that questions become in effect highly structured, although the candidates were never told this. As they are now capable of being objectively marked, they should perhaps never have been written in that form.

Another approach lies through the discussion of a sample of scripts by examiners in order to reach an agreement about possible answers to the questions. Many teachers have become familiar with this process in recent years. But perhaps the most useful approach of all is what is called multiple marking. All answers, or a sample of them, are marked by one or more markers additional to the original marker. The intention is that the difference in the judgments, upon say relevance and fluency, made by the individual markers will be balanced out. There is evidence[3] that multiple marking of open-ended questions can produce a set of grades or marks which are almost as reliable as sets produced by more objective methods of marking.

Despite these different approaches, there seems little doubt, however, that open-ended questions produce marks or grades which are intrinsically more unreliable than those produced by the use of objective question types. The justification for continuing to use open-ended questions in assessment procedures lies in their difference from other question types. The abilities assessed by open-ended questions are extremely difficult to assess by the more objective questions which intrinsically remove the opportunity for the exercise of content sampling by the candidates. It is important also to consider the 'backwash' effect of assessment techniques upon teaching. It is likely that an assessment made up of a number of different techniques will lead to a greater variety in teaching and to the development of a wider range of abilities in pupils.

It is a very great pity that comparatively little effort has gone into the development of open-ended questions. The Secondary School Examinations Council said in its Examinations Bulletin No. 3 published in 1964, that a great deal more was known about objectively marked questions than about open-ended ones but that the latter could probably be improved by careful study and development work. Yet it is probably true to say that the overwhelming majority of development work since 1964 has been upon objectively marked questions. The projected changes in the examination system both at 16+ and 18+ provide another opportunity to undertake development work in open-ended assessment procedures; procedures which are particularly concerned with fluency and dexterity in the handling of ideas. It is to be hoped that it will be taken.

**References**

[1] J. Ward, 'On the Concept of Criterion—Referenced Measurement'. *British Journal of Educational Psychology*, 40 (1970), part 3.

[2] P. Hartog and E. C. Rhodes, *An Examination of Examinations* (London, Macmillan, 1935), p. 132.

[3] J. N. Britton, N. C. Martin, and H. Rosen, 'Multiple Marking of English Compositions'. *Schools Council Examination Bulletin, No. 12* (London, HMSO, 1966).

# 2 Structured Questions

## J. C. Mathews

**What are they and why have them?**

Examinations and examination questions, indeed the whole concept of assessment itself, can be judged from several aspects. Are they reliable, do the objectives match the teaching objectives, does the content properly sample the content of the curriculum, can they be used to estimate future performance? These and other questions are already the subject of research and reform. But there is another, equally important criterion by which assessment techniques can be judged: the extent to which the *activities* in which the students are engaged in their assessment match the activities in which they were engaged during their learning and will be engaged in the future. One of the purposes of the structured question is to meet this criterion.

The essence of modern teaching is to allow children to experience and respond to a wide variety of situations: to practical situations at the laboratory bench, to dramatic situations in the theatre, to social situations such as those experienced in some recent Humanities curricula, to the visual arts (both creative and critical), to problem solving in mathematics, historical situations, environmental situations and so on. The variety of educational experiences is infinite, but they all have two things in common: a situation and a response to that situation.

What is the modern teacher's role? The time when teachers were simply purveyors of information is passing. No longer do teachers simply give information one day and demand that it be repeated the next. Rather do they make it possible for their pupils to experience appropriate situations and then guide them to appropriate responses. Guided discovery is a much used, sometimes misused, phrase in modern teaching: but it summarizes rather well recent trends in education. The difficulty arises in deciding what situations the pupils should experience, how much guidance they should be given, how much they should be told and how much they should discover for themselves. Some situations, indeed most situations, are complex, and to leave children to respond to them in a completely open-ended and unassisted manner may well produce no response or nonsensical responses. What teachers do (and herein lies the greatest art of teaching) is to indicate the structure of the situation, show the pupils that the complexity can be broken down into parts, a knowledge of which makes the whole more understandable, and then to ask the pupils to respond to the parts separately.

Perhaps this idea can be better explained by an example. Suppose that the situation to be experienced is a local stream. Two extreme teaching/learning activities are possible: in one the teacher could simply describe the various features of the stream and require his pupils to learn them for repetition on a future occasion; in the other, the teacher could say 'Go and find out what you can about the local beck'. A more likely compromise nowadays is that the teacher will first *structure* the situation; he would indicate the main features which would be worthy of study: its width, depth, rate of flow, source and end, the nature of the water, the nature of the bottom, its flora, fauna, usefulness, dangers, beauty or ugliness. Having done so, his guidance comes in the form of questions or suggestions: 'What is its rate of flow? Where does it come from? What is the pH of the water? How does the pH affect the incidence of fresh water shrimp? If you find it beautiful, write a poem about it. Identify and paint the water-loving flowers which grow at its verge.'

The degree to which teachers break down complex situations will depend on several things; the nature of the situation and its complexity, the level of learning of the pupils and their individual ability. The more complex the situation or the less able the pupil, the greater must be the degree of structuring. The less complex the situation or the more able the pupil, the more the response can be left free and open-ended.

So it is in modern teaching and learning and so should it be in modern assessment. The sort of situation in which the pupil finds himself when being assessed should not be fundamentally different from that in which he has been when learning. One of the functions of the structured question is to enable this closer relationship between teaching, learning and assessing to be achieved. The pupil is asked to study information given in the stem of the question, and, as in a lesson, this information should be stimulating and, in part, unfamiliar. He is then required to respond to the information by answering a series of questions which progressively test his understanding of the situation into which he has been placed, just as he would in the classroom.

## Some examples

Having outlined the basic function of structured questions, it now may be profitable to discuss an actual example in some detail. The question is taken from the Nuffield O-level Biology Paper I (1969) and is reproduced by permission of the Joint Matriculation Board.

The information on which the candidate has to work is in three different

EXAMPLE I

Diatoms x 500

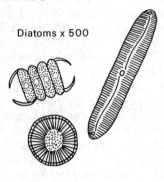

Crustacean x 20

The figure shows some organisms which float near the surface of a lake. Diatoms contain chlorophyll. The population of these diatoms increases rapidly each spring.

(2) (*a*) List **two** factors in the environment whose change may be responsible for the increase in the diatom population and say how the factor may be acting to cause the increase.

| Factor | Change in Factor | Effect of change on diatoms |
|---|---|---|
| 1. ..................... | ..................... | ..................... |
| | ..................... | ..................... |
| 2. ..................... | ..................... | ..................... |
| | ..................... | ..................... |

(2) (*b*) Crustaceans eat diatoms. Using the information given in this question show, by adding a further curve to the graph below, how you think the crustacean population might change.

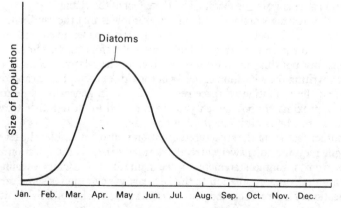

forms: diagrammatic, graphical, and in words. It is partly contained in the introduction (stem) to the question and partly in the sub-question (b). The latter could have been transferred to the main stem of the question but the authors presumably thought it better to introduce the information in two stages rather than all at the beginning. (This is exactly what the thoughtful teacher might have done.) Some of the information is direct: 'Crustaceans eat diatoms'; some has to be deduced: the relative size and complexity of the function of diatoms and crustacea. The authors of the question have succeeded in presenting a good deal of information concisely and yet in a stimulating manner, and, presumably, some of it will be unfamiliar to the particular group of candidates. Of course, there are limitations arising from the traditional assessment format of an examination paper. In the classroom and laboratory the teacher could well have done much more by way of stimulation using actual samples under the microscope, slides, film (real and animated) and so on. In mass examining this limitation on the form of presentation of material may remain, but in small scale assessment, for example, that of an individual teacher in a mode 3 examination, there is every opportunity to vary the form of presentation from that which is possible on the printed page and thus bring the assessment situation even closer to that encountered in actual teaching.

And now to the questions themselves. It would be possible, as in traditional questions, simply to say 'Write an essay on the relationship between diatoms and crustacea', and this could be appropriate at some levels of education. But at this level such questions have tended to give rise to the potted, pre-digested answer, repeating previously learned information; simple to set, but giving rise to all sorts of marking problems. In our example, the authors have structured the responses; that is they have broken down the responses into parts which correspond to the *main educational themes* in the situation. First of all into two main parts: (a) the factors which cause change in the population of diatoms; (b) the effect the change in population of one species has on the population of a dependant species. Then there is further sub-division in (a) into the factors themselves—the direction of change of the factors, and the effect of the change.

Another feature worthy of note in the example is that the candidates are required to give their responses on the question paper itself and so are guided as to the amount they should write on each part. (In some examinations, but not this one, indication is given of the relative weight of each part by writing the allocation of marks at the side of each.) Some candidates may find the limitation of space restrictive, but in general it is better to know approximately how much you are expected to write rather than be left in doubt whether it is one word or an essay.

Another feature of the structured question is also noticeable: the level of thought required to answer correctly normally rises as the question proceeds from a simple statement of the name of two factors causing an increase in diatom population to the last part which requires some careful application of information and principles to arrive at a hypothesis about the trends in crustacean population. Again, this is typical of the treatment a teacher would give to the material in the classroom.

It is likely that the answers will be easily marked. In an essay the marker would have either to search amongst a mass of material for the specific points for which marks could be awarded, or would judge the whole by subjective impression. The answers to a structured question are set out in a fixed pattern and sequence; each answer is of similar and limited length and, since each part question gives rise to one point or a very small number of points in the answer, a precise mark scheme can be used, thus increasing the objectivity of the assessment.

Example 1 is relatively short and simple; Example 2 is at a higher level and is designed to be answered in about 1 hour (taken from Engineering Science—Paper 1 (J.M.B.) and reproduced by permission of the Joint Matriculation Board).

EXAMPLE 2

*Comprehension Test*

Read the passage headed 'Infrared and Optoelectronics at the SRDE' carefully and then answer as many of the questions which follow it as you can. If you experience difficulty with a particular question proceed to the next question.

## Infrared and optoelectronics at the SRDE

1. The U.K. Signals Research and Development Establishment, Christchurch, Hants., has recently declassified much of its work on night-vision systems and optical communication, and is emphasising the possible civil applications of this work.
2. Night-vision systems fall into three categories—those which amplify the very low light levels reflected from a night scene; those which use near-infrared detectors in conjunction with illumination of the scene from an infrared source; and those which use a far-infrared detector to locate an object by the difference in temperature between it and its background.
3. Image intensifiers fall into the first of these categories; those developed under SRDE contracts by Mullard and the English Electric Valve Co. have a gain of about 40000, and require no external illumination or power supplies (they operate from 6V batteries). An image intensifier operates by focusing the available light through a large-diameter objective onto a photocathode, where it is converted into electrons; these electrons are accelerated through a potential difference of 15 kV onto a phosphor screen, where they form a brighter image of the original scene. Apart from their potential uses in navigation, reconnaissance, nature study, security, etc. image intensifiers have been used in hospitals to intensify X-ray images on fluorescent screens.

SRDE'S optical transceiver uses a modified pair of binoculars.

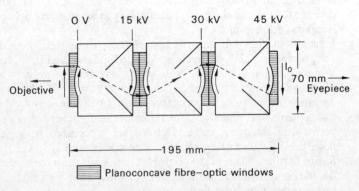

Planoconcave fibre–optic windows

3-stage image intensifier: the images are transferred from the phosphor screen of one stage to the photocathode of the next through fibre-optic faceplates.

4. 'Active' infrared devices required that the area to be viewed is bathed in infrared radiation either from a source on the device itself or from permanent infrared lamps set up to illuminate the area; the observer uses a viewer incorporating an image-converter tube. Such systems have already proved useful for the observation of animals' night-time activities, surveillance work by London's river police, the detection of art forgeries, and the examination of the human eye in its 'fully open' condition. Active devices shown at the SRDE include infrared binoculars with unity magnification and a wide field of view, and a viewer with its own near-infrared source attached. A commercial model of the latter device is now available.

5. Devices operating in the far-infrared region of the spectrum have been used for some years in missiles for locating aircraft engines by the thermal radiation emitted; SRDE workers have now developed a compact version of one of these devices which is claimed to be able to detect a man at a distance of over 100 m. The device detects very small temperature differentials between an object and its background; whether the object is warmer or cooler than the background is immaterial. A fairly simple set-up, with the infrared detector set up as an intruder alarm, was demonstrated at the SRDE; a moving mirror is used to scan the field of view, and the device can be linked to a remote alarm or counting device.

6. Optical-communication work declassified by the SRDE includes development of systems working at both infrared and visible-light frequencies. SRDE workers have developed a simple two-way communication system by fitting near-infrared (0·9 μm wavelength) transceivers to standard pairs of binoculars. Two-way line-of-sight voice communication can be obtained between two such transceivers over distances of up to 800 m; transmission is over a 20 kHz pulse-frequency-modulated beam from a gallium arsenide lamp in one half of the binoculars, while the receiver is a silicon photodiode in the other half. It is estimated that each transceiver could cost between £50 and £70; potential civil uses could be for communication on construction sites or between ships.

7. A similar system demonstrated at the SRDE enables an operator to communicate freely to receivers located anywhere in a room; such a requirement might exist in a vehicle such as a tank, where it is important that the messages are not received elsewhere, or in conference systems in large halls. In this system, the gallium arsenide transmitter is fitted to the ceiling, and operators wear headphones incorporating silicon diodes.

8. The advent of lasers and efficient optical detectors has stimulated interest in communication at visible-light wavelengths, and SRDE work is aimed at finding efficient ways of modulating light for communication purposes and transmitting it over large distances.

9. The Earth's atmosphere is an inherently bad medium for optical

transmission because of the obscuring effects of clouds, fog, rain, etc. and some way of eliminating these problems is desirable. SRDE engineers believe that the best medium for optical transmission is an optical wave guide, consisting of a very fine di-electric fibre (usually glass).

10. A fibre with a $1\mu$m-diameter core supports only three or four modes of transmission, and a very high bandwidth (up to 10GHz over 1 km) is obtained, making it ideal for use in wideband single-channel systems such as the interconnection of computers or trunk telephone exchanges. For the 80 $\mu$m-diameter core under detailed study at the SRDE, there are hundreds of possible modes and the bandwidth is only about 5 MHz over 1 km; this type of fibre is more suitable in applications where many separate channels are needed, e.g. in television conference networks. Suitable glasses for these fibres are being investigated by the SRDE in conjunction with British glass manufacturers; the loss obtained at present with normal optical-quality glass is about 200dB/km, whereas 70dB/km would be necessary for communication purposes.

11. The SRDE has built an experimental system using a gallium arsenide laser and a silicon detector, in which pulse-code-modulated speech signals are transmitted over a 36 m length of 80 $\mu$m-diameter fibre containing many bends; the transmitter and detector both operate at room temperature, are solid state and compact, and require no lenses. The small size of the fibres allows 200 of them to be 'bundled' in a cable only 2·5 mm in diameter.

12. One limitation on the amount of information that can be carried by such a system is the fact that the gallium arsenide laser has to be operated in a pulse mode. A continuous-wave laser circumvents this difficulty, but the output light has to be modulated by passing it through a crystal of electro-optically active material such as ammonium dihydrogen phosphate (a.d.p.), which responds to changes in the applied electric field by amplitude-modulating the light passing through it. At the SRDE an a.d.p. modulator, driven at about 200V by a transistor circuit, is being used in conjunction with a gas laser to transmit television-picture signals. A similar system is commercially available.

*Questions*
1. What does the abbreviation SRDE represent?
2. How many of the larger diameter optical fibres can be contained in a cable of 2·5 mm diameter? (Para. 11)
3. From your reading of the article what do you understand by the following terms?
   (*a*) optoelectronics
   (*b*) transceiver
   (*c*) optical communication

4. The three categories of night vision systems use different wave length ranges. From your knowledge of electromagnetic radiation shade in and label on the given wavelength scale the approximate range of each category.

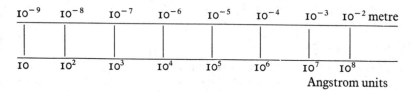

5. In relation to the devices described in the article, what is the meaning of the phrase 'a gain of about 40000'? (Para. 3)
6. State, for each of the three night vision systems described, **one** application which has been developed and operated:
   (a)
   (b)
   (c)
7. Explain in simple language, assuming that the reader has little knowledge of technical terms, the opening section of paragraph 5: 'Devices operating in the far-infrared region of the spectrum have been used for some years in missiles for locating aircraft engines by thermal radiation emitted.'
8. If the earth's atmosphere is a poor medium for optical transmission, why is a glass fibre better for this purpose? (Paras. 9 and 10.)
9. What are the main differences in the transmission properties of glass optical waveguides of 1 $\mu$m and 80 $\mu$m diameter? (Para. 10.)
10. What main limitation exists at present to the practical use of glass optical waveguides?
11. Describe in your own words the method of operation of the first stage of the image intensifier shown in the diagram.
12. Explain in your own words how information is transmitted by the binocular system illustrated in the photograph.

It should be noted that questions 11 and 12 demand miniature essays; as such, they are not really suitable as part of a set of structured questions, and in some respects they ask for the same information as earlier questions. (In subsequent years the set of questions was limited to ten.)

Example 2 is called the 'Comprehension Test' in the Engineering Science examination, but it contains the essential features of a structured question: unfamiliar material upon which to work, the breakdown of the responses into small parts, an increase in the level of response from responses 1 to 12, the recording by candidates of their answers on the question paper (answer spaces are omitted here to conserve space), the likelihood of reliable marking. The stem of the question is also structured and numbered to guide the candidates. (A minor criticism would be that the use of the same notation in responses and stem could cause some confusion.) Similar examples may be found in other subjects, particularly in English and General Studies examinations and they illustrate well the versatility of this form of question, both in range of subject and level of ability: it is likely that they would be equally effective at the Further Education level.

## How to write them

It would be idle to pretend that one of the advantages of structured questions is that they are easy to devise. Far from it; they require experience and skill greatly in excess of that required to set traditional questions or even objective test items. But they are being used more and more in public examinations and, inevitably, teachers will wish to devise them for internal use in schools. The best general advice—as in so many other contexts—is to practice and learn by one's mistakes. Some specific guidance is however, possible and the main points are set out below.

(1) Be continually on the look-out for material which is suitable for the question stem. Sources include: books, journals, newspapers, films, slides, tape-recordings, tables of data, graphs, histograms, photographs; all may be fruitfully used in internal tests in schools. The word 'continual' is used advisedly. It is no good hoping to sit down the night before an examination and expect all the ideas for structured questions to appear from nowhere.

(2) Having got a suitable situation for the question stem, analyse it both from the teacher's and the learner's viewpoint. Look for the main points which one would emphasize if the material were the basis for a lesson: what essential themes in the subject does it illustrate; what skills and abilities would the pupils require to work on the material?

(3) Determine the *sequence* in which the material would be studied in class. There are two factors to be considered here: the logical development of the material and the need to start with easy questions and finish with the more demanding questions. Sometimes these two factors are in opposition; but, normally, the sequence should be as near to the natural teaching sequence as possible, and the level of ability required should rise from the start to the finish.

(4) Think of the *answers first*. This may appear to be illogical, but this is how teachers frequently work: they first decide what response (or responses) is appropriate and then frame their question in the form most likely to elicit that response. (This does not apply to situations in which the response is to be free or discursive.) Similarly in the structured question: decide what responses you wish the candidates to give and then phrase the questions. How successful you have been will appear later when the scripts are marked. Inevitably you will receive responses different from those expected. Except to the most simple of questions, a single correct answer is never possible. Nevertheless, if the marking is to be reasonably objective, precision in the

question is desirable in order to avoid a number of differing responses, a situation which might occur if candidates have not understood what it is that the examiner wants them to do.

(5) It follows from 4 that the draft mark scheme is written at the same time as the questions. Of course, it cannot be the final scheme. When a sample of answers has been marked, the mark scheme will have to be amended and, nearly always, considerably expanded to take note of how the candidates actually responded, rather than the way in which you thought they would respond.

(6) Except for the lengthy comprehension test, a maximum of seven or eight sub-questions is sufficient and each should give rise to one, two or three—at the most four—points in the answer to which marks can be allocated. For ease and objectivity of marking this is important. (Parts 11 and 12 of Example 2, although perfectly proper questions, would not be so readily marked in this way.)

(7) Leave sufficient lines on the question paper for the answer to be written. Be generous to allow for the spreading or verbose writer; but not to such an extent as to invite a diffuse answer. *Precision in both question and answer is essential if objectivity is to be achieved.*

(8) Indicate the relative weighting of each part by stating the number of marks to be awarded and make this number equal to the main points which are expected in the answer.

(9) *Mark positively.* That is look for things to reward rather than faults to penalize. It is normal in an examination paper of structured questions to require candidates to attempt all the questions and all the parts of each. In these circumstances candidates are forced to 'have-a-go' and hence the need for sympathetic marking.

(10) In school examinations the normal time allowed to answer all the parts of a structured question is fifteen or twenty minutes. Examples 1 and 2 indicate the extreme lower and upper limits. Rarely would the total time for a structured examination paper exceed two hours.

(11) Although all the sub-questions should relate to the same material in the question stem, they should be independent of each other—a correct answer to one part should not depend on the correct answer to a previous part. Sometimes, in calculations for example, this is not possible, but then allowance should be made in the mark scheme so that credit can be given for an incorrect answer arising from a previous error.

(12) Experience has shown that question writers tend to make their structured questions too difficult. The reason is that to the writer the material of the question and the expected responses are familiar and have been studied at leisure. To the candidate it is all unfamiliar and responses cannot be made at leisure. So—and this is perhaps the most important advice of all—try to see the information and the questions *through the eyes of the candidates.* The most likely people to do this are practising teachers, and this is why it is so important to get teachers trained in this particular assessment skill.

## The future of structured questions

Reference has already been made to the need for closer links between the teaching/learning situation and the assessment situation, and a function of the structured question is to help bring this about. In any good teaching situation the teacher hopes to get *some* response from *all* members of his class. From the weakest, response may come only to the simpler aspects of the situation and the easiest questions; the most able may understand and respond to the whole. The teaching of groups of mixed ability is increasing and the demand for examinations which will cover a wider ability range arises from it; hence the move towards a single examination system at 16. Well written, precisely phrased and appropriately sequenced structured questions will do much to meet this demand. The least able should be capable of responding correctly to some of the sub-questions, if only the first one or two. At the other end of the scale, only the most able should be able to get full marks.

The fulfilment of all these conditions is asking a lot of any type of examination question and no one would pretend that the structured question is the only and ultimate question form; it lacks, for example, the absolute objectivity of the multiple-choice question; nor does it allow much freedom of response or divergence of opinion; the effort required to devise them is prodigious. Nevertheless, here is a versatile form of assessment which, in the hands of those who are experienced both as teachers and examiners, can contribute much to assessment in the future.

# 3 Short Answer Questions and Objective Items

## B. Argent

'Testing as part of teaching', 'testing and teaching objectives' and 'the efficiency of testing' are those major themes of the book which form the framework of this chapter. Short answer questions and objective items provide an effective means of ensuring that testing contributes to the teacher's task of encouraging and guiding learning. Their use enables the teacher to integrate testing with teaching because they provide the feedback essential for effective teaching and learning. Skilfully prepared questions and items can test reasonably accurately many aspects of learning in terms of subject matter, abilities and levels of difficulty. They do not take long to answer and mark and thus provide relevant information quickly. This can be used either for 'readiness testing' when pupils are beginning a new area of study which requires the use of skills and knowledge acquired at an earlier stage, or for 'progress testing' where regular information regarding performance helps to illuminate some pupils' darkness and rewards the efforts of others, or for 'completion testing' where some measure of final attainment is required perhaps for examination or course evaluation purposes.

This chapter attempts to provide through description and example foundations upon which to develop skills in the preparation of these forms of questioning. When acquired these skills need to be allied to knowledge of subject matter, experience and understanding of pupils, plus perseverance and imagination.

### Description and examples of short answer questions

Short answer questions are at the opposite end of the spectrum from open-ended essay questions. They attempt to ask questions requiring exact answers and although taking many forms they share these distinctive features.

(i) They usually takes less than five minutes to read and answer, many take less than a minute.

(ii) They include some guidance on the extent of the answer required, e.g. the size of answer space or specific instruction such as 'In not more than 20 words. . . .'.

(iii) The answer is supplied by the pupil, not selected as in objective questions.

They can be grouped into two broad categories: (a) extended answer and (b) insert and completion.

The extended answer version includes questions which require pupils to write a brief description, draw a map, make a list, perform a calculation, translate a sentence, write down a definition or formulae and so on. They are probably the commonest form of question used in schools and are frequently used by examining boards. They are deceptively easy to set and usually difficult to mark with any degree of speed and consistency.

*Examples*

1.  Give the titles of *two* Shakespearian comedies and for each the names of *three* of the principal characters.

    *Play title* ...........................     *Play title* ..............................

    .............................................     .............................................

    *Characters*                *Characters*

      (i).....................................     (i) .....................................

     (ii).....................................     (ii) ....................................

    (iii).....................................     (iii) ...................................

2.  Describe briefly *two* factors which contributed to the outbreak of war between Germany and Great Britain in 1939; write no more than about *thirty* words about each factor.

3.  List the stages in the life cycle of the dragon fly, and state for each stage its approximate duration in weeks, and a typical example of the type of environment in which it occurs. Arrange your answer in columns like this:

    | *Stage* | *Duration* | *Environment* |
    | --- | --- | --- |
    | | | |

4.  On the line to the right of each symbol write what it stands for when used on Ordnance Survey maps.

    ✛
    ●     ..............................................................................

    т     ..............................................................................

.................................................................

.................................................................

+ − + − + ......................................................................

5. Name the *two* types of chemical compound which combine to form salts, and then name *one* inorganic and *one* organic salt.

6.

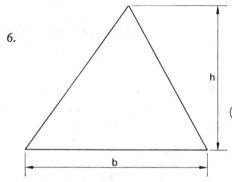

(i) What is the formula for the area of the triangle in terms of its perpendicular height h and length of base b?
(ii) Calculate the area of a triangle in $m^2$ where h = 6 m and b = 4 m.

7. Make sketches, each approximately 2″ × 2″ to show the structure of

(i) chipboard
(ii) blockboard
(iii) plywood

8. Write a sentence containing the words 'eminent' and 'imminent'.

*Note*: There are many more variations but they all share the common feature of many possible forms of correct answer, e.g. correct but misspelt, correct but poorly drawn, correct but with additional irrelevant material, and the like. This makes reliable marking difficult and time consuming, and suggests that although this type of question has many uses for 'progress testing' they can with advantage be replaced by objective items for 'completion testing'.

In many cases questions presented in an extended answer form can be rewritten to advantage in insert or completion form. This often results in the questions being clearer to the pupil and this in its turn eases the task of the marker.

The commonest form of completion question is one where the pupil is required to add one or two words to complete an incomplete statement correctly. Where the missing words are in the body of the statement to be completed it is usually called an insert type. A completion type is where the words are required at the end of the statement. The use of insert or completion questions is not, however, limited to written statements and can be used to prepare extremely good questions based on incomplete maps, drawings, diagrams, formulae, calculations, and the like.

*Examples*

1. On the journey from Edinburgh to London on the A1 the first English county entered is called ......... About half-way the road bypasses Newark which stands on the river ......... in the county of ......... After passing through ......... shire the road enters Greater London, the total distance being about (to the nearest 50) ......... miles.

   (This type of question can be prepared for many types of subject matter, and has the advantage of bringing together numerous pieces of information.)

2. In the human eye light enters through the (1)....... (1) ......, which is surrounded by a coloured part called the (2) i .... As the amount of light increases this part (3) ......, but (4)...... again when the amount of light decreases. On reaching the (5) ...... at the back of eye the light stimulates two types of nerve cell called (6) r ..... and (7) c ......

   (1).....................
   (2).....................
   (3).....................
   (4).....................
   (5).....................
   (6).....................
   (7).....................

   (The clues are not essential, nor is the provision of the right hand answer spaces. The latter does however make the marking of insert questions much easier.)

3. Complete the missing words in this paragraph.
   That night there was so little hotel a ....... tion that they had to take an expensive s .... of rooms. After paying the bill they were almost p .... less.
   (A useful technique for testing vocabulary and spelling.)

4. Complete the following formulae
   ammonia: N—
   sulphuric acid: $H_2$——
   sodium carbonate: —$CO_3$
   (Incompleteness of formulae can be adjusted in accordance with what is to be tested.)

5. Complete the expansion
   $a(a + b)^2 = a^- + \_b^2 + 2a^- b$

6. The first person to fly alone across the Atlantic was

       C.........                      L.........

## Description and examples of objective items

In general terms an objective item is one which eliminates the subjective element in the marking. This means in practice that the items require pupils to indicate or choose an answer and not 'put pen to paper' other than to mark an answer sheet.

There are three main types of objective items: multiple-choice, true–false, and matching block.

Although true–false are really a special version of multiple-choice and matching block can also be presented in multiple-choice format, they are described separately because they do have certain advantages and their own preparation problems.

MULTIPLE-CHOICE

A multiple-choice item consists of three parts, a stem, a key and a number of distractors. The key and distractors together are often referred to as options. The stem can be either a direct question or an incomplete statement; the key is the correct answer and the distractors are plausible but incorrect answers. Some of the many varieties of multiple-choice items are shown below, with the first one labelled to identify the components.

*Examples*

1. *Direct question.*

| | | |
|---|---|---|
| STEM | What is the essential characteristic of an objective item? | |
| DISTRACTOR | A It is written to test a specified learning outcome | |
| KEY | B No subjective judgment is required in its marking | PROBLEMS |
| DISTRACTOR | C It is based on a verifiable fact or principle | |
| DISTRACTOR | D Its subject matter and wording are unambiguous. | |

2. *Incomplete statement.*

Objective questions are so called because

    A   they are written to test specified learning outcomes

    B   no subjective judgment is required to mark them

    C   they are based on verifiable facts or principles

    D   their content is chosen objectively.

3. *Multiple-completion.*

   Using a table of specifications (blueprint) can contribute to the validity of

   1—objective tests
   2—oral tests
   3—in-course assessments
   4—practicals
   A 1 only
   B 1 and 2 only
   C 2 and 4 only
   D 1, 2, 3 and 4

   (An extremely useful form of multiple-choice since it can be applied effectively to many situations 'where there is more than one correct answer'.)

4. *Substitution.*

   <u>The writing of items</u> is an art of which <u>to thoroughly master</u>
          (i)                                      (ii)
   requires practice as <u>well as</u> patience.
                     (iii)
   For each of the underlined sections choose either the original or one of the alternatives as suitable.

   (i) A The writing of items
      B Skill in the writing of items
      C Item writing
      D Preparation of items

   (ii) A to thoroughly master
       B to master thoroughly
       C thoroughly to master
       D thorough mastery

   (iii) A as well as
        B and
        C or
        D not

5. *Incomplete options.*

   Which expression when completed correctly is the seat of government in the United Kingdom?
   A The H        of P
   B The T        of L
   C B          P
   D The M      H

Dr Johnson's biographer's surname began with the letter

A    'P'
B    'A'
C    'B'
D    'W'

(The incomplete options form can often be used when giving the options in full would make the answer too obvious, or for testing vocabulary where the recognition element may make the items invalid.)

*Note*: There are many other varieties of multiple-choice, two of the most common being classification and assertion/reason. The former offers some economy of wording in some cases and when skilfully employed the latter can probe quite deeply into reasoning ability and understanding. It is, however, best to concentrate on the more direct forms of multiple-choice as illustrated before attempting the more involved versions which often fail to work well because pupils have difficulty in following the rather involved instructions which are usually necessary.

### TRUE–FALSE

As its name implies the basic true–false item requires the pupil to select either 'true' or 'false' as his answer. It is usually written in the form of a statement which the pupil must decide is either 'true' or 'false' or alternatively choose between other word pairs relating to the statement such as 'greater than—less than', 'plus—minus' 'often—rarely' 'same—different' 'faster—slower' and so on. It is the possibilities offered by these other pairs which make the true/false form a particularly useful one.

Within the category of true–false can be included another variety of alternate answer items. This provides three or more possible answers not differing in kind as in multiple-choice but simply occupying different positions along a true/false, positive/negative scale. Common examples of such answers are 'always true—sometimes true—always false', 'greater than—equal to—less than'. There are many possible developments on this theme. One is to couple the category of answer with a reason or supporting statement thereby testing some aspect of understanding. A possible answer structure for such an item which could make use of a variety of material is:

A (True)—The statement is supported by reference to the evidence.
B (?)—There is no evidence one way or the other to support or refute the statement.
C (False)—The statement is not supported by reference to the evidence.

Often more than three 'scaled answers' of this type can be useful but to go beyond five answers usually places too much of a burden upon the pupil's memory in relation to the wording of the answer categories.

*Examples*

1. For each of the pairs of values listed below circle G if the first is
   *greater*, L if it is *less*, and E if they are *equal*.
       (i) density of ice/density of water at o°C      G—L—E
       (ii) mass of a moon car on earth/mass of
          the same car on the moon      G—L—E
       (iii) speed of sound in air/speed of sound
          in water      G—L—E
       (iv) velocity of radio waves/velocity of
          light waves      G—L—E

2. For each of the following statements:
       (a) circle T if it is true, and F if it is false;
       (b) for each false statement underline the word or words which
          make it false.

       (i) Member countries of the E.E.C. are signatories of the
          Treaty of Paris.      T—F
       (ii) France and Spain are members of the E.E.C.    T—F
       (iii) The United Kingdom became a member of the E.E.C. in
          1972      T—F

3. For each of the following statements:
       (a) circle TT if both parts are true;
       (b) circle FF if both parts are false;
       (c) circle TF if the first part is true and the second part is false;
       (d) circle FT if the first part is false but the second part true.

       (i) The authorized version of the Bible was commissioned by
          James II and is still in use today      TT/FF/TF/FT
       (ii) Samuel Pepys is famous for his diaries which he wrote
          while secretary to Oliver Cromwell      TT/FF/TF/FT
       (iii) In the seventeenth century London was ravaged by the
          'Great Fire' and the 'Black Death'.      TT/FF/TF/FT

4. For each of the statements below:
       (a) circle 'T' if there is conclusive evidence to support it;
       (b) circle 'F' if there is conclusive evidence to refute it;
       (c) circle '?' if there is no dependable evidence to support or
          refute it.
       (i) Eating carrots improves the ability to see in the dark   T/F/?
       (ii) Vitamin C deficiency causes scurvy      T/F/?
       (iii) People with red hair are on the whole worse
          tempered than other people      T/F/?

       (Although set in a 'science' context this type of question is
       equally applicable to the 'explanatory' aspects of other
       subjects such as history and geography.)

5. For each of the pairs of philosophers below circle '$+$' if the first tended to take a more optimistic view of human nature than the second, and circle '$-$' if the opposite is the case.

    (i) Hobbes and Locke                          $+/-$

    (ii) Rousseau and Voltaire                 $+/-$

    (iii) John Stuart Mill/Malthus            $+/-$

        (This question illustrates a useful technique for gauging general overall grasp of a concept, principle or trend, before more detailed teaching or testing.)

MATCHING BLOCK

The matching block format consists of two lists and the pupil is required to relate correctly one or more entries from one list with one or more entries from the other. Usually one list contains more entries than the other so that correct matching by elimination is impossible.

The commonest forms of matching exercise are based upon inter-relationships such as those shown below:

| *Typical List I Entries* | *Typical List II Entries* |
| --- | --- |
| word meanings | words |
| descriptions of discoveries, inventions, historical events, etc. | names of discoveries, inventors, dates, etc. |
| properties of chemical substances | common names or chemical formulae |
| habitats and habits of animals | names of animals |
| descriptions of operations | names or sequence of operations |
| function and purpose of apparatus, equipment, tools, instruments, materials | names or typical uses of equipment |
| passages from books or poems | titles or authors |
| nutriment composition in relative percentages of protein, carbohydrate, fat | names of foods |

The other major variety of matching-block is generally presented as one list and the other 'list' in a number of letters in alphabetical order representing a sequence, for example; most to least dense, earliest event to most recent event, faster growth rate to slowest growth rate, greatest distance to shortest distance.

*Examples*

1.  List I Landmarks    List II Locations
    1 Nelson's Column    a Berlin
    2 Statue of Liberty    b Rome
    3 Brandenberg Gate    c Paris
    4 Colosseum    d New York
    5 Acropolis    e London
        f Athens
        g Vienna
        h Cairo

Indicate the city in which each of the landmarks in List I is located by completing the match-panel.

LIST I

| 1 | 2 | 3 | 4 | 5 |
|---|---|---|---|---|
| e |   |   |   |   |

LIST II

The matching-block can be presented in multiple-choice form but offering the pupil completed match-panels as options, *viz*:

A

| 1 | 2 | 3 | 4 | 5 |
|---|---|---|---|---|
| e | b | a | f | c |

B

| 1 | 2 | 3 | 4 | 5 |
|---|---|---|---|---|
| e | d | g | b | a |

C

| 1 | 2 | 3 | 4 | 5 |
|---|---|---|---|---|
| e | f | g | 1 | b |

D

| 1 | 2 | 3 | 4 | 5 |
|---|---|---|---|---|
| e | d | a | b | f |

2.  List I    List II
    *Historical Events*    *Century A.D.*
    1 The French Revolution    a 15th
    2 Spanish Civil War    b 16th
    3 Jacobite Uprising    c 17th
    4 The Glorious Revolution    d 18th
    5 Reunification of Italy    e 19th
        f 20th

In the match panel below enter the letter from List II to indicate the century of each event in List I.

| 1 | 2 | 3 | 4 | 5 |
|---|---|---|---|---|
|   |   |   |   |   |

(This application of matching block rapidly tests knowledge of sequences and similar 'frameworks')

3. | List I | List II | List III |
|---|---|---|
| *Adjectives* | *Words with Similar Meanings* | *Words with Opposite Meanings* |
| 1 benign | A bare, empty | (i) dense |
| 2 demure | B well-mannered | (ii) brazen |
| 3 sparse | C lost, wandering | (iii) boisterous |
| 4 prodigal | D wasteful | (iv) parsimonious |
|  | E sober, composed | (v) faithful |
|  | F thinly populated | (vi) malignant |
|  | G gentle, gracious | (vii) dammed |

Show the meaning of the words in List I and your choice of words with opposite meanings by putting the appropriate letters and numbers in the match-panel.

| *List I* | *List II* (A–G) | *List III* (i)–(vii) |
|---|---|---|
| 1 |  |  |
| 2 |  |  |
| 3 |  |  |
| 4 |  |  |

(This is a useful extension of the matching block method, which is best marked by allowing one mark for each correct match, i.e. in this example there are eight correct matches.)

## Preparation of short answer questions and objective items

The basis for the preparation of 'good' questions and items can be acquired by following a few straightforward guidelines. Increased skill will come with plenty of practice and the use of imagination. This section deals first with guidance which applies to both categories and then considers parts which apply to one or the other specifically.

GENERAL GUIDANCE

The commonest faults in any form of question are irrelevance and triviality. The only certain way of avoiding both is to ensure that all questions are related to previously established operational course objectives and that they are used to test something when it needs to be tested and when the information gained can be used.

This is a two-way process since writing questions helps in stating course and learning objectives more clearly. A careful review of question content, marked answers and, where applicable, marking schemes can lead to a more down-to-earth idea of what objectives really are attainable in practice. It is likely to suggest also that some 'objectives' are perhaps better seen as long-term aims and aspirations towards which the humbler course objectives may be stepping stones.

In order to keep the relationship between subject matter areas and objectives clearly in mind it is useful to have a 'question writing specification'. This shows for a course or part of a course the overall pattern of relationships as between subject matter and objectives and can prevent questions being written which are based upon inappropriate objectives/subject matter matches. The specification or writing plan is best prepared in two parts. Part 1 is a simple grid as shown below and outlines those subject matter area/course objective combinations which require questions and those which do not.

| Subject matter areas \ Course objectives | (1) Understanding terminology | (2) Understanding of fact and principle | (3) Ability to explain or illustrate | (4) Ability to calculate |
|---|---|---|---|---|
| A Open–ended questions | ✕ | ✕ | ✓ | ✕ |
| B Structured questions | ✓ | ✓ | ✓ | ✓ |
| C Objective items | ✓ | ✓ | ✓ | ✓ |
| D Oral questions | ✕ | ✓ | ✓ | ✕ |

Key: ✓ Questions required
✕ Questions not required

Part 2 is a more detailed statement of the specific, detailed, learning objectives to be tested. For example: in Part 2 C/1 and 2 might read 'The pupil should be able to

(i) distinguish between examples of objective items and non-objective questions;

(ii) describe and give examples of multiple-choice, true–false and matching block items;

(iii) decide if non-objective questions can be converted to objective form and make satisfactory conversions;

(iv) detect and correct faults in poorly constructed objective items,'
and so on.

In addition to content relevance there is also relevance for purpose. It is essential to know whether questions are to be used at the readiness, progress or completion stages of learning, and that their main function is to provide feedback for you and your pupils. Questions for readiness and progress are mainly diagnostic—aimed at detecting strengths and weaknesses in pupils' acquisition of subject matter. Questions for progress testing should also encourage pupils, by being relatively easy at first, perhaps with cues to direct them towards the correct answer. For completion testing questions must concentrate on terminal objectives and give valid, reliable measures of pupils' achievement.

Thus, question content is influenced by four factors which can be illustrated as follows:

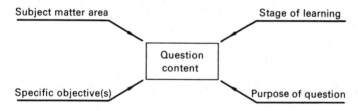

Often questions do not do what they were designed to do because of inexactness and ambiguity in the wording. Remember that for the pupil the question is a request and he is more likely to fulfil that request if he understands it precisely. Typical examples of inexactness are:

| *Words used* | *Request intended* |
|---|---|
| 'Explain.........' | 'Give two reasons for.........' |
| 'Describe how.........' | 'List the four stages in.........' |
| 'Discuss briefly the advantages and disadvantages of.........' | 'Give three advantages and three disadvantages of.........' |

In order to check the wording of a question thoroughly it must be seen in conjunction with an acceptable answer and marking scheme. Careful inspection of the last two will often show that words used in the question do not quite result in the request intended. Careful question preparation should involve the following stages:

| | | | |
|---|---|---|---|
| 1 | writing | 5 | first use |
| 2 | presentation | 6 | performance appraisal |
| 3 | editing | 7 | reviewing |
| 4 | first revision | 8 | storage or banking |

In the final instance the best check is how well the question worked in practice as revealed by the pupils' answers. A large part of question preparation is concerned with being ready to study answers and amend questions before they are used again. The following general principles also apply throughout:

CO-OPERATION

At many points the successful preparation of questions requires the help of other teachers, e.g. editing, and sometimes other schools, e.g. pre-testing. The views of other teachers are invaluable not only for wording but as a help towards clarifying course and testing objectives.

Any extensive use of multiple-choice items would be facilitated by the use of simple machinery for marking and question analysis. Although one school may not be able to afford such equipment, several could easily share the cost.

Such mutual co-operation could lead to the development of shared storage facilities for questions and items, an excellent method of avoiding undue duplication of effort and a great saving in time, as well as a way of communicating teaching approaches and course interpretation.

PUPIL PARTICIPATION

Pupils are a teacher's most important asset in question preparation. Their assistance in writing, editing and performance appraisal will not only improve questions but will also enable them to see that questions and testing are an aid to learning and not just occasional hurdles to clear or stumble over as chance may dictate. Particular examples of pupil participation are:

(i) writing draft questions as a test of their grasp of the subject;
(ii) class editing of questions presented on the board or overhead projector;
(iii) trial marking of each other's questions and discussion of marking schemes.

ATTITUDE AND TIMING

Good ideas for questions do not come just because you sit down for an hour or so to write them. A good approach is to keep a 'question possibilities' notebook in which to jot down ideas as they occur, especially during lesson preparation and teaching. When you do write questions it is best to settle down to it for two or three hours. It is a creative exercise requiring half an hour or so for warm up and then about two hours real productive work before ideas start to flag or repeat themselves.

Each of the preparation stages is now dealt with in turn.

WRITING

When writing the extended version of the short-answer question a list of acceptable answers and a mark scheme should be prepared at the same time. The question itself should indicate whenever possible the length of answer required by the use of such phrases as 'in about 20 words'. Alternatively, a suitably sized space can be left on the answer sheet.

In the marking scheme it is usually best to give either '1' or '0' for each part of the answer which receives marks. Usually giving '½' marks is unnecessary and leads to inconsistency in awarding marks to different pupils.

Where questions are used for diagnostic purposes it should be possible for pupils to follow the marking scheme and if required mark their own questions with assistance when required.

For the completion and insert form it is particularly important to leave large enough answer spaces to accommodate variations in size of writing and it is usual to indicate the type and/or extent of answer required. For example

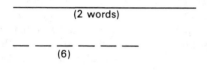

This means the word required has six letters, sometimes one or more of the letters might be given.

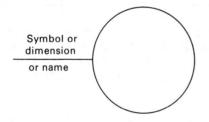

Used for blanks on maps, diagrams etc.

The following specific points should also be noted when writing short-answer questions:

(i) Do not leave blanks at the beginning of sentences.

(ii) Omit only key words, ensure that what is omitted does not make what is left incomprehensible.

(iii) If the blank requires an answer in units, specify the units.

(iv) Although definitions, rules, principles and relationships can be converted to good insert or completion questions it is best to give their title in full.

(v) Avoid the temptation to write insert questions based on passages taken direct from books or notes.

(vi) Try to frame insert questions having more than two or three sentences with a blank in each so that an incorrect insert in one place does not lead to other mistakes.

For multiple-choice items the rules for writing stem, key and distractors are best considered separately.

Stems can be direct questions or incomplete statements; neither has any special advantages. Use whichever form comes most naturally to you at the time.

Do not worry too much about the exact wording of the stem at your first attempt; concentrate on framing a purposeful, relevant question. The wording can be improved later.

The key must answer the question posed in the stem. It should be expressed in such a way that pupils with the necessary knowledge see it as such while not presenting incidental clues to those who do not know the answer. Such clues take three main forms:

*Length*: Often the key in an item as initially written is the longest of the options. If this is the case throughout a number of items length may become a clue. To avoid this the best policy is to vary key lengths so that they are sometimes longer, sometimes shorter and sometimes the same length as the distractors. Although it may be possible to change the length of the key it is often just as effective to lengthen the distractors.

*Word associations*: If the key contains the same significant word or words as the stem this may act as a clue.

*Stereotyping*: Use of direct quotations of rules, definitions etc as keys tend to act as clues. They can be used if the distractors are similarly stereotyped.

Distractors should be written as incorrect answers which will appear as correct to pupils who do not have the knowledge to answer the question. Writing good distractors requires a thorough knowledge of the real errors and misconceptions that do occur, and a readiness to put oneself in the place of the pupil, i.e. at his level of acquaintance with the subject matter. All too often perfectly good ideas for distractors are abandoned because the writer finds them personally implausible. They may well, however, be perfectly plausible to the less knowledgable pupil.

Good distractors can often be formed by including in them those features which should be avoided in the key namely length, word associations and stereotyped wording.

The time required to write distractors is usually at least as long as that required to write stem and key. This is reasonable since they are equally essential to the quality of the item. Do not expect always to produce all the distractors for an item at the first attempt.

It is often better to leave a blank than to put in a weak distractor. When the item is looked at again later it is often easier to produce a good distractor if you are not reminded of an earlier unsatisfactory one.

As a general rule most people find it possible to write three good distractors for each item, and although it can be shown that questions with four distractors tend to be more reliable this is not the case if one or more of them does not work. In practice, therefore, four option, three distractor items are a good workable proposition.

Many people are deterred at first by the time it takes to write good multiple-choice items; but, with practice a certain skill rapidly develops and a rate of six to ten satisfactory items an hour is quite possible.

A good quick check a day or two after you have written the items is to read each stem, with all the options covered and write down the answer. If you cannot do this or if your answer is markedly different from the key or rather like one of the distractors the item needs improving. The check is of course not applicable to stems which deliberately direct you to the options, e.g. 'Which one of the following .........?'

Another useful quick check is to cover the key and look carefully at the remaining options to see whether any of them might conceivably be correct. This is not a foolproof check but a useful guide.

With each item it is good practice to note down the subject matter area and ability (or objective) tested and indicate which is the key option.

As well as the above general principles the following specific points apply

(i) Avoid negatively worded stems. Pupils adopt an answer set for positive stems and are often put-off by negative ones. Where a negative stem is the only way, or the least cumbersome way of expressing a question emphasize the negative by underlining or otherwise highlighting the negative words, such as none, no, not, least, except,

(ii) Arrange numerical options in ascending or descending order.

(iii) Watch for overlap between options. This is easy to spot on numerical answers, but is less so with written answers where it can also occur.

(iv) If the same word or words occur at the beginning of each option consider placing them in the stem if it is an incomplete statement or as a common preface to the option set if the stem is in question form.

(v) Remove from the stem all information such as instructional asides and elaborate scene setting, which are not necessary to the question.

(vi) Avoid using 'none of the above' and 'all of the above' as options. If they are keys it can be argued that logically any of the other options is correct. It is usually possible in any case to find better distractors.

(vii) With incomplete statement stems especially make sure that the options follow-on grammatically.

(viii) Remember that items which turn out to be too easy or too difficult can often be changed by amending the distractors rather than the stem.

The following ten items illustrate some of the faults which can occur in multiple-choice questions if the above principles are not followed.

1. An objective test
   A can be marked quickly and accurately
   B is not suitable for slow readers
   C should contain one type of item only
   D works best when attempted by a large number of pupils

*Comment*

The stem does not pose a question. Apart from being undesirable in itself this has led to a mixed-bag of options which is also a feature to be avoided. This would not have occurred if the stem had, for example, asked specifically for a suitable use, an essential feature or particular advantage of the objective test. Sometimes this type of item can be presented as a series of 'True/False' statements.

2. In a one-hour geography test consisting of fifty, 4-option multiple-choice items a pupil scores 35. What is his score after guessing correction is applied?
   A 15
   B 20
   C 25
   D 30

*Comment*

This item contains 'window dressing', i.e. irrelevant material about duration and subject matter, and also assumes the application of one form of guessing correction. A better item can be prepared by using a stem which concentrates on the assumption made when applying the guessing correction. For example

'In applying the guessing correction (CR)

$$CR = \left\{ \text{number correct} - \frac{\text{number incorrect}}{(\text{number of options} - 1)} \right\}$$

What assumption is made about the incorrect responses?'

3. Short-answer and essay questions are sometimes referred to as 'supply questions' because the answer is supplied and not selected as in the case of objective items. Which of the following is also an essential difference between objective items and 'supply questions'?

   A objective items are written to match a test specification
   B no subjective judgment is required in marking objective items
   C supply questions can test higher level abilities
   D objective items take much longer to write

*Comment*

The item begins with a piece of information, an 'instructional aside' or 'lead-in' which is not required, and moves on to using an imprecise description, i.e. 'essential difference' as the core of the question. It can be improved by removing the aside and concentrating directly on some defined point of difference between the two types, e.g. 'Why can objective items be marked more reliably than supply questions?'.

*Note*: Quite often 'window dressing', 'instructional asides' and 'lead-ins' are useful in the first draft of an item because they help the writer. They should, however, be removed eventually because in addition to taking up the pupil's time they can be confusing to him.

4. A test which is unreliable will also be invalid because
    A the questions or items will be based on the wrong objectives
    B reliability is a necessary, although insufficient condition for validity
    C it will not be comparable with tests in the same subject area
    D the marks will be spread too widely

*Comment*
Option B is written in formal language which distinguishes it from the other options. Such items can be improved by writing the other options in equally formal terms.

5. In a matching-block item it is advisable to have more entries in one list than in the other so that
    A to start with pupils have a wide choice of possibilities
    B correct matching by elimination is avoided
    C the difference between the lists is quickly recognized by pupils
    D there is room for answers under the shorter list

*Comment*
Use of the word 'matching' in option B serves as a clue. This can be overcome either by rewording option B, or by including the word 'matching' in each option.

6. What is the major contribution that preparing and using a test specification can make to test construction?
    A it ensures a well proportioned marking scheme
    B it encourages a consideration of all relevant objectives
    C it describes the intended test content and thereby serves as a check on content validity
    D it highlights the relative importance of objectives

*Comment*
Option C is considerably longer than the other three, and is thereby heralded as the likely answer; in such cases either shorten the key or lengthen the distractors.

7. Which of the following does not contribute to marking inconsistency?

    A the 'halo' effect
    B unexpected forms of correct answer
    C failure to test appropriate objectives
    D pupils' writing style

*Comment*

The stem is negative and would be improved if the 'not' was printed in bold type or italics. Where the use of negative stems is unavoidable, it is often best to use the word 'except' at the end of the stem, e.g. 'Each of the following contribute to marker inconsistency *except*'

8. Efficient test evaluation begins

    A with a consideration of its validity
    B by careful analysis of its reliability
    C comparing item by item performance of high and low scorers
    D calculating its mean and standard deviation

*Comment*

This is a typical 'first draft'; the item can be improved by recognizing that each option describes an operation and can be shortened by transferring this aspect to the stem, *viz.*

Efficient test evaluation should begin with a consideration of the test's

    A mean score
    B standard deviation
    C reliability
    D validation

9. The following are required to calculate a test's standard error of measurement

    A its mean score
    B its duration and number of items
    C its standard deviation and reliability
    D its item analysis

*Comment*

Only options B and C follow grammatically from the stem, and the items as a whole could be improved by organization in multiple-completion form, *viz.*

Which of the following are required when determining a test's standard error of measurement?

    1 its reliability
    2 its mean score
    3 its standard deviation
    4 its item analysis

A 1 and 3 only
B 2 and 3 only
C 1, 3 and 4 only
D 1, 2, 3 and 4

10. The major advantage of objective items is
    A pupils are not penalized for working slowly
    B ways in which they sample more course content in less time
    C marking time
    D wide ranges of ability tested

*Comment*
This item has many faults. The stem is imprecise. Words like 'major', 'chief', 'most important', usually need qualifying, e.g. 'The major contribution to reliability in objective tests is derived from .........' In many instances it is better simply to ask for 'an advantage', 'one reason', 'a cause', in the stem. Because 'major advantage' is not qualified any of the options could be considered correct, although the undue length of option B suggests that the writer had this in mind as the key, and the imprecision of option C would make it ineffective as a distractor. None of the options follow grammatically from the stem. First attempts at item writing often produce this type of item. Rather than trying to improve the stem and options piecemeal it is best for the writer to ask himself exactly what it is he is trying to test and then construct a new item around that. In this case the essence of the item is an advantage of objective items, knowledge of which could be tested like this:

One potential advantage common to objective items when compared with essay questions is that
    A they can be edited and pre-tested
    B for certain abilities they can provide a more comprehensive coverage
    C they encourage more systematic teaching methods and study habits
    D when used in tests statistical information about their performance can be obtained

11. Of the following which is the most comprehensive and up-to-date account of educational testing published in the United Kingdom?
    A *Educational Measurement* edited by R. L. Thorndike
    B *The World Year Book of Education: Examinations* edited by J. A. Lauwerys and D. G. Scanlon
    C *Developments in Educational Testing* edited by K. Ingenkamp
    D *The Essentials of Educational Measurement* by R. L. Ebel

### Comment

The writer of this item has succumbed to the temptations of TOT (Tricks, Opinions and Trivia). Writers of any type of question or item must beware of these temptations; they are, however, particularly strong when writing multiple-choice items. The stem is based partly on a trick, only options B and C are published in the U.K. It involves opinion, on what basis is 'comprehensiveness' to be judged? By 'up-to-date' does the author mean most recently published or containing the latest views and information? Then overall the item is trivial. What matters is that the books exist; to test knowledge of their contents, their treatment of particular topics, or even the difference in emphasis on certain subjects might be worthwhile for some purposes. Testing date and place of publication is probably not. Even a bookshop assistant would consult a catalogue rather than commit such information to memory.

Provided that the general principles of item writing outlined earlier are applied then good true–false and matching-block items can be prepared. The following more specific points are also relevant. For true–false items:

(i) Remember that 'true–false' is only one of the possible word pairs that can be used and that in many instances 'scaled answers' are also applicable.

(ii) Truth or falseness (or any of the other extremes) must be demonstrable as matters of fact or by reference to some authority, and not merely be matters of opinion.

(iii) Make sure that the statements used are qualified where necessary so that the pupils see clearly under what conditions or what circumstances a statement is to be judged as true or false. True–false items are often answered incorrectly by more able students because necessary qualifications have been omitted.

(iv) Avoid words such as 'all', 'always', 'never', 'invariably', 'none', 'no' etc which tend to be used to make statements false, and words like 'generally', 'sometimes', 'may' and 'could' which tend to be found in statements which are true.

(v) Do not make statements false by the addition of trivial or irrelevant detail.

(vi) Do not use negative statements.

For matching-block items:

(i) Always state the basis for the matching even if this appears to be obvious, and give a title to each list.

(ii) Make one list longer than the other but avoid any lists with more than ten entries.

(iii) Arrange the lists vertically down the page, side by side preferably with the list containing the longer entries on the left-hand side. This assists the pupil because he is led naturally to the reading of the long entry first. This can then be held in mind while the right-hand list is scanned.

(iv) Use letters for the entries in one list and numbers for the entries in the other.

(v) Where appropriate use a match panel for the answer, e.g.

| *List I* | A | B | C | D | E | F | G |
|----------|---|---|---|---|---|---|---|
| *List II* |  |  |  |  |  |  |  |

or leave a space beside the letters in list I for the pupil to enter the numbers from list II. Match panels are easier to mark.

PRESENTATION

Even when the wording of an item seems just right it can be improved further by good presentation. Pupils tend to find it easier to read quickly and understand what is required if an item is arranged systematically. For example this question 'Name two species of wild duck which nest in the British Isles and give for each distinctive details of the plumage of male and female and whether they migrate in winter' can be put over more readily to the pupil as follows:

(a) Name two species of wild duck which nest in the British Isles.
(b) For each
   (i) give distinctive plumage details of the male and female
   (ii) state whether it migrates in winter.

It could also be set in table form as follows:
Complete the table below for two species of wild duck which nest in the British Isles.

| | *Duck*–A | *Duck*–B |
|---|---|---|
| *Name* | | |
| Distinctive plumage features — In male | | |
| Distinctive plumage features — In female | | |
| Winter migrant— state Yes or No | | |

Good presentation and organization have two aims. One is to avoid giving the pupil more work than necessary in order to demonstrate his knowledge or lack of it, the other is to enable the answers to be marked as quickly and accurately as possible.

All short-answer questions can be answered either on the paper given to the pupil or on separate answer sheets. Even with extended answer forms, completion and inserts it is well worthwhile having separate answer sheets, suitably lined up or tabled for the answers so that (a) they can be easily marked and retained for question appraisal and (b) the question sheets can be re-used or questions presented on a board, overhead projector or slide projector. Quite often the use of colour is a great advantage in question presentation and the use of transparencies or slides is an economical way of doing this.

For objective items, especially multiple-choice, separate answer sheets are invaluable if pupils' responses are to be used for detailed analysis (see Chapter 4). Nothing elaborate is required provided pupils receive sufficient practice in their use and guidance on how to indicate answers is clearly given. For tests with ten or more objective items it is sensible to have a reminder after each fifth item for pupils to check that they are indicating their answers correctly on the answer sheet.

For multiple-choice items allow a two-line or three-line space between the stem and the first option and begin each option on a new line with a one line space between them.

Use letters not numbers to label the options. Upper case A, B, C and D without brackets is a popular format. If the stem is a question the last word should be followed by a question mark and each option punctuated in accordance with standard English practice. If the stem is an incomplete statement there is no need to put colons or dashes at the end.

Where more than one item refers to the same figure etc the group of items concerned should be prefaced by some such guide as 'Items 4–7 refer to the map and description on page 9'.

Perhaps the greatest drawback to producing realistic items is the attempt to confine the content of the item to a short written statement. This is not necessary; questions or items should make use of additional materials such as photographs, charts, large-scale maps and models. They can equally well be written to be used in conjunction with films, video tapes, sound recordings, and outside activities such as visits to factories, nature trails and any other educational activity which provides suitable opportunities for pupils to show their knowledge and understanding in ways not possible within the limitations of the classroom.

EDITING

Every question writer has to be his own editor in that he must check the relevance and wording of his questions. It has, however, been found especially with multiple-choice items that an independent check by someone else is essential. The writer himself being too familiar with his intention and product will not on occasion spot even obvious faults or possibilities for improvement.

Part of any effective approach to question preparation is working in conjunction with other teachers for question editing. Some editors should be qualified in the subject matter of the course and familiar with its objectives. Others should come from different disciplines and so provide a fresh insight on wording and expression which pupils may find difficult.

Editors should be asked to check systematically both the content and construction of questions. For this a checklist can be developed listing those aspects requiring review.

An extract from a typical checklist for multiple-choice items is shown below. Similar lists should be prepared for all other types of questions and would in the case of short-answer forms require some reference to the marking schemes.

| *Multiple-choice items editing checklist* | |
|---|---|
| *Content* | *Construction* |
| (1) Is the question relevant to the course? | (1) Does the stem present one central question, clearly and concisely? |
| (2) Does it test (*a*) the subject matter (*b*) the ability stated? | (2) Is the key the correct answer? |
| (3) Is it technically accurate? | (3) Are there any clues in the key? |
| (4) Is it suitable for the purpose stated? | (4) Could any of distractors be considered as correct? |
| (5) How difficult is it likely to be? e.g. on the hard side, on the easy side or about average. | (5) Are any of the distractors unlikely to be plausible? |

For systematic editing it is advisable to prepare a simple comments form such as

| *Editing comments form* | | |
|---|---|---|
| *Question No.* | *Content* | *Construction* |
| | | |

Above all it should be remembered that question editing is an opportunity to share knowledge, experience and opinions. A writer may well not agree with the editors' views but usually discussion on questions resulting from editing gives both writers and editors new insights into course content and objectives.

FIRST REVISION

Editing usually results in a writer wishing to make some changes to his questions, which should as far as possible be made before the questions are used. If, however, this is not possible, or a writer decides not to change his questions the editorial comments should be retained and looked at again when questions have been used and it is possible to make some appraisal of how they worked in practice.

FIRST USE

Ideally all questions would be trial tested before being used operationally. In practice, however, a teacher is not likely to be able to do this and it is more realistic to suggest that he uses the information obtained from the first real use for review and amendment.

This means keeping pupils' answers to questions and gauging their reactions to them. Pupils who have just answered questions are often good judges of ambiguity and in the case of multiple-choice items can very readily be encouraged to explain how it was that some distractors make perfectly good keys, and to suggest ideas for better distractors.

On the basis of such first impressions it is possible to make a more systematic evaluation of question performance.

PERFORMANCE APPRAISAL

In Chapter 4 a full account is given of some techniques for the analysis of objective items and non-objective questions. For the moment it is sufficient to mention the following.

(i) Questions which result in answers which are completely off the point or too long have failed.

(ii) Questions and items which are answered well by less able pupils but which confuse more able pupils are probably ambiguous.

(iii) Multiple-choice items with distractors which attract no responses probably need better distractors, or they may be suitable for use earlier in the course.

It is worth mentioning here that using multiple-choice items early in a course can indicate the effectiveness of distractors better than using them towards the end. Such items still have a use for readiness and progress testing although they may not be suitable for completion testing.

REVIEWING

Once questions have been used and some data collected on their performance they can be reviewed, that is considered for entry into the question bank, to be available for re-use when required.

Provided one is satisfied that questions do test relevant content in a satisfactory manner they can be accepted for future use. If possible, use a short list of criteria so that your reviewing is systematic, e.g.

(1) content                   acceptable/unacceptable/borderline
(2) effectiveness for purpose   acceptable/unacceptable/borderline
(3) facility                  acceptable/unacceptable/borderline
(4) discrimination         acceptable/unacceptable/borderline
(5) performance of distractors   acceptable/unacceptable/borderline
     (multiple-choice only)

Provided questions are acceptable for (1) and (2) they might still be retained, bearing in mind that on their first use they were only exposed to a small number of pupils and may well work better next time.

STORAGE

Questions can be arranged and catalogued in such a way that they can be quickly located and selected for use in teaching.

Each question should be written out on a firm card about 8" × 10" so that all information relevant to its use can be stored with it. This information should include:

(1) a reference to the subject matter covered and the ability tested;
(2) performance record;
(3) acceptable answer and marking scheme when required;
(4) purpose of question, e.g. whether for readiness, progress or completion testing.

To make the best possible use of a question store an 'entry record' and 'contents summary' are required. The record is simply a list of all questions stored in the following form:

| Entry number | Subject matter area | Ability tested | Type of question | Purpose |
|---|---|---|---|---|
|  |  |  |  |  |
|  |  |  |  |  |
|  |  |  |  |  |

From the entry record, contents summaries can be prepared to indicate how well the store is stocked for any particular course or area of subject matter. For example a simple table like this could be used.

| Subject matter areas | Number of questions | | | Matching block |
| | Short answer | Multiple-choice | True/false | |
|---|---|---|---|---|
| A | 6 | 21 | 9 | 4 |
| B | 20 | 10 | 2 | 3 |
| C | 7 | 32 | 12 | 8 |
| etc. | | | | |

This approach provides the basis for general purpose storage of questions for classroom use. A more detailed discussion of more refined procedures for question banking is presented in Chapter 13.

Although the stages described earlier are adequate for question preparation it is desirable to apply a more rigorous approach to preparing and storing questions and items for use in completion testing if this is to be used for course evaluation or examination purposes. The chief differences being that:

(1) they must be pretested under conditions as near as possible to those under which they are eventually to be used. This means using a test compiled in accordance with a test specification upon a sufficiently large number of pupils representative of the population who will take the real test;

(2) they must be analysed in a statistically reliable manner so that their performance parameters, e.g. facility values, discrimination values and, where relevant, distractor popularity can be used for more exacting revision than has been discussed in this chapter.

These matters are discussed more fully in Chapter 4 'Item Analysis and Question Validation' and Chapter 13 'Question Banking'.

## Use of short-answer questions and objective items

### GENERAL PRINCIPLES

Other than the ability actually to write, sketch or otherwise put an answer down on paper there is very little in terms of subject matter or objectives which can be tested by short answer questions that cannot also be tested by objective items. In the same time both types can cover about the same amount of subject matter, although there is some material which either true/false or matching block items can cover much more quickly than other varieties. The only real difference between them is that short answer questions tend to take less time to prepare than objective items; this may not always be the case when compared with true/false and matching block but is almost so when compared with multiple-choice. The time saved in preparation is, however, usually more than occupied with marking. Overall time requirements are much the same and the more often an objective item is used instead of a short answer question the more marking time is saved. Short answer questions cannot, moreover, be marked as consistently as objective questions.

These factors do not mean that ones whole effort should be turned towards objective items. On the contrary, it is best to proceed with a policy of preparing and using both. There are several reasons for this.

Good short answer questions can be reasonably quickly prepared and are particularly useful for progress testing where the exact nature of misunderstandings, mislearnings etc needs to be probed.

Used in this context they and their answers provide excellent materials upon which to base objective items, particularly multiple-choice. Here pupils' answers to short answer questions make good starting points for distractors. In fact a good practice when writing multiple-choice items is to set only the stems to a class in the first instance. This not only helps you find out if the stems are clearly worded but usually provides a good crop of draft distractors.

In this way short answer questions can be put to good use for readiness and progress testing where reliability is not at a premium and can be used to help prepare good objective items some of which will be suitable for completion testing where usually a fairly high level of reliability is required.

From the point of view of pupils' learning it is also necessary to avoid complete reliance in an objective format. The short answer question does call for and provide practice in an essential skill of recalling and using knowledge. This is necessary during the acquisition (progress) stage of learning even though it may not be appropriate in attainment tests at the completion stage.

Of the objective items multiple-choice is the most versatile in terms of the abilities it can test and the levels of difficulty at which it can be pitched. Anyone becoming proficient in question writing is bound to eventually make greater use of multiple-choice items than any other type.

For speedy surveys of simple factual material, however, the true/false item is better provided one does not expect the test scores to be particularly reliable.

Although the matching block item is ideal for testing knowledge of classifications, and relationships and can be presented in multiple-choice format by having different already completed match panels as options, it cannot usually test the more complex levels of understanding.

QUESTIONS OR TESTS

Questions can be used to provide feedback either when used singly, in groups or in tests. The use of questions singly or in groups during teaching is just as valuable as their use in tests. This is where a well stocked store of questions and items can be most useful in providing just the right ones for any particular teaching requirement. Although stored questions may be written or typed onto cards they can also be on OHP transparencies or slides so that they are available for immediate classroom use. Marking schemes and answer keys can also be kept in this way, thus enabling pupils to check their own answers if this is wanted.

When pupils are working at different speeds or working through different aspects of the subject matter they can be given the entry number of questions to be drawn for self-testing when required. When questions are to be used in tests the tests can be compiled in either of two ways (a) in accordance with a carefully prepared test specification or (b) by selecting a complex of subject matter/objective combinations that require testing and drawing out questions to match it. The former method is usual for completion testing.

*Postscript*

Short answer questions and objective items provide real opportunities for integrating testing with teaching and learning. Their preparation and use and the development of a 'question bank' for everyday use is an investment of time and effort which will show considerable interest in terms of more effective, and perhaps even more enjoyable learning.

# 4 Item Analysis and Question Validation

## R. B. Morrison

Assessment is basically a measuring process in which the test or examination performs the function of a measuring instrument. A rigorous and systematic approach to assessment requires the same kind of disciplined approach as is to be found in measurement in the sciences, engineering, building and other areas which call for the design and use of appropriate measuring instruments. Such instruments need to be both valid and reliable* in operation if the feedback they provide is to be of value in assessing the situation under consideration. We therefore need to ask two important questions about a test or examination. First, what are the specific abilities or skills the test is designed to measure? Second, does the test measure such abilities or skills reliably, i.e. is it consistent?

The design and eventual production of an assessment instrument, be it an objective test, a written examination or a practical test, are important parts of the procedure for measuring abilities. It is in these initial stages that answers are sought as to the specific abilities or skills the test is being designed to measure. This is not simply a matter of ensuring adequate coverage of the content topics of a syllabus, but also of making sure that the educational objectives of the particular course of study are being assessed. The specification for the assessment needs to mirror faithfully the specification for the course of study or training. In so far as one can render articulate the syllabus topics and the educational objectives which accompany them, just so far can one hope to achieve a desirable degree of validity in the assessment instrument under construction.

Equally important with the design stage, however, is the provision of feedback to the test constructor or examiner as to how the assessment instrument has behaved. To be useful, such feedback needs to provide more detailed information than simply the frequency distribution of marks or scores for the candidates. An uncalibrated and unreliable speedometer

* Validity and reliability are discussed in more detail in Chapter 8. Further reference to reliability will also be found in Chapter 1.

in a car may still provide a speed distribution for a journey, but it will not be a valid record of what actually occurred. To be useful, assessment feedback needs to provide information on how the various items or questions comprising the assessment succeeded, or failed to succeed, in achieving what they were designed to assess. Although the overall frequency distribution of marks may appear to be satisfactory, certain individual items or questions making up the test might be far from satisfactory. A detailed analysis for each item or question is required. An assessment instrument is like any other measuring instrument in that each component needs to be doing its proper job and functioning harmoniously with the other components in the system. One weak component and the performance of the instrument becomes suspect and its validity questioned.

In this chapter we are concerned with certain analytical techniques which provide assessors with useful feedback when using the two most common modes of assessment of cognitive skills at the present time, namely objective tests and choice-type written examinations. The feedback for objective tests is provided by item analysis, and this technique has been known for some time. Comparable feedback for choice-type written examinations has only emerged fairly recently. The question synoptic chart technique, developed at the University of Reading by the author and his colleagues, has been found to be useful and intelligible to teachers and examiners and is the technique described here. The interested reader is referred to *British Examinations: Techniques of Analysis* by D. L. Nuttall and A. S. Willmott and published by the National Foundation for Educational Research for a more comprehensive review of the question synoptic chart technique and other analytical methods which have been developed in this area of assessment.

## Item analysis

As described in Chapter 3, objective test items may take on various forms depending to a large extent on the type of ability one wishes to assess. The most common and most comprehensive form, however, is the multiple-choice type item consisting of a situational stem and four or five options, only one of which is appropriate or correct. Item analysis provides statistics of performance for each and every type of item, and in the case of the multiple-choice item it provides additional information on how the various options behaved. In what follows, the more comprehensive analysis as it is applied to multiple-choice items will be described; the more general statistics will be found to be applicable to other item types.

The first piece of useful information is to know how easy or difficult the candidates found the particular item. This is provided by the *Facility Index* ($F$). It is defined as the percentage of all candidates who gave the correct response to the item. Thus if 80% of those taking the test gave a correct response to a particular item in the test, the facility index for the item would be 80%. This suggests a fairly easy item. An item with a facility index of 20%, however, errs on the side of being difficult. An item with a facility index between 40% and 60% indicates an acceptable item as far as facility is concerned in that it has achieved a reasonable level of difficulty for those taking the test.

The second piece of useful information is to know how the items discriminated between the candidates. Has the item discriminated in the same way as the test as a whole? If 35% of the candidates gave a correct response to an item, did they all comprise the top 35% for the test as a whole? If this were to be the case, then the item has discriminated perfectly and is functioning harmoniously with the test as a whole. It is rare to achieve such perfect discrimination, but one would expect a reasonable degree of harmony between the way an item discriminates and the way the test as a whole discriminates. This degree of harmony is measured by the *Discrimination Index (D)*.

The most rigorous statistic used for the discrimination index of an item is the point biserial correlation coefficient, $r_{p\,bis}$.

$$r_{p\,bis} = \frac{M_p - M_q}{\sigma} \times \sqrt{pq}$$

where, $p$ is the proportion of candidates giving a correct response to the item and $M_p$ is their mean score on the test, $q$ is the proportion giving an incorrect response and $M_q$ is their mean score on the test and $\sigma$ is the standard deviation for all candidates' test scores.

The point biserial correlation coefficient varies between $+1 \cdot 0$ through zero to $-1 \cdot 0$. A value of $+1 \cdot 0$ means perfect discrimination with the item discriminating in the same way as the test. A value of $-1 \cdot 0$ means perfect discrimination in exactly the opposite way to the test. In our example earlier, it would mean that the 35% who gave a correct response to the item were all to be found comprising the bottom 35% for the test as a whole. The vast majority of items in practice have values between zero and $+0 \cdot 6$, zero suggesting poor discrimination and the higher positive values denoting improving discrimination. In general, items would be considered acceptable if the facility index were satisfactory and the discrimination index exceeded $0 \cdot 25$, although a discrimination index in excess of $0 \cdot 4$ would be better.

The facility and discrimination indices may be found for any type of objective item once the response sheet of candidates to items is obtained. In the case of multiple-choice items, it is important to know how the various options behaved. Let us suppose that a multiple-choice item consisted of five options A, B, C, D, E, and that the correct response or key was D. The candidate/item response sheet for such items should list what each candidate scored as the 'correct' response. It is therefore possible to list the percentage responses for each option. We shall suppose these to be A (15%) B (16%), C (6%), D (52%), E (8%) leaving the remaining 3% who omitted to answer the item at all. The reader will note that the facility index for this item is 52%. The facility index on its own, however, does not tell us how the incorrect responses were distributed. The extended analysis provides this information. Thus, in our example, few were distracted by options C and E, whilst A and B proved to be reasonable distractors. The item writer may wish to look at options C and E to determine whether they might be improved, for options which attract a very small percentage of responses are proving ineffectual and reducing the five option choice item to a four or even a three option item.

The teacher who is designing and using objective tests in school may wish to employ a simpler method for obtaining the facility and discrimination indices for the items in a test. Such a method is described in detail in *Objective Testing* by H. G. Macintosh and R. B. Morrison (University of London Press). It is based on analysing the item responses for the top and bottom 27% groups as determined by the total test scores. For a particular item we shall suppose the top 27% to have given $N_H$ correct responses and the bottom 27% to have given $N_L$ correct responses. Let the number of candidates comprising a 27% group be $n$. Approximate facility and discrimination indices can then be calculated as follows:

$$\text{Facility Index } (F) = \frac{N_H + N_L}{2n} \times 100\%$$

$$\text{Discrimination Index } (D) = \frac{N_H - N_L}{n}.$$

The facility and discrimination indices, together with option behaviour for multiple-choice items, provide the item writer with basic useful feedback as to how the item has behaved and enables the test constructor to decide as to its suitability for the test under construction. Because these item analysis statistics depend upon the sample taking the test or pre-test, it is important that the sample so used should be representative of the population for which the test is being designed. Neglect of this precaution will nullify the usefulness of the feedback and militate against the eventual validity of the test. Further, there are many commercially available objective test items which have not been pre-tested and subjected to item analysis. If such items are used in classroom testing an item analysis should be carried out to ascertain their appropriateness for the test it is desired to carry out. Such items may be quite unsuitable for the group of pupils one has in mind, and only a proper item analysis can settle this.

There are a number of ways in which the reliability of a test may be measured, and the reader is referred to standard texts in educational measurement such as *Statistics in Psychology and Education* by H. E. Garrett (Longman) for a full discussion of these. Broadly speaking, a test-retest with the same group of candidates can show how reliable the test is from the point of view of giving consistent results. The split-half method of calculating reliability provides a measure of the test's internal consistency. The scores obtained on all the odd numbered items are correlated with the scores obtained on all the even numbered items. In effect this is a correlation based upon half the test and may be represented by $r_{\frac{1}{2}}$. The reliability coefficient, $R$, for the whole test is obtained using the Spearman–Brown formula:

$$R = \frac{2r_{\frac{1}{2}}}{1 + r_{\frac{1}{2}}}.$$

The Kuder–Richardson reliability of a test is often calculated, and this also provides a measure of the test's internal consistency. A variant of this reliability may be found using the number of correct responses in top and bottom $27\%$ groups by using the formula:

$$R = \frac{k}{k-1}\left\{1 - \frac{2n\sum(N_H + N_L) - \sum(N_H + N_L)^2}{0 \cdot 667[\sum(N_H - N_L)]^2}\right\}$$

$k$ is the number of items in the test and the other quantities have already been defined.

Properly constructed tests usually give reliability coefficients of $0 \cdot 8$ or higher, whilst short classroom tests average about $0 \cdot 6$. Generally speaking, the longer the test the more reliable it is likely to be.

## Question Synoptic Chart analysis

In the case of an objective test, the candidates are expected to answer all the items in the test. No choice is allowed, although certain candidates will omit to answer some of the items. As objective tests are not designed to be speed tests, the majority of candidates may be expected to answer all the items in the time available, and it is, therefore, usually found that the number of omits is small. This means that the ability spectrum for those answering each item is basically the same and is also that of the whole entry. This is not the case for the choice type examination where the ability spectrum for those answering a particular question depends upon the sub-group from the total entry which decides to answer that question. As a result, the ability spectrum may and often does vary from one question to another. Some questions are answered by below average ability sub-groups, whilst others are answered by above average ability sub-groups.

The existence of choice means that additional feedback is required for the examiner who designs a choice-type written paper. In addition to knowing how easy or difficult the question turned out to be, and how discriminating it was, the examiner needs to know the popularity of the question and some measure of the ability of those who chose to answer it. A question which is decidedly unpopular means a restriction in the actual choice provided and this should be known. Equally, if it is established that certain kinds of question appeal to the below average part of the entry, the subsequent deletion of such questions will inevitably handicap the choice of these candidates. Similar considerations apply to the above average part of the entry.

The *Choice Index* (*C*) of a question may be defined as the percentage of the total number of candidates who chose to answer the question. In practice this index has been found to vary over quite a wide range, most questions having an index between 30% and 80%. The existence of popular and unpopular questions is well established and the choice index permits their identification in quantifiable terms.

The *Mean Ability Index* ($M_T$) for a question is defined as the mean total percentage mark obtained in the examination for those candidates choosing to answer the question. The assumption underlying this definition is that $M_T$ is a close approximation to the ability of the sub-group answering the question. This will certainly not be true for an invalid examination, and it may not be true for a first examination design, but profitable use of feedback leading to improved validity will automatically improve the justification of the assumption. In any case, as the first step in an iterative process $M_T$ is the only appropriate index of ability available. The mean ability index provides a quantifiable indication of the ability of those candidates who chose to answer a question.

The definition of a facility index for a question is not as simple or straightforward as the definition of a facility index for an item in an objective test. The mark for an item is one or zero according to whether the response was correct or not. The mark for a question may be anywhere on a scale of marks, the maximum being the maximum mark assigned to the question. A first consideration might be to suggest that the facility index for a question might be defined as the mean mark for that question expressed as a percentage. This might be reasonable if there were no choice, but the effect of choice makes this definition untenable. A mean mark of 70% may suggest an easy question, but an average difficulty question may provide a mean mark of 70% if the sub-group answering it happened to be of decidedly above average ability. The same average difficulty question may provide a mean mark of only 30% if the sub-group answering it were of below average ability. The mean mark for a question is thus a function of the ability of the sub-group answering the question. It can also be a function of the leniency or severity of the marking in those cases where there is not a tight mark scheme. This latter complication does not enter into objective test marking. A satisfactory facility index for a question on a choice type paper needs (a) to make allowance for the ability of the sub-group answering it, and (b) to be independent as far as possible of the leniency or severity of the marking.

The author has suggested that a suitable *Facility Index* (*F*) which meets these two requirements may be defined as

$$F = 50 + (M_Q - M_T)\,\%.$$

$M_Q$ is the mean percentage mark obtained for the question, and $M_T$ is the mean total percentage mark obtained in the examination for the sub-group answering the question, i.e. the mean ability index.

The assumptions underlying this definition are that $M_T$ is a close approximation to the ability of the sub-group answering the question, which has been discussed above, and that $(M_Q - M_T)$ is reasonably independent of the leniency or severity of the marking. The latter assumption holds if the lenient or severe marker is consistently lenient or severe, for in this case both $M_Q$ and $M_T$ will be affected equally and the difference between them will remain constant. This will not be the case if the marking is erratic, but the only remedy for this kind of error is to ensure that it does not take place.

The facility index as defined above has been extensively tested in recent years within the Educational Measurement Research Unit at the University of Reading. There is sufficient evidence now to show that the index does make reasonable allowance for the ability of those choosing to answer the question. Further, quite different groups of candidates answering the same questions and marked according to the same mark scheme have yielded much the same values for the facility index. This suggests that the facility index is reasonably sample free. The requirement for a representative sample is not therefore as important here as it is in item analysis, where the facility index for an item is sample bound. Recently, M. S. Rothera of our Unit has shown operationally that different markers marking the same scripts have produced reasonably equal facility indices even where marked discrepancies in leniency and severity have been observed. It would appear, therefore, that the assumptions made are to a large extent justified.

It will be noticed that a facility index of 50% is obtained for a question when $M_Q = M_T$, whatever the value of $M_T$. This may be taken as a facility datum in that such questions are matched to the ability of the candidates answering them, i.e. candidates are getting the same mean percentage mark for the question as for the examination as a whole. If candidates get a higher mean mark for the question than for the examination as a whole, this would suggest an easier question, or possibly a case of isolated lenient marking of a question. This is reflected in a higher facility index. Given consistent marking, however, a high facility index suggests an easy question, a low facility index a difficult question just as in item analysis. Using a similar convention as for objective test items, questions with facility indices between 40% and 60% would be acceptable as being of reasonable difficulty. In practice, it has been found that most questions from a variety of examination papers have facility indices covering the range of values from 30% to 70%.

A corresponding discrimination index for a question may be defined on the basis of a correlation coefficient analogous to the use of the point bi-serial correlation coefficient used in item analysis. The *Discrimination Index* (*D*) for a question may be defined as the product–moment correlation between the marks for a question and the corresponding total marks gained by the candidates on all *other* questions. Thus, if $X_Q$ is any candidate's mark on the question and $X_T$ is the candidate's total mark for the examination, the discrimination index is given by the product–moment correlation coefficient between $X_Q$ and $(X_T - X_Q)$ for all the candidates choosing to answer the question. As in item analysis, the discrimination index may assume values between $-1\cdot0$ and $+1\cdot0$, and should preferably be greater than $+0\cdot4$. It has been found, using the definitions given, that the discrimination indices for choice type questions are generally higher than for objective test items.

The results of question analysis may be summarized in the form of a table, a specimen from a larger table being given below. The first column gives the choice index ($C$), the second column the mean percentage mark for the question ($M_Q$), the third column the mean ability index ($M_T$), the fourth column the facility index ($F$) and the fifth column the discrimination index ($D$). All are expressed as percentages except the discrimination index.

*Question Analysis Table*

| Question | $C$ | $M_Q$ | $M_T$ | $F$ | $D$ |
|---|---|---|---|---|---|
| 1 | 53 | 37 | 43 | 44 | 0·41 |
| 2 | 72 | 57 | 40 | 67 | 0·51 |
| 3 | 29 | 43 | 45 | 48 | 0·32 |
| 4 | 65 | 49 | 39 | 60 | 0·46 |
| 5 | 49 | 30 | 47 | 33 | 0·30 |

(Mean percentage mark for total entry = 41%)

Consideration of the question characteristics shows the following. Questions 1 and 4 are acceptable. Question 2 is on the easy side and question 5 on the difficult side. Question 5 also has poor discrimination which applies to question 3 as well. Questions 2 and 4 were the most popular and question 3 the least popular. Questions 3 and 5 were answered by the above average part of the entry, or avoided by the below average part. Question 4 seemed to appeal to the below average part of the entry, or had no appeal for the above average part. Question 2 proved to be the easiest and question 5 the most difficult. It cannot be stressed too much that such feedback needs to be considered in conjunction with the content and wording of the questions themselves as well as with the mark schemes if possible reasons for their performance and likely improvement are to be realized.

A clearer appreciation of the question characteristics may be gained by plotting the mean percentage mark for a question ($M_Q$) against the mean ability index ($M_T$) for that question providing what has been called a *question synoptic chart*. Such a chart provides a synoptic view of the examination as a whole. The question synoptic chart for the questions above is given below.

The Facility Datum line for $F = 50\%$ is marked on the chart. All questions falling on this line will have a facility of 50%. The boundary facility lines for 40% and 60% are also marked. Vertical separation of the questions is a function of their facility, the higher the question on the chart the easier it is and vice versa. Similarly, the horizontal separation is a function of the mean ability of those choosing to answer the questions, questions to

## Question Synoptic Chart

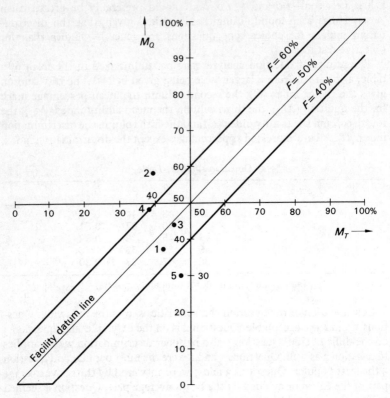

the left being preferred by the lower ability candidates and those to the right by the higher ability candidates. The discrimination indices may be marked on the chart alongside each question plot as may also be the corresponding choice indices.

The reliability of the choice type examination is not an easy statistic to calculate and the interested reader is referred to the contribution by J. K. Backhouse and others in *British Examinations: Techniques of Analysis (loc. cit.).* A modification of the Kuder–Richardson reliability coefficient, $R$, using the facility and discrimination indices found from question synoptic chart analysis has been suggested by the author, namely

$$R = \frac{k}{k-\mathrm{I}}\left\{\mathrm{I} - 6\frac{\left[\Sigma\left(\frac{F}{\mathrm{100}}\right) - \Sigma\left(\frac{F}{\mathrm{100}}\right)^2\right]}{[\Sigma D]^2}\right\}.$$

$F$ and $D$ are the facility and discrimination indices respectively for the questions making up the paper, and $k$ is the number of questions on the paper. It has been found that this coefficient is itself reasonably reliable where the number of questions on the paper or papers is large ($k \geqslant 15$). It becomes rapidly unstable for shorter question papers and should not be used in these cases. This may not be surprising in that a choice type examination employing only a few questions is a poor sampling of the course content and is therefore subject to the errors resulting from question spotting, last minute revision and increased anxiety on the part of the candidates.

A disquieting feature of the choice-type written examination has been the almost complete lack of awareness of any need for feedback. Questions have been set by examiners based largely on their intuitive judgment as to what was a 'good' question. The performance by candidates on individual questions has influenced examiners only where it has proved extreme. This may be contrasted with objective testing where the candidates' performance has always been an integral part of the decision as to what constituted a 'good' item. This is not to argue that the item writer in writing an item is any less subjective or intuitive than the writer of questions, but simply that one subsequently uses feedback and the other does not. It is to be hoped that the analytical methods now available for choice type examinations will be used increasingly in the future to provide this feedback. The intuitive judgment of the assessor needs to be coupled with a knowledge of the behaviour of the assessed if the validity of assessment is to be improved.

# 5 Aural and Oral Assessment

## B. Park

### Introduction

Schools Council Examinations Bulletin No. 4 published in 1964, makes the point that 'all examinations should employ as nearly as possible the same medium of expression as that in which the pupil or student will eventually make use of his attainment'. Since most pupils after leaving school spend more time speaking than they do writing, one might have expected to see a considerable extension of oral and aural assessment in public examinations. This has not happened, however. Moreover, even in those subjects such as English where a considerable extension of oral assessment has taken place in recent years, the techniques used at the secondary level follow a fairly similar pattern. There is nothing, for example, in current GCE or CSE examinations as interesting or as original as the 45 minute completely taped test developed by the Association of Recognized English Language Schools which aims to test spoken English in six basic areas.

It is probably fair to say that it is in Modern Languages that most work has been carried out recently in this country in relation to oral and aural assessment taken together. It is largely for this reason, therefore, that this chapter concentrates almost entirely upon Modern Languages, although brief reference is made to oral assessment in English and to aural assessment in Music. Another reason for this decision is limitation of space. In a book which aims to cover a wide range of topics as this one does, each chapter must obviously be limited in length. This means that a particular topic can either be dealt with by providing practical advice for teachers in relation to a comparatively limited area or by describing in outline the possibilities over a wider range of subject matter; both can hardly be done adequately. In this chapter the former course using Modern Languages has been adopted as being the most useful. The examples quoted will be in French since this is the most widely taught foreign language in Britain.

It is true, of course, that the detail which follows is applicable to any second language learning including English as a foreign language. Whittaker, moreover, in Chapter 6 covers oral assessment in relation to practical work and Deere indicates its possibilities in Chapter 7 as part of the assessment of project work. Nevertheless, the range of possibilities for these techniques of assessment have not been as fully explored as they might have been and interested readers, particularly if they are concerned with assessment in this area in English, should supplement their reading by reference to some of the works mentioned in the bibliography at the end of the book.

## Aural tests of Modern Languages

'Define before you assess and try to assess only that which you have defined.'

This simple rule might appear to be self-evident, for it is clear that unless it is strictly adhered to, one can never be certain to what extent one has assessed the skills one has set out to assess. For example, if, in order to test Aural Comprehension in French, a passage for dictation is set, how far can one be sure that errors made are due to failure to comprehend or inability to spell or ignorance of the rules of grammar? Although no one would claim that the different skills which make up competence in a foreign language are taught in isolation, it does follow from the first statement that in a testing situation the skills should be isolated as far as possible. Mixed skill tests in any subject are almost always unsatisfactory because it is inevitable that one skill will impinge upon another and one can, therefore, never be sure of precisely what one is testing.

(A) THE DEFINITION

This is often the most difficult task in any scheme of assessment. It is, however, essential to have a clear notion of what one means by 'aural comprehension' even if to some degree this means stating the obvious. The definition might read: 'Pupils should be able to understand a native speaker, speaking at rather less than his natural speed over a limited range of topics.' There would have to follow a list of topics which were appropriate for the listening situation, for example:

Shopping
Buying a meal
Going to the cinema, theatre
Listening to a newscast or station announcement
Making travel arrangements by bus, train or plane
Arranging to meet someone
Listening to a simple narrative.

Three further points must be made about the above type of definition:

(i) The reference to 'less than his natural speed' is deliberate, since it is a reflection of the aural tests used by all GCE and CSE boards at the time of writing. If, through the greater use of audio-visual and audio-lingual courses, the general standards of aural comprehension improve significantly, then clearly this statement would need modification.

(ii) The type of list used above might be replaced and/or supplemented by a detailed list of structures and vocabulary.

(iii) The list is not intended to be absolute and is intended merely to illustrate the need to define; it could easily be extended.

(B) THE TECHNIQUES

The table which follows gives a brief summary of the techniques used currently by GCE and CSE boards, together with those used by other testing organizations such as the National Foundation for Educational Research, the Schools Council Modern Languages Project, Educational Testing Service—Princeton, New Jersey and the Pimsleur Proficiency Tests—published by Harcourt, Brace and World, Inc.

| Technique | User |
|---|---|
| Single passage or dialogue with Question/Answer in French | 2 GCE boards, 1 CSE board |
| As above with Question/Answer in English | 3 GCE boards, 14 CSE boards |
| Dictation | 7 GCE boards, 11 CSE boards |
| Nacherzälung (Aural Reproduction) | 3 GCE boards, 2 CSE boards |
| Multiple-choice questions in French, based on a series of passages or dialogues | 2 GCE boards, SCMLP, ETS |
| Shorter multiple-choice items of the following types: | |
| Who is speaking? Where are they? What are they doing? | 2 GCE boards, SCMLP |
| Appropriate rejoinder (See page 65) | SMCLP, ETS, Pimsleur |
| Multiple-choice questions based on sets of 4 pictures | NFER, SCMLP |
| As above, based on blocks of 9 pictures | SCMLP |
| True/False statements based on a series of passages or dialogues | SCMLP |

Naturally each technique has its advantages and disadvantages, but it is worth reiterating the point made earlier that in making his selection, the teacher must choose a technique which assesses a particular skill in the way in which he intends. There is a distinction to be made between teaching and testing, and although the one should be a natural extension of the other, it does not follow that the same techniques can be used for both. Let us look briefly at the techniques listed.

Dictation, Passage or Dialogue with Q/A French and Nacherzälung all test a mixture of skills, chiefly writing and listening. For this reason they are not satisfactory as aural tests. In other words they are good for teaching but not for testing.

The single Passage or Dialogue with Q/A English is good in that it tests what it sets out to test, but suffers from the defect that one passage of, say, 300 words inevitably revolves around one linguistic area and may place some pupils at a considerable disadvantage if, for example, they do not know certain key words. Moreover, great care has to be taken over the construction of questions, since they may well be capable of two or more interpretations, each of which may be valid to a greater or lesser degree. To quote a simple example:

'Cet après-midi Paul va prendre l'autobus pour aller en ville. Il veut visiter le musée.'

It might be thought reasonable to ask the following question:

What is Paul going to do this afternoon and why?

In all there are three pieces of information which might feature in an answer: catching a bus, going to town, visiting the museum. A pupil might answer using all three pieces of information or any combination of two. Alternatively, he might begin with the third piece of information and then have to invent an answer to the question 'why?'. The question needs rephrasing in order to remove the ambiguity and should perhaps read:

What is Paul going to do this afternoon? (Mention three points in your answer.)

The example chosen was deliberately kept at a simple level. It follows that the more complex the language being tested, the more difficult it is for the teacher setting questions to spot possible sources of ambiguity or misinterpretation. Setting good questions in English is by no means as easy as it looks.

Multiple-choice and True/False questions in French have the advantage of complete objectivity in the marking. Moreover, because pupils spend less time noting down their answers, it is possible to increase considerably the amount of language that they listen to. A well-constructed multiple-choice test should contain a suitable balance of long and short passages or dialogues and in this way the danger of pupils performing badly through ignorance of one or two key words is kept to a minimum. However, the chief disadvantage of these questions is that they are more difficult to set than open-ended questions in English, particularly those based upon longer passages or dialogues. Care has to be taken that the questions are based only on the salient points for comprehension and do not depend upon insignificant details. The language of the multiple-choice options must be simple and short and easier than the material which is being tested. Finally, for a public examination, pre-testing is essential, and this involves finding a suitable trial population and conducting a thorough item analysis. However, this is not to say that teachers should automatically rule out multiple-choice items from a class test. The shorter multiple-choice items are easier to write than items based on long passages. The same also applies to True/False questions. The Who? and Where? items are inevitably restricted to a limited number of topics, but the What? and Appropriate Rejoinder items offer much wider scope.

Multiple-choice questions based upon pictures are very suitable at an early stage of language learning, particularly for pupils who are not familiar with the written word. The chief difficulty is the provision of suitable pictures, but since simple pictures are always the best (pin-men are often ideal) this is not an insuperable problem.

True/False questions based on a passage or dialogue are much easier to set than multiple-choice questions. However, because theoretically half the questions can be answered by random guesswork, a larger number have to be set. For example, in a test of twenty multiple-choice items, where four options are provided, a pupil can score one quarter of the marks by guessing randomly, perhaps by selecting option A every time. Marks on the test might be expected to range from 5 to 20. If a comparable test of True/False questions were set, then 40 questions would be needed. About half might be answered by random guessing, giving a potential mark-range of 20–40.

In practice, random guessing appears to be extremely rare and in fact many weak pupils will score less than the figure they could have scored by 'choosing letter A'. The evidence of the SCMLP Tests suggests that the majority of children make a conscious attempt at selecting the correct answer. There is a vast difference between making an intelligent guess, which very often depends on a simple word association, and making a purely random guess, which is simply an attempt to defeat the system. As soon as children start making assumptions about the language being tested then they are responding to the test in the manner for which it was designed. The test constructor has to ensure that the questions set are of an appropriate degree of difficulty and that there is a sufficient spread of marks available to permit him to distinguish between the different levels of ability within the class or group being tested. If one views the problem of random guesswork in this light, it is possible to keep it in its proper perspective.

(C) THE CLASSROOM AURAL TEST

Let us look first at an aural test suitable for a class of mixed ability, i.e. one covering the top 60% of the ability range, after 12 months' study of an audio-visual course.

It is assumed that by now the aims have been defined and that the topic areas and/or linguistic structures to be tested have been drawn up on a simple grid. Since the amount of language covered in one year will be fairly limited, it is likely that pupils will have had little exposure to the written word. The test should, therefore, use pictures wherever possible and exploit the spoken word, preferably with the use of the tape-recorder. It is divided into three parts:

Part 1—Vocabulary test based on pictures;
Part 2—Multiple-choice questions to test specific structures;
Part 3—True/False statements based either on pictures or on dialogues of 50–70 words.

*Part 1—Vocabulary test based on pictures*

The 'traditional' multiple-choice method is to have a set of four lettered pictures. A simple phrase is spoken twice, and the pupil selects the appropriate picture, noting his answer on a separate answer sheet.

EXAMPLE

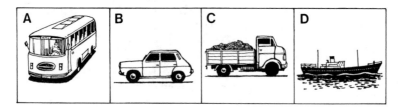

The pupil hears: 'Indiquez le camion', and indicates his answer by ringing or underlining letter 'C' on his answer sheet.

The advantage of this method is that the provision of four reasonable options will ensure effective discrimination. The disadvantage is that it is rather wasteful of pictures. A method which experience suggests is just as effective at this level and much more economical in its use of pictures is to use six questions set on a block of nine pictures, which should be grouped in word families and lettered in sequence. For instance, a group based on transport might be set out as follows:

Question 1 would be: 'Indiquez l'avion'. Pupils would be expected to indicate letter 'H' on an answer sheet.

Another technique which is economical of pictures is to say four things about one picture. This could be a simple test based on nouns or verbs.

EXAMPLE

After hearing a suitable instruction, framed in English for the sake of clarity, pupils should first hear and then work an example. The text for the above picture might read:

'Numéro un—A Il se lève.
B Il se lave.
C Il marche.
D Il court.'

Clear instructions are absolutely vital in this type of test and although the techniques are straightforward pupils tend to panic, particularly in an examination, if they are the least bit uncertain as to how to tackle a new and possibly unfamiliar type of question. It is, therefore, worth going into some detail in order to avoid possible confusion. An instruction for the six questions on nine pictures could read:

'Look at page 1 of the pictures. You are going to hear a number of sentences. Each sentence refers to one of the pictures. Decide which picture is referred to and then ring the appropriate letter on your answer sheet. Here is an example:

Numéro un—Indiquez le train. (Repeated)

The correct answer is "D" so you would ring that letter on your answer sheet:

A B C ⒟ E F G H I

Now try this example for yourself.

Numéro deux—Indiquez le taxi. (Repeated)

You should have ringed letter "F".

If you wish to change an answer, cross out your first choice clearly and ring the correct letter. Each sentence is repeated. Note your answer after the second reading. If you have any questions ask them now. There must be no interruptions once the test has begun.'

The text of the test would then be read out or played back on the tape-recorder and would run as follows:

'Numéro un:      Indiquez la moto.
Numéro un:      Indiquez la moto.
Numéro deux:   etc.'

A 5-second gap after the second reading of each question allows sufficient time for pupils to answer.

*Part 2—Appropriate rejoinder questions*

Of the multiple-choice techniques in common use, this particular one is recommended for the following reasons:

(1) It is extremely flexible and well suited to testing common idioms and structures.

(2) Unlike the Who? and Where? items, it is not restricted to a fairly small linguistic area.

(3) Of the different types of multiple-choice item, it is among the easiest to write.

(4) This particular technique has been shown to discriminate as well if not better than most others in tests of aural comprehension.

(5) The four suggested answers, or options are deliberately kept short and do not have to be written down in some kind of pupil's booklet. This cuts out any element of reading comprehension, which could well be inappropriate for children who have only studied a foreign language for one year.

*The form of the item*   An appropriate rejoinder item takes the form of a question, to which four answers are suggested, only one of which is correct, the remaining three being fairly plausible but clearly incorrect.

*Example*

Où vas-tu demain, Jean?
   A Oui, demain.
   B Avec Marie.
   C En ville.
   D Par le train.

The points to note in the construction of this type of item are:

(1) The correct answer, C, can only be arrived at by complete understanding of the stem and the option.

(2) Each of the other options is plausible to a pupil who misunderstands or partially understands the question. For instance, 'Demain' will attract less able pupils, who will remember hearing the word in the stem. In option B, 'Où' will be confused with the English word 'Who', by weaker pupils. In D, there is a link between 'train' and 'vas' which is plausible if the whole question has not been fully understood.

(3) The questions and options are kept as brief as possible in order to avoid placing too great a strain on the pupils' memory.

(4) The correct answers are distributed randomly so that the same letter is not used all the time to indicate the key.

Experience with the SCMLP Tests suggests that children of 12–13 years of age can cope with up to 20 questions of this type, in one session, without undue strain.

*Part 3—True/False statements based on dialogues or on pictures*

The important thing to remember about this type of question is that the terms 'True' and 'False' are always related to a context, in this instance a linguistic context or a visual context. The pupil must always be presented with information which either supports or contradicts the statement on which he has to pass judgment. Here are some examples:

*First example—based on a dialogue*

—Je te vois à sept heures ce soir, Marcel, devant le cinéma Rex? Le film commence à sept heures vingt.
—Non, non, Pierre. L'autobus n'arrive en ville qu'à sept heures dix.
—Alors, à sept heures et quart.
—Oui, d'accord.

1 Pierre va au cinéma avec Marcel.
2 Marcel va arriver en ville à sept heures.
3 Il va venir en autobus.
4 Il va voir Pierre derrière le cinéma.
5 Il va voir son ami à sept heures dix.

*Second example—based on a picture*

1 Le monsieur prend une tasse de café.
2 Il est très vieux.
3 Il porte une chemise noire.
4 Sa cravate est noire.
5 Il écoute la radio.
6 Il mange un oeuf.

Points to note in the construction of these types of item are as follows:

(1) The True/False statements are kept as brief as possible, thus avoiding the need to write them down in some form of answer booklet for pupils to read as they listen. Reading comprehension and memory are not intended to play too great a part in the production of the correct answer. Where dialogues or narratives are tested, emphasis should be laid on comprehension of the text, not of the statements made about it.

(2) When statements are based on some text, they should be made in

chronological order according to that text and care should be taken that one statement does not contain information which permits pupils to work out the answer to another.

(3) All the material should be repeated, using the sequence: Text plus statements, text plus statements.
To sum up, the following break-down of questions is suggested:

*Part 1.*
4 blocks of 9 pictures, with 6 questions per block making a total of 24 questions.
6 multiple-choice questions of the type 'four statements on one picture'.

*Part 2.*
10 appropriate rejoinder items.

*Part 3.*
4–6 short dialogues or narratives (60–100 words each) with 6–10 True/False statements on each.
This would give:

    Part 1—30 questions
    Part 2—10 questions
    Part 3—40 questions
    Total —80.

Allowing for repeats, the whole test should last for about 40–45 minutes and for this reason it would be best to run it in two sessions, with a break of five minutes between.

If we look now at the techniques suitable for testing a mixed ability group after the fifth year of an audio-visual language course, there are two points to keep in mind, namely the limitations of the use of pictures and also of True/False statements.

The problem with pictures is that they inevitably limit the language tested to items which can be portrayed visually. It is likely that after five years' study pupils will be able to understand language which is too complex to be assessed purely by visual means. This is not to say that pictures have no place in language testing at this level. In Speaking and Writing—the productive skills—pictures have an invaluable role, both as a stimulus and as a control. However, in testing comprehension, it seems likely that they are less useful at this level because the complexity of the language inevitably means that the pictures themselves become more complex. This in turn means that we are faced with a 'mixed skill' situation, with the difference that the two skills are not both linguistic. Aural comprehension is one of them, but the other is the ability to interpret the picture, in purely visual terms.

As for True/False statements, although suitable for use at an early stage of language learning, they are less suitable in the later stages. Their chief disadvantage is that in order to set a sufficiently large number of questions upon a given text, every detail has to be tested, or else an inconveniently large number of texts have to be chosen. Experience is limited in this field but it seems likely that True/False may yet be suitable for less able pupils, even at the age of sixteen and after five years' study of a language. However, for potential GCE pupils the technique is probably unsuitable, for the two reasons quoted.

The test is again divided into three sections and a balance is maintained of long and short items.

*Part 1*

A combination of Who?, Where? and What? items, examples of which are given below.

*Part 2*

Appropriate rejoinder items.

*Part 3*

Three dialogues or narratives, of 50, 100 and 150 words respectively, tested either by open-ended questions in English, or possibly by multiple-choice questions in French or in English.

Parts 1 and 2 would contain 10 questions each and Part 3, 12 to 15 questions in all. As with the earlier test, it could run in two sessions, each lasting about 20 minutes. Points about the construction of the different types of question are given below.

*Who?, Where? and What? items*

These should all be written around common everyday situations and the different techniques introduced with an example and a simple, clear instruction. For example:

'You are about to hear a series of short conversations. After each one you are to indicate who you think is speaking, by choosing one of the four answers suggested.

—Écoutez. Qui parle?
—Bonjour, madame. Vous désirez?
—Deux truites, s'il vous plaît. Et est-ce que vous vendez de l'huile?
—Non, madame, mais si vous allez chez l'épicier en face du commissariat, vous en trouverez.

A Un pêcheur et une touriste.
B Un marchand de poissons et sa cliente.
C Un agent de police et une touriste.
D Un épicier et sa cliente.

The correct answer is B, and you should have ringed that letter on your answer sheet. If you have any questions, ask now. There must be no interruptions once the test has begun. The rest of this section is spoken in French.

—Écoutez. Qui parle?'

Although the instructions may seem to go into great detail, it is worth taking that extra amount of care to ensure that no child is penalized through failing to realize precisely how he has to answer the question. As with the appropriate rejoinder item quoted in the first test, care has to be taken with the distractors. It would be pointless for them simply to consist of a miscellaneous selection of professions. There is a deliberate link between each distractor and a part of the text, which is either more or less plausible to pupils who misunderstand or only partially understand the text.

In answering a Where? item, the pupils are given the question 'Où se trouve la personne (ou les personnes) qui parle?' together with an appropriate instruction.

A typical example might run as follows:

—Passe-moi la serviette, Charles.
—La voici.
—Merci. La mer est trop froide pour moi, ce matin. Je veux me rhabiller, et ensuite nous irons prendre quelque chose au café.

A Sur la plage.
B Dans la mer.
C A l'hôtel.
D Dans un café.

An interesting point emerges in the construction of this particular item, which is, however, applicable to item-writing in general. It would have been wrong from the point of view of technique to begin option C with 'Dans', because this would have then drawn attention to the first option as being the only one beginning with 'Sur'. Although A is the correct answer, had it been allowed to stand out in this way, many pupils would choose it for the wrong reasons. It would also almost certainly have been wrong to use as a distractor, 'Au café', since these are the last two words of the text and would distract very heavily.

Coincidentally the same text could be used in a What? item, in which pupils are asked the question 'Que fait la personne (ou les personnes) qui parle?' The options would then read:

A Il s'essuie.
B Il se lave.
C Il mange quelque chose.
D Il boit du café.

The main point to note in the construction of this type of item is that the text must either be spoken almost entirely by one person, as in the example, or be spoken by two people who are both involved in the activity concerned.

*Appropriate rejoinder items*

These would take exactly the same form as in the earlier test, with the obvious difference that the language level would be more demanding.

69

*Techniques of Assessment*

For example:

—Mademoiselle, pourriez-vous me dire pourquoi le vol de Londres va arriver avec dix minutes de retard?

A Parce qu'il y a du brouillard, monsieur.
B Oui, à dix heures, monsieur.
C C'est dommage, monsieur.
D Oui, j'arrive de Londres, monsieur.

### Dialogues or narratives

The suggested techniques are open-ended questions in English and multiple-choice questions in either English or French. In order to select which is most suited to a given teaching situation, it is worth looking briefly again at the pros and cons.

### Open-ended English

They are the easiest of the three to set, but inevitably involve a subjective element in the marking. They occupy more pupil-time, because answers have to be written out.

### Multiple-choice English

They are easier to write than multiple-choice French, can be marked objectively and avoid the danger of testing Reading Comprehension. On the other hand, care has to be taken that the distractors do not hinge on the finer points of the pupils' English vocabulary and some teachers may object to the introduction of a comparatively large amount of English into a French examination.

### Multiple-choice French

These items are the hardest of items to set and are more difficult to write than the shorter multiple-choice items already mentioned since one is working to a fairly well defined context. The language of the text imposes constraints upon the item writer which are more limiting and less easy to manipulate than in the construction of the shorter items. However, properly constructed, they have all the advantages of objective items, plus the additional face-validity of being written in the language tested.

### (d) GENERAL POINTS OF TECHNIQUE

There remain one or two general points which apply to almost any aural test of a modern language.

(i) *Use the correct register.* In other words, make sure that the language tested is appropriate, in this case, for speech. A literary passage, for instance would be completely inappropriate. Dialogue is the most natural form to use since spoken language consists largely of conversation. Monologues are appropriate only in the form of short factual utterances, such as station announcements, newscasts or in accounts of personal experiences.

(ii) *Use a variety of material and techniques.* Five texts of 50 words will discriminate between the more able and the less able pupils more effectively than one text of 250, because the five can cover different topic areas and be of different levels of difficulty. Moreover, they will avoid the problem of a pupil being unable to understand a vital key-word and so failing to do himself justice in the test as a whole.

(iii) *Use of visual material.* Where pupils cannot read or write the foreign language, the teacher must make intelligent use of pictures. These should not be elaborate and above all should illustrate clearly the linguistic point being tested. If duplication of pictures is a problem, then flash-cards or slides for an overhead projector might be used as alternatives. Out-of-date mail-order catalogues or a sympathetic Art department can be very useful sources of supply.

(iv) *Record the test.* Unless you happen to be bilingual, have the test recorded by a native speaker or speakers whose enunciation is clear. You may have to make one or two trial runs before you achieve an acceptable recording, but it is well worth the effort. The language used will sound more natural and authentic and by using a recording the teacher is left free to concentrate on administering the test.

(v) *Repeat the material.* Whether you record the test or read it aloud, always repeat the material. If, in a real-life situation, a pupil mishears something, he can always ask for it to be repeated. One would not wish his performance in a test to be affected simply because his neighbour blows his nose at an inopportune moment. Providing a second chance reduces the danger of unforeseen interruptions affecting performance and makes it more certain that where errors occur, this is due to failure to comprehend.

(vi) *Share the work.* If at all possible, where multiple-choice items are to be used, it is best to share the work out amongst two or three teachers, who should write items and review each other's work. Simple item analyses can be carried out with the aid of tables such as those produced by Nuttall and Skurnik (see 'Suggestions for Further Reading'), which were specifically designed for this purpose, and items can then be banked for future use.

## Aural tests of Music

The principles outlined at the beginning of the chapter remain the same. Define before you assess, and assess only that which you have defined.

The aim may be couched in fairly broad terms such as the recognition of differences of pitch and rhythm, of different instruments and voices, or even of excerpts from certain works. On the other hand, it helps to be more specific. For example in the 1974 Music syllabus of the Yorkshire Regional Examinations Board* we find:

* Reproduced by permission of the Yorkshire Regional Examinations Board.

Candidates may be required:
(a) to recognize the sound of instruments or voices heard alone or in ensemble;
(b) to recognize 'traditional' (Dixie-land), 'main stream' and 'modern' jazz;
(c) to recognize styles of various periods; classical, romantic and modern;
(d) to recognize which of the following is being performed: solo concerto, symphony, chamber music;
(e) to recognize the following dance forms: minuet, gigue, gavotte; and the following vocal forms: chorale, madrigal, aria;
(f) to recognize whether a rhythm is duple or triple;
(g) to recognize whether music is in the major or in the minor mode.

The simplest way to test recognition in this field is to prepare a tape. Provided excerpts from gramophone records are of less than 30 seconds' duration and the material recorded is used only for the test, there should be no problem of infringement of copyright. Pupils can then be asked factual questions about what they hear, writing their answers on an answer sheet. The questions should also be recorded, so that the sequence is: question, musical extract, pause for answering and so on. Care must be taken with the questions so that no ambiguities exist. Where groups of items are being tested, for example in (b), the same question can be repeated. For a question on jazz the recording 'script' might run:

*Question 2*
You will now hear four pieces of jazz. State on your answer sheet whether the jazz you hear is traditional, main stream or modern.
(a) Is this traditional, main stream or modern jazz? (Musical extract)
(b) .........
and so on.

One point to remember is that where there are three elements in the group tested, at least four questions should be set, where there are two elements, at least three and so on. If only three questions are asked about three different types of music, some pupils may answer the last question by a process of elimination. By deliberately setting more questions than there are 'elements' and by stating this at the beginning of the section, this problem is avoided.

The extracts selected must be clear, unequivocal examples of the type of music being tested, and should not be works with which the pupils are known to be familiar.

## Oral tests of Modern Languages

(a) THE DEFINITION

Inevitably oral and aural skills overlap since the ability to hold a conversation presupposes the ability to understand what the other person is saying! Nevertheless it is worth trying to specify two broad areas, *viz*:

the ability to answer questions, using certain structures and covering certain topic areas;

the ability to ask questions and obtain information.

Within these it is possible to define sub-divisions which are useful when making the actual assessment. The chief ones are:

fluency;

pronunciation and intonation;

use of vocabulary and idiom;

command of structure.

(b) THE TECHNIQUES

| Technique | User |
|---|---|
| Reading aloud | 7 GCE boards, 12 CSE boards, ETS |
| Prepared questions | 2 GCE boards, 1 CSE board |
| Conversation on prepared topics | 3 GCE boards, 4 CSE boards |
| General Conversation | 8 GCE boards, 11 CSE boards |
| General questions | 7 CSE boards, Pimsleur |
| *Narration of story based on picture sequence | 1 GCE board, 4 CSE boards, SCMLP, ETS |
| *Role playing | 2 CSE boards, SCMLP |
| Questions based on pictures | 8 CSE boards, SCMLP, ETS, Pimsleur |

*These techniques have also been used with the special Ordinary level examinations worked by pupils using the Schools Council Modern Language Materials.

### Reading aloud

As a test, this is of doubtful value since it involves a special skill which for practical purposes is virtually useless. Undoubtedly, reading aloud can be assessed as reliably, indeed perhaps more reliably, than general conversation. However, it is quite noticeable that pupils who read poorly do not always have poor accents, so that the ability to read aloud with the appropriate inflections and histrionic nuances is not always a reliable guide to a pupil's pronunciation.

### Prepared questions

The advantage for the pupil is that he knows what is coming to him in the oral test. The disadvantage is that pupils can be trained to respond like parrots. Weaker pupils may not even understand the answers they give. Abler pupils will find the technique too easy and it will not discriminate adequately amongst them.

### Conversation on a prepared topic

To some extent this has the same disadvantage as the pre-learnt questions, in that weaker pupils can learn off a set text by heart and simply regurgitate it parrot fashion, in the test. However, it is more demanding than the pre-learnt questions, and will discriminate better if pupils are allowed to develop their ideas in some form of spontaneous conversation.

## General conversation

The great advantage of this technique is that if the conversation is conducted properly, it can be adjusted to the level of ability of the individual pupil. Its disadvantage is that it demands considerable skill on the part of the interviewer to keep a pupil at his ease and talking. At the same time he must vary the questions constantly to permit the able pupil to show his knowledge of different structures and to prevent the weaker pupils from lapsing into the all too familiar periods of excruciating silence.

## General questions

Provided care is taken over the construction of the questions, this can be a very suitable technique for testing basic structures.

## Narration of story based on picture sequence

This is a demanding test, in which the pupil is given about 5 minutes to prepare the narration of a story told by pictures. Great care has to be taken with the pictures, in order to ensure that they are clear. The pupil is placed in a situation where he is forced to create language spontaneously, but at the same time the picture provides a control over the language so that all pupils are given the same task, which assists the marking considerably. The examiner's role is to say as little as possible, just to introduce the odd leading question or remark to prevent any awkward gaps in the pupil's narrative.

## Role-playing

This technique is explained on pages 75 and 76. Its chief advantage is that it tests a different and vital area from the other techniques, namely the ability of the pupils to initiate language in a real life situation, by asking questions in order to obtain information. Teachers find this a valuable teaching technique and pupils enjoy it because they can appreciate its relevance in language learning. The difficulty lies in the conduct of the test, since the teacher's role in it is fundamental and may well affect the pupil's performance. Careful preparation by the teacher of both questions and answers is therefore essential.

## Questions on pictures

Pictures are always a good stimulus for conversation, and if they are carefully drawn can provide, in addition, a useful means of controlling the language produced, so that pupils are set tasks of parallel difficulty. It is a good idea to begin an oral test with a few simple questions on pictures, just to get the pupil talking and give him confidence. The easier the question, the better, to start with. The harder questions can follow!

(c) CONSTRUCTION OF THE TEST

As in the case of the aural test, it is assumed that the teacher knows what he wants to test, i.e. which structures and which topic areas, and that he will make out a detailed grid so that he can ensure that they are covered.

In oral testing, there is an additional limiting factor, and that is time—the time it takes to give every pupil an individual examination. Usually, with a class of thirty children it is impossible to allow more than 10 minutes per candidate, which inevitably restricts the number and type of questions to be asked. Much depends on whether the main aim of the test is diagnostic—finding out what structures have been mastered—or achievement, i.e. producing an order of merit. If the aim is purely diagnostic it might be possible to split the class into say three groups carefully matched for ability and give each group a thorough test of different structures. Taking the group performance as being representative of the whole class it would be possible to cover the syllabus fairly widely. In an achievement test ideally the whole class should perform the same tasks, answering either the same questions or alternatively, sets of questions which have been carefully balanced to ensure as far as possible that all sets are of equal difficulty.

Let us assume a class of pupils who have completed five years' study and that the test is an end-of-year achievement test.

The techniques will look at the following aspects of speaking.

| *Technique* | *Testing aim* |
| --- | --- |
| (1) Role-playing situations | To test ability to ask questions and initiate language exchange. |
| (2) Questions on pictures | To test basic structures. |
| (3) Brief conversation | To test genuine conversational ability. |

(1) *Role-playing situations*

As has been said already, the idea behind this technique is to place the pupil in a real life situation in which he has to ask questions in order to 'survive'. He may be in the street, asking the way, in a shop buying food or at a railway station asking about train times. He should be able to seek out basic information such as distance, prices, times etc.

The testing technique may appear a little artificial, and it does demand that the teacher has to play an active part in the test, assuming say the role of a shop-keeper, ticket-collector or passer-by. Experience suggests that these disadvantages are more than off-set by the enthusiasm with which most pupils tackle this type of activity and the conviction shared by teachers who have tried it out that in language-learning terms 'role-playing' is something that requires to be carefully taught but which is well worth the effort.

In a typical role-playing test the pupil is given a card with some instructions in English and is allowed two minutes to prepare. The card might read as follows:

You are at the Gare St Lazare in Paris. Your teacher is a railway official.
(a) Ask for a return ticket to Lyon.
  (He gives you the ticket)
(b) You pay for the ticket, explaining that you only have a 100 franc note.
  (He gives you change)
(c) Ask what time the 10 o'clock train from St Lazare arrives in Lyon.
  (He tells you and you thank him.)

For the sake of clarity, it is essential to give the instructions in English. However, it is equally vital for the teacher to begin the test in simple French, creating a language 'bridge'. For instance the teacher might begin the above example as follows:

Eh bien, Pierre, nous sommes à la gare St Lazare. Vous êtes un passager et moi, je suis l'employé des chemins de fer.
—Vous désirez, monsieur?

This helps the nervous pupil and encourages him to think in French from the outset.


## (2) *Questions on pictures*

The technique is fairly self-evident. The important thing is to have a good selection of straightforward pictures, portraying a strong, unequivocal image. It is better to ask one or two questions about each of five pictures than to ask ten questions about one picture, since in order to provide the answers to ten questions, a single picture would have to be rather large or complicated or both. It might then easily create visual problems for the pupil rather than linguistic ones. It is a good idea to carry out a simple pre-test of the pictures to be used, simply by asking a colleague or another pupil the appropriate questions, in English, to see if the pictures suggest the answers that you would expect from candidates for the test.

The other important criterion in selecting pictures is that collectively they must permit the sampling of different structures. With a little care it is quite possible to test different question forms:

que? quand? où? qui? pourquoi? combien?

and also to sample a variety of tenses besides the present.

It is also possible to vary the question forms by asking a supplementary question about each picture, using the second person.

Consider the following:

(a) Ce monsieur, qu'est-ce qu'il va faire?
(b) Et toi, comment es-tu venu à l'école
    ce matin?

(a) Ce garçon, qu'est-ce qu'il a fait?
(b) Et toi, si tu casses une fênetre, qu'est-ce que
    tu fais?

A more demanding pair of questions for this picture
would be:

(a) Ce garçon, il a cassé la fenetre, n'est-ce pas?
    Qu'est-ce qu'il faisait probablement avant de
    casser la fenêtre?
(b) Et toi, si tu cassais une fênetre, qu'est-ce que
    tu ferais?

The main problem with pictures is that they normally have a strong
connotation of the present time for most pupils. Unless, therefore, the
teacher has access to a good supply of carefully drawn pictures he is better
advised to keep to the present tense in this section of the test and concentrate on different question forms.

(3) *General conversation*

The aim here is not just to talk. Properly conducted this is easily the
most difficult part of the test for the teacher. He has to try to allow the
candidate to follow his own interests but at the same time has to make sure
that the pupil is continually being extended to reveal his control, or otherwise, of a variety of structures. The examiner has to be extremely sensitive
to every response the pupil makes and carefully lead him on to more
demanding linguistic areas without forcing the pace too much yet without
giving away too much in the way of key-words and structures.

Preparedness, as always, is the watchword and it is a good idea to have to
hand a prepared list of half-a-dozen questions of varying degrees of difficulty, for each topic area, which can be used as the occasion demands.

For instance talking of holidays the following set of questions might be
useful.

Où vas-tu passer les vacances cette année?
Tu aimes la mer? Qu'est-ce que tu aimes faire là?
Pourquoi préfères-tu la mer à la campagne?
Si tu avais dix mille francs, où irais-tu passer les vacances? Que ferais-tu?
Est-ce que beaucoup de touristes français sont allés à Londres l'année
dernière? Pourquoi?

It is far safer to have a set of questions to use as a framework for the oral.
In this way one can ensure a proper degree of control without having to
invent too many questions on the spur of the moment.

(d) CONDUCT OF THE TEST

Let us assume that the test will consist of three sections:
(1) 2 role-playing situations                                    (2 minutes)
(2) 10 questions based on pictures                               (4 minutes)

77

(3) Conversation on an everyday topic such as school/
holidays.                                                                            (4 minutes)

Ten minutes approximately should be allowed for each pupil to work the test. In addition, pupils will need about 2–3 minutes' preparation time for the role-playing situations. The usual order for events is for the first pupil to prepare the roles, then he starts his test. At the same time the second pupil starts to prepare his two roles. Pupil number 2 is then examined whilst pupil number 3 prepares and so on.

## The examiner's role

The main point to bear in mind is that the object of the exercise is to get the pupil to speak. The examiner has as far as possible to keep in the background. He has to keep the test flowing along, trying to smooth out awkward gaps if they occur, tailoring his language to meet the situation, but taking care that in an effort to help pupils produce the required language he doesn't inadvertently give away too much, thereby invalidating the test.

There are therefore a few simple rules.

(1) *Put the pupil at his ease.* That means smile at him, even if you are feeling more nervous than he is! If you are recording the test, keep the tape-recorder out of sight, on a chair or on the floor—only the microphone need be visible.

(2) *Conduct the test in simple French.* Encourage pupils to think in French by using the language as much as possible. Only if there is a danger of a total breakdown in communication should you use English.

(3) *Do not mark and test at the same time.* It is impossible to assess a pupil fairly and accurately when one is trying to administer the test. This is particularly true of a more sophisticated technique such as role-playing, where the teacher's responses are of vital importance to the proper conduct of the test. There are two possibilities, therefore: one is to record the test and mark the recording, the other is to have two examiners present, one to conduct the test and one to assess.

(4) *Be prepared.* Have a written note of all the answers you expect for Parts 1 and 2, and have a written list of basic questions for each of the topic areas you wish to cover in Part 3.

### (e) MARKING THE TEST

There are broadly speaking two approaches to marking oral work, a detailed structured scheme and an impression mark. The detailed scheme is less subjective and more inflexible, and is particularly useful when a group of teachers or examiners wish to ensure that they are all marking to the same standard. An impression scheme is more subjective and therefore more flexible. If it is used sensibly it can be as reliable as a detailed scheme.

The mark schemes suggested for the Specimen Oral Test are as follows:

Part 1. *Role Playing*
> Structured or impression.

Part 2. *Questions on pictures*
> Structured.

Part 3. *Conversation.*
> Impression.

*Part 1—Structured scheme*

Assuming that we are dealing with the specimen role, the pupil's answers to (a) could be marked on a 3, 2, 1, 0 scale as follows:

| | |
|---|---|
| Correct, fluent response | 3 |
| Response with one major error (e.g. in the verb) or marred by excessive hesitation. | 2 |
| Response with more than 1 major error and/or excessive hesitation | 1 |
| Completely unsuitable response. | 0 |

For example:

| | |
|---|---|
| Un billet, aller et retour, pour Lyon s'il vous plaît. | 3 |
| Un billet à Lyon, aller et retour. | 2 |
| Pour Lyon. | 1 |

This scheme gives a total of nine marks per role and therefore eighteen for Part 1.

Its defect is that it weights grammatical accuracy rather heavily. Another method would be to consider each role *in toto* and mark in categories, 0–4, on an impression basis. The following categories could be used:

Pronunciation.
Fluency.
Accuracy of communication.
Accuracy of language.

The definitions of the points on the scale are:

4. Well above average for the group.
3. Above average.
2. Average.
1. Below average.
0. Well below average.

Important points to remember are:
(1) Marks are given by limiting comparisons to that of the group as a whole and not to some abstract, indefinable concept of 'excellence'.
(2) All the points in the scale should be used. '4' is not perfection, nor is

'o' abysmal failure. The advantage of using 0–4 instead of say 1–5 is that the average mark is 50% of the total, whereas 3/5 represents 60%, and may possibly have an adverse effect on the overall mark-weighting.

*Part 2.*

The structured scheme would be virtually identical to the structured scheme for Part 1.

*Part 3.*

The categories for this impression scheme would be:
Pronunciation.
Fluency.
Use of vocabulary and idiom.
Accuracy.
Ability to communicate ideas.

## Oral tests of English

It is assumed in the following remarks that the pupils concerned have English as their mother tongue and that for this reason the approach to testing their command of spoken English differs from that outlined in Section 1 of Oral Assessment. Clearly where English is the second language, much, if not all, of what has been said already about Modern Languages will still apply.

(a) THE DEFINITION

A definition of aims in English presents problems, since it is not usually relevant to relate them to a list of specific structures or even topics. The aim is to assess the pupil's ability to communicate orally, taking into account his range of vocabulary and idiom, and the lucidity with which he expresses his thoughts. It would normally include the ability to answer questions and to deliver a short speech, lasting 2–3 minutes.

(b) THE TECHNIQUES
*Reading aloud a prose or verse passage*

This is a fairly simple test to set and administer. It is possible to mark the pupil's pronunciation and intonation, though both will be affected by his ability to interpret and comprehend the text he reads. It can be criticized on the grounds that in itself it is an activity which is largely irrelevant to the pupil's needs and everyday experience.

*Conversation on a prepared topic*

Assuming that the pupil has chosen and prepared the topic well in advance, this has the advantage that it is geared to the pupil's own interest. Its disadvantage lies in that, as with a foreign language, there is a tendency for pupils to learn a piece by heart and reproduce it parrot-fashion. Moreover, the teacher needs to be warned beforehand of the nature of the topic, so that he has time to prepare a suitable range of questions.

### Conversation on an 'unprepared' topic

Here the teacher has a selection of half a dozen topics and offers the pupil a choice of two. The pupil is then given 5 minutes to prepare a brief talk, and then the teacher can ask questions. The advantage to the teacher is that he has a smaller number of topics to handle. It is therefore easier to frame a balanced range of questions and he himself can decide whether or not a topic is suitable, for assessment purposes. Clearly, it can be argued that by restricting the pupil's choice, one is perhaps reducing his motivation, but against that argument one can point out that the greater the choice of topic and therefore of question, the less reliable the test. Some topics are intrinsically more difficult than others and it is well-nigh impossible for the teacher to make appropriate allowances for these difficulties when he has to award a mark. In the long run it is fairer to the pupils to restrict the choice.

### Conduct of the test

It is assumed that the test consists of a talk on a topic 'prepared' or 'unprepared'. Much of what has already been said about oral testing of foreign languages is very relevant. For the pupil the test is a confrontation. The examiner's prime responsibility is to put the pupil at his ease, and encourage him to talk.

It is a good idea to ask one or two simple questions at the outset to break the ice and then lead the pupil on to his topic. For the rest, there are a few simple 'do's' and 'don'ts'.

Do *not* fire a string of questions right from the outset. Once the pupil has launched into his topic, give him his head for two or three minutes.

If, however, there is a gap in the conversation, plug it with a simple observation or a prompting question, simply to enable the pupil to collect his thoughts.

Once the pupil has spoken long enough to enable you to assess his ability to express his thoughts, and has given you some idea of his range of vocabulary and structure, move on to the second part of the test, the ability to respond to questions and maintain an intelligent conversation. Here, one must remember that the examiner is not merely holding a conversation. His task is to probe and assess. Questions must be carefully selected, and tailored to meet the ability of the candidate. One has to be prepared to ask searching questions to allow the more able candidate to develop his thoughts and yet be ready to switch the type of question if a pupil is clearly becoming confused or is perhaps unable to answer because he does not know the facts. As with the foreign language 'conversation' it is best to have a written list of questions, pitched at varying degrees of difficulty. This enables the examiner to control to some extent the language produced, to present all pupils with a task of similar difficulty and avoids the problem of having to invent questions on the spur of the moment.

*Marking the test*

The skills involved are so complex, that a detailed structured marking scheme would be self-defeating. It is best to keep in mind the general principles behind the assessment, that one is assessing communication (i.e. not accent), and bearing in mind lucidity of thought, range of vocabulary, the ability to respond to questions and maintain a flow of intelligent conversation. Marking would then be done by impression on a scale of 1–10.

As with all impression schemes, it is important to use all points on the scale, and to remember that '10' does not represent perfection, but the highest level attained by individual pupils within a group. Similarly 1 represents the lowest level within the group. Because an impression scheme is used exclusively, it is best to double mark even a class test. If more than one class and teacher are involved, then double-marking is essential to ensure comparability of results.

## Conclusion

An attempt has been made in this chapter to point to the principles of testing and relate them to the assessment of aural and oral skills. Throughout the emphasis has been placed on definition and control. Without definition, assessment is impossible; without control, it is unreliable. Definition and control are not, however, intended to be restrictive influences upon the teaching. The definition of aims should be the first step in devising any teaching programme, for unless it is taken, how can one hope to assess progress or achievement? Control is necessary for the construction of a satisfactory test. It can be achieved by closely structuring the pupils' responses or by some form of multiple-marking. One thing above all stands out, namely that although testing should be regarded as a necessary complement to teaching, the same techniques can rarely be used for both. The tendency in the past has been for an examination to consist of a few teaching techniques linked together in the hope that their use will provide a suitable order of merit. In fact as much thought and attention to detail must be devoted to the construction of a test as to teaching the programme which it is designed to assess.

# 6 The Assessment of Practical Work

## R. J. Whittaker

One of the most interesting features of teaching in English schools has been the tradition of practical work carried out by individual pupils; this characteristic has been particularly evident in respect of the teaching of science subjects; practical work has been seen to constitute an important element in the teaching/learning process and the development of practical skills has been established as an important desirable outcome of courses in many subjects. This chapter is concerned with a discussion of the ways in which practical work can be assessed but before the techniques can be considered it is necessary to relate the assessment of practical work to the general context of subject-based examinations.

Although this chapter is included in that part of the book which deals predominantly with techniques, the reader will find that much of its content is devoted to a consideration of certain problems and the discussion of certain principles. The first part of the chapter is concerned with a discussion of the nature of practical work, its place within the context of individual subjects and the factors which should be taken into consideration when devising methods of assessment. The later sections of the chapter are concerned with a discussion of a variety of assessment techniques or instruments which might be used in the assessment of practical work.

## Why assess practical work?

In the Introduction to this book, assessment has been placed in its educational context. In considering the methods to be used in assessing practical work it is first necessary to establish the place which practical work has in a particular subject and the purpose of its assessment.

It is important to appreciate that the purpose of practical work varies from subject to subject and that there can be a variety of purposes within an individual subject. For instance, some practical work will be carried out in a teaching course with the purpose of introducing, developing or reinforcing theoretical concepts; such work might be regarded as being of importance in the teaching/learning process but as being relatively unimportant in terms of the skills whose development is a major objective of the course. Examples of such work can be found in many of the 'learning by discovery' situations which have been so enthusiastically developed in recent years. Practical work in the form of personal studies or 'projects' can also be included in this category. Their inclusion in any course of study can, for example, provide opportunities to develop student understanding of particular aspects of the subject as well as permitting the demonstration of those practical skills necessary to undertake the work. Other work will form part of a course because the practical skills developed and demonstrated by that work are regarded as being important attributes whose acquisition should form major objectives of the course.

Some subjects are often described as being 'practical subjects', for instance, Art, craft subjects as for example Needlework and Dressmaking, Cookery, Woodwork and Metalwork. This description usually indicates that one of the major educational objectives of the course of study is the acquisition and development of certain practical skills. The term is also used in connection with subjects which are felt to be founded on a practical base, for instance, science subjects such as Physics, Chemistry and Biology; in these subjects practical work is of importance in establishing and illustrating the theoretical aspects of the subject as well as developing necessary and desirable skills which all students of the subject should be required to possess.

Because practical work of some sort is undertaken by pupils as part of their course, it is not an automatic requirement that it should be assessed. If practical work is to be assessed, then the assessment should be concerned with measuring those skills and abilities which have been established as being important and ones which the courses concerned aim to develop. Practical work is assessed because it is important to the particular subject and because it would be unrealistic to provide for a pupil any form of certification of ability or achievement in the subject without including its assessment.

## What is practical work?

This question is raised and discussed here because it is considered to be central to the development of suitable measurement instruments. If what is to be measured is not satisfactorily identified, it is unlikely that the assessment will be successful.

Practical work is often regarded as being the *doing* activities rather than the *knowing* qualities of pupils, but it is not as simple as this. It is as varied as are those purposes of practical work mentioned earlier. The integration of practical work with the factual and theoretical basis of a subject and the development of courses involving open-ended practical investigations rather than routine practical operations, result in a blurring of the distinctions between practical and theoretical work. Much practical work involves the application of knowledge, the use of theoretical concepts and the theoretical evaluation of the results obtained by the practical experience. All such interrelationships between practice and theory raise problems for effective assessment. The author does not intend to suggest that the assessment procedures should be so designed as to eliminate overlap between theory and practice; any attempt to do this would seriously distort the educational process and would deny the essential relationships between practical work and other aspects of the pupil's knowledge and understanding of the subject. What is suggested rather, is that all such interrelationships should be acknowledged and taken into account in the assessment procedures.

It is interesting and possibly significant that the main weight of effort in test development in recent years has been directed towards the establishment of principles for the planning of written tests and to the construction and refinement of questions for such tests (see Chapters 1, 2 and 3). Practical tests and practical questions have attracted far less attention. The work of Bloom, Ebel, Gagné and others in the field of educational measurement, has had great influence on the design of 'purposeful' examinations in which the objectives of the examining process have been clearly defined and the assessment techniques have been designed to achieve those objectives but such work has had its effect mainly in the area of written examinations. Some classifications of the objectives of practical work are beginning to appear. As these are developed further and become more widely appreciated, it should be possible to perceive more clearly what is generally understood by practical work in terms of the educational outcomes of such work and thus set down systematically the objectives of practical assessment.

The specification of the objectives of the assessment is the most crucial exercise in the development of any assessment procedure. Other aspects of a scheme of assessment may appear to be more complicated or may be superficially more difficult to produce but the specification forms the key. It is from the specification that the operational divisions against which the pupil's work is to be measured are derived. All too often assessment schemes, internal and external, give the impression that the specification of the objectives of the assessment has been given insufficient thought and consideration.

The specification of a list of qualities which are to be tested under the heading 'practical work' must take into consideration the effects which the specification is likely to have upon the teaching of the subject. The specification must also take into account the extent to which appropriate instruments of assessment can be devised and administered to test the listed qualities. These qualities must meet the following criteria:

(a) the quality must be one which plays an important part in the work involved in the particular subject and which is relevant to the approach adopted in the teaching of the subject;

(b) the quality must be one which it is reasonable to expect pupils to develop at their particular level in relation to all the other work which they will be carrying out in the subject;

(c) the quality must be one which can be measured in a reliable way by the use of available instruments.

A survey of specifications which have been provided for examining practical work in a variety of subjects, makes it possible to identify certain qualities as providing appropriate descriptions of those aspects of practical work which should be assessed. It is not, however, suggested at this stage that these qualities or the method of specification are necessarily the best statements upon which to base an assessment procedure. Five qualities appear consistently in examination specifications and they also appear to be involved in assessment situations for which no specifications have been provided.

(a) Skill in observation and the recording of observations.

(b) Ability to assess and interpret the results of practical work.

(c) Ability to plan practical procedures and techniques for solving particular problems.

(d) Manipulative skills.

(e) Attitudes towards practical work, including such attributes as persistence, enthusiasm, originality and enjoyment.

The terminology used throughout this chapter is most frequently associated with science subjects but the principles which are discussed are relevant to practical assessment in all subjects. Not all these qualities are included in all existing specifications, nor are they always presented in the same form of words. Not all these qualities can be measured by the same assessment instruments. The remaining sections of this chapter are devoted to a consideration of the procedures which can be used to measure practical work as this has been defined in this chapter. This leads on to the suggestion made at the end of the chapter that practical work presents particular problems of assessment which may make it desirable to adopt a different form of specification from that generally used and described above.

**What instruments of assessment should be used?**

This section is concerned with discussing the instruments or techniques of assessment which might be appropriate for the measurement of those qualities listed earlier as forming the operational divisions for the assessment of practical work. Each of the five qualities will be considered separately. It is hoped that the discussion will result in the emergence of some general principles and will thus make it possible to take decisions as to the most appropriate agencies for the conduct of the suggested assessment.

The success of any scheme of assessment depends upon the quality of the instruments of assessment which are used. Quality here depends upon who asks the questions as well as upon the questions that are asked. It is also dependent upon the choice of appropriate areas of work for assessment. If the instruments are faulty there is little chance that the assessment will be successful. Their suitability can, and should, be evaluated by applying the following criteria:

(a) the assessment used should measure the stated objectives validly and reliably;*

(b) the application of the assessment should not make unreasonable demands upon the available resources such as administration, manpower, finance, time;

(c) the nature of the assessment and its application should not distort the educational process.

It is not suggested that any scheme of assessment or any particular instrument of assessment should be used only if it satisfies all the criteria specified above. If this were to be the case it would be difficult to justify the continued existence of any assessment procedures. The criteria are 'ideals' and should be striven for as such. In particular it should be appreciated that some distortion of the educational process takes place as soon as assessment in any form is introduced and that the third criteria is, therefore, always breached in some measure; what is important is that the distortion should be as insignificant and harmless as possible.

SKILL IN OBSERVATION AND THE RECORDING OF OBSERVATIONS

The purpose of the assessment here is to measure the extent to which in any given situation the pupil observes those things which should be observed and makes appropriate recordings in order that he can subsequently evaluate the results of these observations. Pupils can be presented with specific operations, either as demonstrations or as exercises to carry out themselves, and be required to make their records of what has happened. The assessment will lean heavily on the ability of the pupil to report his observations and it is inevitable that the assessment will often take the form of awarding marks for written records of observations.

If specific exercises are set to test this quality, it is important that the setter has a clear idea of what will result from them and thus of what can be observed. This is necessary because it is not always possible for the assessor to check that what the pupil reports has actually taken place. Where quantitative results are involved, tolerance limits can be set and a scheme of marking devised to take account of them.

In addition to the assessments of written reports, the laboratory situation makes it possible for oral reports by the pupil to be taken into consideration. This is an important aspect of the testing of this quality as the oral report is made simultaneously with, or immediately following, the event. The pupil's oral report of his observation will thus not be affected (or not

* For definitions of these terms see Chapters 4 and 8.

affected to the same extent as his written report) by considerations of what he felt he ought to have seen.

There will obviously be degrees of complexity involved in the observations required and their recording. In some circumstances a full account of everything which takes place might be required, in others the assessment might be concerned with the extent to which the pupil has exercised discrimination in identifying the important or relevant features of the particular situation.

THE ABILITY TO ASSESS AND INTERPRET THE RESULTS OF PRACTICAL WORK

Here the purpose of the assessment is to measure the extent to which the pupil can evaluate the results obtained by practical work. This quality involves the application of factual and theoretical knowledge to a specific situation and the use which the pupil makes of his observations and recordings.

Several levels of activity can be included under this general heading. The pupil can be required to carry out calculations, to identify unknowns, to determine particular characteristics of the material under practical investigation. The pupil could also be required to interpret the results of a particular piece of practical work in the light of other practical experiences and to relate different experiences to the particular situation with which he is faced.

Many practical examinations require the pupils to draw conclusions from practical work. This requires an explanation of the processes involved or a development of the situation, or both. It must always be appreciated that the success of the assessment here is dependent upon the extent to which the pupil has obtained the results which would lead to the correct interpretation. If the assessment is based upon a situation in which a practical exercise is undertaken, its results are tabulated and conclusions are drawn, then the pupil who fails to obtain the desired (expected) results will be unable to make the appropriate inferences. This problem becomes particularly acute if assessment of this kind is being administered externally. In such circumstances the assessor is in no position to judge the actual data upon which the interpretations were made.

It may well be that where this quality is to be measured, steps ought to be taken to eliminate the dangers of consequential errors. One way of doing this would be to present all pupils with common data. It may even be that this quality is one which should not form a major part of practical assessment since written examinations provide a situation in which it can be tested much more satisfactorily. If, however, this quality is considered to include the extent to which a pupil adopts an analytical approach to practical work and reacts to unexpected results, its assessment must be based upon which the pupil actually does under practical conditions.

ABILITY TO PLAN PRACTICAL PROCEDURES AND TECHNIQUES FOR SOLVING
PARTICULAR PROBLEMS

The purpose of the assessment here is to measure the extent to which the pupil is able to plan a procedure of practical work. The quality can be measured by presenting the pupil with a practical problem and requiring him to evolve an appropriate method of undertaking a practical study of the problem. In devising the situation with which the pupil is to be faced, it is essential to ensure that the task is within his competence. This means taking account of the likely practical and theoretical knowledge and experience of pupils at the relevant level. If the ability to plan is to be validly tested it is important that the pupil should not be presented with the design of some practical procedure which is already familiar to him. The situations used to test this quality should be such that the basic procedure is well known to the pupil but has to be adapted or modified in some way to take account of new or unfamiliar materials or apparatus. The assessment of this quality often involves the pupil in attempting to anticipate problems which are likely to arise in carrying out the procedure. This has its disadvantages since a more important quality may be the ability of the pupil to recognize the shortcomings of the procedure he is considering; this will only happen, however, when he begins to obtain practical results which he recognizes are unsatisfactory and then realizes the need to modify the procedure.

Exercises can be devised to test this quality but they need to be devised with extreme care. The pupil must be made aware of the facilities and apparatus available and the purpose of the practical work must be clearly stated to ensure that he knows exactly what he has to plan in order to achieve his end. If an exercise is to be planned which the pupil then has to carry out it is most important that the plan is evaluated by the assessor before it is put into operation so that any fundamental weaknesses can be eradicated. Unless this is done the pupil may be doubly penalized for faults in the experimental design.


MANIPULATIVE SKILLS

Here the purpose of the assessment is to measure the extent to which the pupil can carry out the range of manipulative skills which are felt to be appropriate to the particular subject at the particular level. Most practical examining assumes that the manipulative skills are being measured by exercises in which the pupil is required to perform specified operations and report results. The danger here is that the pupil's efficiency or inefficiency in the mastery of specific skills is often hidden in the overall result obtained. In an extreme case, for example, all the manipulative skills may have been correctly performed but an error in recording leads to an incorrect result which gains no marks. This is, of course, bad assessment but it can easily happen if proper care is not taken. Manipulative skills are always best assessed in situations in which the specific skill can be isolated for attention.

It is also important to decide what is the most important aspect of manipulative skills for assessment purposes; for example, to what extent should the concern be with 'results obtained' or with 'how the particular operation was carried out'. If the latter is considered to be of importance the assessment situation must be one in which the pupil's actions are actually observed by the assessor.

ATTITUDES TOWARDS PRACTICAL WORK

Here one is concerned with such things as the pupil's approach to the subject, the extent to which the practical basis of the subject is accepted by the pupil and the way in which the pupil's enthusiasm for the subject and for particular aspects of his practical work is shown by his methods of working. In terms of the educational development of the individual these are extremely important qualities and are likely to form part of the objectives of many courses of study. It would seem, therefore, desirable to assess them if one can. The whole topic of the assessment of attitudes is considered in much greater detail in Chapter 10* but in the context of practical work external measures of assessment would appear to be of doubtful value even if they can be constructed. A more useful and valid approach would seem to be through continuous observation on an impression basis. If this is done then the teacher would be the only person in a position to undertake the assessment.

The last section has drawn attention to the existence of a variety of ways in which the five suggested general qualities can be assessed. In the section which follows further consideration, albeit brief, will be given to the following approaches to the assessment of practical work:

   (i) set exercises;
  (ii) project work;
 (iii) course work;
 (iv) oral questioning;
  (v) assessment by impression.

All these approaches have, of course, a wider application to assessment in general and three of them form the subject of separate chapters (The Project Chapter 7, Course work Chapter 9, and Orals Chapter 5) while reference is made to the other two on several occasions throughout the book.

While the pages that follow will suggest that some of these approaches are more appropriate than others for specific purposes, those constructing and using assessment must always make this decision for themselves in the light of their objectives, their courses of study, their resources and their pupils.

* It is also referred to in Chapter 9.

(i) *Assessment through set exercises*

The use of set exercises for the assessment of practical work is a well-established feature of both public examinations and courses of study. While it is perhaps rather an over-simplification to suggest that its use in the latter is a direct consequence of its use in the former, it is important to recognize that the use of any particular approach to assessment has direct implications for teaching practice. At the very least teachers must ensure that their pupils have some training in the type of exercise which examinations require them to undertake.

The use of set exercises has much to commend it for assessment purposes. All pupils are presented with the same practical problem and can be required to work under similar conditions in respect of, for example, time and apparatus. The exercises can be made self-contained and given an appearance of realism which gives the pupil a sense of purpose. In order to obtain these advantages it is of course necessary to present the exercises in a form which makes this purpose clear to those taking them. The pupil must always be given clear guidance both in the instructions and in the questions.

If this is done, not only will the likelihood of pupils giving the wrong answer for the wrong reason be diminished but the assessor will also benefit from the introduction of some control into the nature and form of the responses which he is required to judge. Both pupil and assessor will also benefit from the deliberate attempt to assess defined qualities in practical work.

A major disadvantage of set exercises is that they tend to place too much emphasis upon the results which pupils have or say they have obtained. This makes it difficult to provide direct specific assessment of the qualities which were suggested as forming an appropriate basis for objectives in practical work. It can be argued, of course, that if the stated results are correct at any particular stage then the practical operations involved up to that stage will have been carried out correctly; it can also be argued that it is the results which matter and not the way in which they have been obtained.

The intent of this chapter has, however, been to establish that assessment ought to be directed at measuring particular qualities and it is suggested, therefore, that the use of major set-piece exercises to test specific qualities is not desirable even if there is a high correspondence between results and techniques. There are too many variables involved in a practical exercise for an assessor to be able to discover the causes of error from the evidence of a written report. If the exercise is being marked by someone who is able to observe the pupil at all stages of the work then specific qualities can be assessed without dependence upon the written report. It may, however, be impracticable to ask teachers, who are the only people who can act as continuous observers apart from fellow pupils, to devote the time necessary to watching the detailed work of one pupil over a large exercise for this purpose.

Set exercises are also subject in their formulation to a number of restricting factors. They have to be capable of being carried out by large numbers of candidates. The results must be able to be reported in a way which makes standardization of marking possible by people who have not watched the work being carried out. Exercises that have been set externally cannot take into account variations in facilities between schools and laboratories. The materials and apparatus used are, therefore, limited to those which can be readily obtained or are known to be available. All these factors can result in a degree of uniformity and predictability which leads to stereotyped assessment. In extreme circumstances it may indeed produce a situation in which the means of assessment are not closely related to the kind of practical work which schools think to be important. When this situation is reached the validity of the assessment is in question in that teachers may well be obliged to direct their teaching towards work with which they are not in sympathy or which they would oppose on educational grounds.

The discussion on set exercises so far has been confined to those which are most frequently set in practical examinations and which require thirty minutes or more for their completion. There are, however, many situations in which smaller-scale exercises can be used to test specific qualities. Such exercises can, for example, involve measurements, the taking of readings, the setting up or the connection of a piece of apparatus and the carrying out of a specific operation. They involve a very small amount of time but can test agreed qualities effectively and discretely. A test battery including several such exercises could be given in sequence to a number of pupils who could, if required, be assessed upon the same material and under the same criteria.

### (ii) *Assessment through project work*

Another means of assessing practical qualities is through projects involving practical work. Where such a procedure is used it is important to bear in mind that the finished project may not of itself make a major contribution to the assessment but rather that it may form a vehicle for the assessment of certain practical qualities which have gone into its 'making'. These qualities must, as always, be spelt out clearly for the benefit of both pupil and assessor.

In assessing work through projects two important factors must be borne in mind; they do not of themselves make project work unsuitable for this purpose but they may limit its usefulness at certain levels. First, that the choice of the project itself plays an important part in determining the qualities that can be demonstrated; the choice of qualities to be assessed does not, therefore, necessarily rest with the assessor. Second, success on a project, particularly a fairly substantial one, may hinge upon the pupil's ability to integrate a whole range of practical skills which will thus require to be well developed before the work can be successfully undertaken; it may thus not be a suitable instrument for assessing the development of these same qualities in isolation.

As with the set exercise so with the project; the major undertaking may not yield the greatest return. Small-scale projects carried out by pupils as investigational studies can form useful instruments of assessment without raising the kind of problems referred to earlier.

### (iii) *Assessment through course work*

Practical work can be assessed by measuring agreed qualities over the whole of the course followed by the pupil. Such assessment would involve the use of records kept by the pupil in the form of notebooks, laboratory books, homework and classwork records, as well as the assessment of performance in practical work over the same period.

The problems of relying on course work as an instrument of assessment are those which have been mentioned previously in connection with reliance on written reports. It should also be appreciated that course work as the basis of assessment conflicts, to some extent, with the concept of assessment as providing a measure of achievement at a given point in time. It may, therefore, be necessary to devise procedures which place greater emphasis for assessment purposes on the evidence provided by the course work of the standards reached by pupils during the later stages of their courses.

If course work is being considered as the only means of assessment it must be appreciated that there may be an undesirable 'backwash' effect on the work done by pupils. The teaching/learning situation ought not to discourage pupils who make mistakes and the records kept by pupils during the course should be working records reflecting problems encountered and progress made. If pupils are aware that such records are going to be used for assessment purposes it is probable that they will be prepared with that objective in view, being written-up for assessment rather than to meet the needs of the particular educational situation; 'clean copies' will be used to compile the pupil's dossier rather than the 'real' records of work. The assessor may be faced with the difficult task of interpreting the information and of devising some way by which the agreed qualities can be applied to a mass of material which does not lend itself to assessment under such terms.

### (iv) *Assessment by oral questioning*

As was indicated during the discussion of the qualities which might form the operational divisions, use could be made of oral examining in measuring several of these qualities. It is suggested that the oral situation could play an increasingly important part in the assessment of practical work. The situation is not artificial as the teacher is constantly involved in using the oral question-and-answer technique during normal classroom/laboratory activity. The observational skills of pupils can be tested effectively and quickly by such a process and it can also be used to supplement most other forms of testing.

The pupils and teacher are frequently involved in dialogue about varying aspects of the course, and discussion of the methods and results of practical work are fundamental to the teaching situation. At several points in this chapter comment has been made on the shortcomings of the written report; if the assessment situation can include an element of oral assessment the pupil could be given the opportunity to explain results or actions and to discuss interpretations. This could be used to confirm assessments made by other means or to pursue particular points in directions which had not been anticipated by the pupil in a written answer or by the assessor in constructing a question or an exercise.

Oral assessment also makes possible the use of group discussion as part of the evidence upon which the assessment of practical work can be based. Where such discussions are taken into consideration care has to be taken to ensure that reticence on the one hand and vociferousness on the other do not affect the outcome of the assessment. Oral techniques can also be useful in the assessment of those qualities which are generally included under the heading of attitudes as well as for the other purposes mentioned above.

### (v) *Assessment by impression*

Many of the separate qualities discussed earlier in this chapter could be assessed by impression during the normal conduct of laboratory/practical work. Although it would be possible to devise exercises or simple tests to measure some of the qualities and to use schemes of marking for making the assessments, this could be wasteful in terms of time and could interfere with the running of practical work. An assessment by impression of particular qualities in relation to practical work will often be the best that the teacher can do if he is not to create specific, and probably artificial, assessment situations which would interfere with the course.

When impression marking is being used the teacher should concern himself with one quality at a time. Assessment by impression could take place at the same time as the pupil is being assessed on some other quality by a different technique. Notes should be kept of the results of assessment by impression; these are of additional value to teachers in giving indications of progress and as pointers to aspects of the assessment which may require further attention.

## Should the assessment be internal or external?

In considering whether the teacher or an external examiner should act as the assessor two factors must be taken into consideration: the objectives of the assessment and the techniques to be used. In relation to these the person best able to carry out the assessment effectively should be chosen. In general terms both the 'external' examiner and the 'internal' teacher/assessor have their advantages and disadvantages and these may be summarized in relation to practical work as follows.

ADVANTAGES OF EXTERNAL ASSESSMENT

(i) It provides an independent assessment whose results are more likely to be accepted by the users of examination results.

(ii) It provides for uniformity of practice and standards with all pupils being assessed upon common qualities by common criteria.

(iii) It concentrates resources and expertise for setting and marking.

(iv) It enables the assessment of practical work to exert an influence on the nature of the practical work carried out in schools.

(v) It obviates the possibility of any conflict arising between the teacher as a teacher and the teacher as an assessor.

(vi) It provides an assessment procedure unaffected by personal relationships between teachers and pupils.

DISADVANTAGES OF EXTERNAL ASSESSMENT

(i) The means of assessment are limited to those which can be administered by an external agency.

(ii) The assessment may exercise a restricting influence upon the practical work carried out in schools.

(iii) The assessment is limited to the outcomes of practical work and does not include a consideration of how the work was carried out.

(iv) The number of occasions upon which the assessment can take place is limited by administrative considerations.

THE ADVANTAGES OF INTERNAL ASSESSMENT

(i) The dangers of chance failure or success are decreased by making assessment possible on a number of occasions.

(ii) A wide variety of means of assessment may be used covering a wide variety of qualities.

(iii) It makes possible the development of assessment procedures which are suited to the facilities available in particular schools and which are closely related to the courses of practical work devised by these schools.

(iv) It requires teachers to think about assessment in terms of educational and assessment objectives.

(v) It enables pupils to be assessed upon how they undertake practical work as well as upon its outcomes.

THE DISADVANTAGES OF INTERNAL ASSESSMENT

(i) It is less likely to be objective than external assessment.

(ii) It can endanger the relationship between teacher and pupil.

(iii) It can place a severe strain upon the teacher in terms of time, effort and expertise.

(iv) It makes it difficult to relate and compare standards between school and school.

(v) It can give rise to suspicions in the minds of users about the validity and reliability of the results of the assessment.

Many other advantages and disadvantages could be listed but the above should provide a sufficient basis for consideration of what would seem to be most appropriate in any particular situation. From the previous sections of this chapter it should be apparent that if certain qualities are to be included in the assessment of practical work internal assessment must form at least a part of the assessment since an external agency is not able to undertake the necessary observation. It must be appreciated that the choice does not always rest starkly between an internal or an external assessor; there will be situations in which the most appropriate scheme involves some external assessment and some internal assessment.

The point must be made, however, that there is a growing body of opinion which would subscribe to the view that the assessment of practical work should always be carried out internally by the teacher. Internal assessment has been sufficiently widely practised in a variety of subjects and at a variety of levels to support the contention that the teacher—the only person in a position to act as internal assessor—is able, when asked to do so, to take the objective, dispassionate position expected of an external assessor. He must, however, be given advice and guidance in his task in order that his concerns are overcome and the strengths that he can bring to bear as an assessor can be used to the full.

Throughout this chapter stress has been placed upon the need for assessment to be purposeful, for the objectives of the assessment to be carefully devised and clearly stated so that everyone concerned with it is always aware of the objectives and is constantly striving to achieve them. The teacher involved in a scheme of internal assessment is in danger of feeling isolated and cut off from advice and guidance. It is essential, therefore, that such teachers are brought in to the development of assessment schemes, even if only through an invitation to comment on proposals in draft form. The final scheme must always include a statement of the objectives of the assessment, suggestions as to how it might be carried out and advice regarding the standards to be used. Machinery should also be established, formally or informally, to provide a means whereby technical enquiries can be answered and through which the teachers involved in the scheme can consult one another, exchange experiences, seek advice and share ideas. The moderation of standards between schools must be considered and appropriate methods of equating standards be developed and made known to everyone involved in the scheme. (See also Chapter 11.)

Whether the assessor be internal or external it should always be appreciated that assessment is not a one-sided affair. The objectives of assessment and the means designed to achieve these objectives are of equal concern to the teacher, the assessor and the pupil. The interaction between assessing and teaching is receiving a wider appreciation and understanding than was the case only a few years ago. The teacher, whether he is acting as an assessor or not, is vitally concerned with the assessment techniques which are used to assess his pupils. It is important, therefore, that he appreciates the range available and their possibilities and that he is in sympathy with those being used by external agencies. It has already been stated that an examining board has a responsibility to provide a great deal of information regarding schemes of internal assessment; it is also important, arguably even more so, that teachers should be given just as much information about the purposes of and instruments used in external assessment.

## A possible re-appraisal of practical assessment?

In this final section the author has permitted himself the luxury of querying the foundations of practical assessment as described and discussed in the preceding parts of this chapter. It is suggested that the type of specification which is generally used as the basis for the assessment of practical work may have some fundamental weaknesses and that some of the assessment problems which have been discussed may result from the nature of the specification of objectives.

A cursory inspection of the basic specification discussed earlier is sufficient to appreciate that there is a significant difference between that statement and those provided for written examinations. Most statements for written examinations are given in a form in which the various qualities are presented in a hierarchical sequence and it is apparent that any one of the specified skills or abilities involves some, or all, of those which are ranked lower in the hierarchy. Specifications for the assessment of practical work, whether the assessment is to be carried out externally or internally, are rarely structured to the same degree. Any specification of the objectives of assessment should be clear and unambiguous, and, as far as possible, each of the specified qualities should be capable of being assessed independently of the others in the list (accepting that in a hierarchic order the possession of one quality will be dependent, to some extent, on the possession of those qualities ranked below it). Earlier in this chapter it was noted that practical work is closely interrelated with factual and theoretical studies; this relationship must be acknowledged and recognized in the assessment of practical work, otherwise the assessment procedure will distort the teaching and the nature of the subject. There are, however, certain outcomes of practical work which are not shared with theoretical work, e.g. manipulative skills, observational skills and that blend of initiative and intellect which results in the solution of practical problems.

In many specifications the five qualities (or whichever of them have been included in the specification) which have previously been discussed are divided into sub-categories, or are amplified to a greater or lesser extent. Even where this is done, however, no relationship is established between the qualities and no hierarchy is constructed. If the specification could aim at producing a hierarchic taxonomy in which each of the categories is self-contained (discrete) the author suggests that the users of the specification would more readily appreciate what is involved. Purposeful assessments could then be made separately of each category and the sum of the assessments for each category would give a more realistic measurement of practical work than would the assessment of a small number of broad categories.

An example of a highly structured specification is given below; for each category a brief description is given of methods by which assessment could be undertaken.*

## (a) KNOWLEDGE OF APPARATUS

All that would be required under this category would be the ability to name practical apparatus and to state its purpose in terms of use. Assessment could be undertaken by presenting the pupil with pieces of apparatus and requiring him to name them and to describe their use.

## (b) KNOWLEDGE OF PROCEDURES

All that would be required here is basic knowledge of routine procedures, i.e. the extent to which the pupil knows the procedures for carrying out routine practical operations which are basic to the subject. Assessment could be undertaken by using questions requiring descriptions of the procedures.

## (c) KNOWLEDGE OF WAYS OF USING APPARATUS

Under this heading the pupil would be expected to know how to use apparatus involved in carrying out routine procedures and how to handle the apparatus to achieve varying degrees of accuracy. Knowledge and use of safety precautions would also be included.

## (d) THE ABILITY TO USE APPARATUS

Under this heading the pupil would be required to show that he could use apparatus of which he had knowledge. This means that he should be able to combine the aspects of knowledge required under (a), (b) and (c) and to apply some degree of manipulative dexterity in the performance of relevant operations.

Assessment for these last two categories could be undertaken by means of simple exercises involving the use of the particular piece of apparatus. The criteria for judging the quality could be based either on pre-determined results with an allowed margin of error and/or direct observation of the work being carried out.

## (e) THE ABILITY TO IMPLEMENT PROCEDURES

This heading would involve the carrying out of those procedures of which the pupil had knowledge (b).

Assessment could be undertaken by providing simple instructions for the particular procedure and requiring the pupil to perform it. The assessment would take into account the extent to which the pupil carried out any checks necessary to ensure the satisfactory working of the apparatus used and the necessary accuracy of results.

## (f) THE ABILITY TO SELECT APPROPRIATE PROCEDURES FOR A PARTICULAR PRACTICAL PROBLEM

Under all the previous headings the apparatus or procedures have been

* Such an approach would be particularly suitable for profile reporting of results, a topic which is discussed in chapters 8 and 12.

in the limited context of a specific or specified purpose. This heading involves the ability of the pupil to select, by applying appropriate criteria, the most suitable apparatus and/or procedure for a particular practical or experimental task.

Assessment could be undertaken by presenting the pupil with a practical problem and a range of alternative apparatus and procedures. The extent to which the most appropriate choices are made would form the basis of the assessment.

(g) THE ABILITY TO OBSERVE THE MATERIAL UNDER INVESTIGATION

Under this one heading there are two levels of complexity. At its simplest level the ability is concerned with the identification and classification into known categories of the objects or processes which are being investigated, i.e. a descriptive skill based on observation. At a more complex level the ability involves the pupil in the exercise of a degree of discernment in establishing patterns from his observations and systematizing the information derived from them.

Assessment could be undertaken by requiring the pupil to translate his observations into oral or written terms. The criteria adopted for the measurement of the ability would be the extent to which the pupil's observations were comprehensive, systematic and ordered in terms of significance.

(h) THE ABILITY TO OBSERVE CHANGES OR DIFFERENCES TAKING PLACE IN THE MATERIAL UNDER INVESTIGATION

This heading is an extension of (g). There attention was to be paid to the general method and effectiveness of the pupil's observation; under this heading is included the extent to which the pupil is able to recognize the changes that take place in the material being studied and, having recognized such changes, to take whatever steps are necessary to examine them systematically.

Assessment could be undertaken by presenting the pupil with a practical situation and requiring him to observe the changes which take place and to identify and isolate the changing factors in such a way that they can be studied more comprehensively, e.g. by refined counting techniques and sampling procedures and by eliminating possible errors and variations resulting from the techniques used or from inherent variation in the material being studied.

(i) THE ABILITY TO RECORD APPROPRIATELY OBSERVED MATERIAL AND THE CHANGES WHICH TAKE PLACE IN IT

This heading covers the ability of the pupil to make and keep records of the activities described in (g) and (h).

Assessment could be undertaken by evaluating the use made by the pupil of the available methods of recording observations. The criteria upon which the assessment is made should include not only the pupil's selection of the available methods of recording but also the extent to which the pupil is aware of possible distortions of the data by the use of different methods of presentation. They should also include the extent to which conclusions drawn from the data arise from the data itself or are conditioned by the method of presentation.

(j) THE ABILITY TO DEVISE NEW APPARATUS OR TECHNIQUES TO MEET THE DEMANDS OF A PARTICULAR PROBLEM

This heading involves the ability of the pupil, when faced with a practical problem which cannot be solved satisfactorily by the use of familiar apparatus and procedures, to make modifications and adaptations to known apparatus and procedures to meet the demands of the new problem.

Assessment here requires that the pupil be presented with a situation in which the apparatus and techniques used and the problem posed are sufficiently within his experience for him to appreciate that the former are insufficient to solve the latter.

(k) THE ABILITY TO PLAN AND CARRY OUT A PRACTICAL INVESTIGATION

This heading involves all the preceding categories and the use of all the pupil's practical experience and skill in the design of practical work and its execution.

Assessment can be undertaken by presenting the pupil with a problem and requiring him to plan an appropriate practical procedure to solve it. The initial plan should be written out by the pupil and evaluated before it is implemented. The assessment should take into consideration the extent to which the pupil has anticipated all the problems which he could justifiably be expected to anticipate at the planning stage. It should also include the extent to which the pupil recognizes problems as they arise and modifies his plan to overcome them. It is therefore not necessary to ensure that the plan is foolproof before the exercise begins but care must be taken to ensure that a plan which has serious faults when first designed, is modified to enable the pupil to proceed with the practical work.

(l) ATTITUDES TO PRACTICAL WORK*

In almost all subjects in which it is felt necessary to incorporate practical work in the overall pattern of assessment one of the most important educational objectives is the establishment of particular attitudes towards practical work. The desirable attitudes here are, for example, 'willingness to co-operate in the normal routine of a laboratory', 'persistence', 'resourcefulness', 'enthusiasm', 'the ability to work as a member of a group', 'commitment to practical work as a worthwhile pursuit without compulsion'. Attempts to assess such qualities are rarely included in public examinations because of the very real problems of making assessments with any degree of objectivity. These qualities, moreover, are those upon which it is

* See also Chapter 10.

particularly difficult for individuals to reach agreement over their recognition and definition and upon the standards to be applied in assessment if they can be identified. It is, however, necessary to note that this area of attitudes is probably the most important of all in terms of teaching objectives. Careful consideration should, therefore, be given to the matter before a decision is taken to include or exclude what in Bloom's terminology are 'affective' objectives.

A study of the twelve categories suggested above will show that the first three are concerned not with 'doing' but with 'knowing about'. These suggest that it is important in the assessment of practical work to include specific and purposeful measurement of the pupil's factual knowledge of the tools and procedures of the laboratory or workshop. The categories have been stated in terms which are generally applicable to all science subjects. They should also be capable of adaptation in order to meet the particular needs of subjects other than the sciences, e.g. workshop subjects, craft subjects and even for subjects such as Geography or History if practical work there was considered an appropriate part of the teaching.

It is appreciated that a specification such as that suggested above has an initial appearance of complexity which could daunt teachers and examiners who might be concerned with its operation but it is suggested that more 'conventional' specifications involve many, or most, of the twelve qualities listed above. It is also suggested that a scheme of assessment using such a detailed specification would, with use, be found to be both practicable and more worthwhile than schemes which have an outwardly less complex appearance. If it were decided that a detailed scheme such as this should not be implemented it is possible to group the suggested qualities in such a way that a smaller number of broader, well-defined categories could form the specification. Whatever specification is eventually decided upon for use in a particular assessment scheme the discussions and deliberations which go into its formulation should take place in terms of the kind of detail which has been suggested. It is only if detailed consideration has been given to the contents of each section of the specification that broad categories will be meaningful to those responsible for carrying out the assessment.

The purpose of the suggestions made in this section is to provoke and stimulate discussion rather than to provide a model or, even worse, imply that the suggested categories should be accepted for use without careful consideration of their relevance to the subject or group for which they are intended. Certain categories which often form part of practical assessment have been omitted from the above list. For example, practical work involves pupils in thinking about, evaluating and using the results of their work; the measurement of their abilities in these directions is thus usually included in the assessment of practical work. While it is appreciated that such activities are important here, the author would suggest that they are better assessed independently of practical work and that it is unwise to include them in the specification of those qualities which are to be assessed under this heading.

# 7 The Assessment of Project Work

## M. T. Deere

The assessment of project work is often thought to be extremely difficult. As examples of extreme views, there are those who will not undertake this kind of activity because they believe assessment to be beyond their grasp; there are also those who believe that project work and assessment are inimical, and who will only undertake the method if it is *not* to be assessed. Whether or not such objections are valid, they are worth discussion, if only because the premises on which they are based are vital to a study of project assessment. In short, to consider objections to project work is to shed light on its assessment. The fact that such opposition comes, often enough, from teachers themselves is significant because the final assessment has to be as much concerned with the attainment of the teacher himself as with the students.

One of the strongest reservations concerns project work carried out by groups. Even when project work is acceptable for an individual, it is argued that to pursue it as a group activity is to raise problems. How does one identify the contribution of a single 'candidate' within the group? The possibility of the 'passenger' is raised as well. This particular issue is chosen first because it encompasses almost all the problems associated with this theme in one gulp. As we shall see, it is not a question of single versus group projects—the one is not simply better, or more difficult, than the other. The real comparison has to rest on which is the better vehicle for developing one's objectives, and it is on these objectives that the structure of assessment must surely rest. In any event, it may be contended that the individual project rarely, if ever, exists, since the individual student must form some kind of group with his teachers. In the final analysis, the teacher will influence—to a greater or lesser degree—the course of the project, however independent the student may appear.

This issue of teacher participation is perhaps the second most common reservation. The straight question is this: 'how much of the final result is due to the candidate?', and one hears it in precisely this form. Yet however direct it may be, the question begs other, more important ones. Is not the very act of allowing the candidate to follow his suggestion for a project a positive teacher-decision? If the teacher provides a theme himself, is this not the more true? More than being mere decisions, are not these actions really pre-judgments on the candidate himself? And these refer to the beginning, before the project has started! There seems to be nothing wrong in teacher involvement of this kind. Indeed, it must be inevitable and proper. Just as correct is the continuing dialogue between teacher and student that is one characteristic of project work itself.

So far, some initial issues have been raised in order to open up the idea of project work as a learning activity. This will help to offer some definitions and thus enable one to move on to consider objectives and assessment schemes. At this point, however, it is not intended to give the impression that the questions raised can lightly be cast aside—we shall see something of their true influence later. The first aim has been to focus attention on the teacher as well as on the candidate. This is done because in project work the teacher is linked firmly into the process, since both his teaching and his (and anybody else's), assessment are interdependent. In the more traditional assessment modes one person can teach and another assess without direct contact. In project work the tripartite relationship of teacher–student–examiner has to be far closer. It may well be that those who argue that assessment wrecks projects do so because they fear the lack of this relationship, or to put it another way, they will not accept a form of assessment designed for one learning mode to be applied to another. If this is the case, the critics are right to be cautious. For the teacher who both wishes to utilize the project, and to assess it—in spite of the critics just mentioned—there is one admonition worth repeating: the inevitability of teacher involvement means that the final assessment is as much a measure of him as it is of his students.

It is time to put some of the problems to work more directly. The main feature of project work that most people will accept as distinguishing it from a lot of other work is that it is an integrating activity. Unlike other themes so far covered, this is not a problem that prevents teachers from adopting the project. Rather it is one that they have to accept because it is this very problem that forms the heart of their objectives. This needs explaining in rather more detail. When we present a candidate with an 'examination' problem—in whatever form—we are asking him to consider a task which is more or less circumscribed, is shorn of most of its ambiguous fringe, and leads to an 'answer' which is fairly tightly defined. Further to this, the task is based on a single packet of subject material. When the project is contrasted with this approach by describing it as 'integrating', one has in mind the knitting together of various packets of material, of various kinds of task, and of the efforts of at least two people. If you like, the number of 'degrees of freedom' implied by a project-type task is greater than that normally associated with the examination-question-type task. Invariably, the result of these extra dimensions is to make possible a largish range of 'acceptable' solutions, and this still leaves the interpretation of 'acceptable' disquietingly open.

In elaborating this problem, a beginning has been made in tackling the task of *defining* the activity that has been called a *project*. However, there is one last issue that needs consideration before further developing this definition. We shall see that one view of a project is that of a simulation of a real situation. In effect the student assumes the mantle of researcher, historian, designer, or development engineer. This is not a bad form of definition, but it can have a rather unfortunate back-lash. In the previous paragraph the existence of a range of 'acceptable' solutions was pointed out. Now it is temptingly easy to argue that if the student plays the role of the professional practitioner, then his end-product may be judged by the same criteria as those used by, or applied to, the professional practitioner. In some ways this is not unreasonable, but in another sense there are snags. We shall be forced to confront them later; it is sufficient to say here that if the resources and experience of the student fall short of those possessed by professionals, it seems scarcely fair to apply a single set of criteria to both classes. The consequence is that the end-product, be it a three-dimensional device or a report, is insufficient evidence on its own, and we need to examine the thought processes that led to it, and the final views of its creator on its status.

Let us now summarize the general problems associated with project work that have been chosen for discussion as an introduction to project assessment. Firstly, an ill-chosen assessment scheme undermines the whole notion of the project activity. Secondly, the project is invariably a group process—no matter how individually-based it may appear—in that it involves the teacher. The task is thus one of recognizing the individual contribution or influence of each member. Thirdly, the teacher's roles as planner, consultant and assessor are all interdependent; unlike other more traditional methods, the relationship between teacher, student, and an external examiner has to be relatively close. Fourthly, the integrating character of the project activity leads to large numbers of variables which in consequence leads in turn to a range of acceptable and often unforeseen solutions. Lastly, the temptation to use the simulating character of the project to justify assessment by comparison with professional work can be dangerous.

We can now consider the meaning of project work. It seems clear enough that there exist several basic ideas, which, while differing quite widely in approach, attach to this much-used term. In the light of this it is probable that many of the points previously discussed are due to semantic rather than to philosophical issues. Equally, each different discipline approaches the activity according to its own ethos. To find a common description among this jungle of attitudes is not easy, and the result is unlikely to be a brief statement. However, an analysis is certainly possible, and will be approached here by considering separately the broad phases, which are three in number: the initiation of the project; its course, as it is pursued by one or more students; and its terminal result.

The basis of project initiation must be the 'brief' (for want of a better term) given to the student at the beginning of the exercise. Put broadly, this is the initial stimulation given in order to concentrate the student's mind on the project. There must be a gradation here, and it is important to assessment. At its simplest, the brief can be a definite target, in the form of a specific device to be produced, or a definite question to be answered. At its most complex, the brief is a mere statement which recognizes a problem situation, or even a bare theme (for instance, that of 'noise' in physics), from which the student has to extract his own target. If these are extremes, there are also a wide range of intermediate briefs, which go some way to delineate a target. There are two further points to consider at this stage. The first concerns the cases where the students are 'self-briefed'. Whereas one might argue that this is the most complex of all, it has immediately to be recognized that a lot will depend on the open-ness *of* the student's brief. The issue is whether the task of the student who self-selects, with no preamble, a device, simple in character, that he would like to design and make is more demanding than that of the student who explores a brief given to him in very wide terms with such insight as ultimately to propose a completely novel study. The second point is that a narrow brief, not requiring extensive study by the student in order to produce a target, does not preclude the possibility of his meeting wider, more extensive demands later on, in the pursuit of the target.

The initiation phase, as just described, can be generally applicable to all projects. Equally, there are characteristics common to all of them, however diverse the range of project activity may be. We have noted already that an 'easy' start does not imply an easy 'journey'. The course of the project accumulates its demands on the student through the requirement for decision, each decision being desirably based on collected evidence which is organized by applying criteria which the student has to seek or generate himself. It is true that the range of decisions can be infinite, but they can at least be classified. Firstly, there is the choice of strategy, or method of approach, seen in the content of the project itself. Secondly, there is the collection of information, which will depend on yet another set of decisions as to the likely sources of information. Thirdly, there are the criteria by which information accumulated is organized, and this is followed by the repetitive decisions which re-consider at intervals the validity of the chosen strategy, and the status of the desired end-product (i.e. is it attainable, beyond current resources, or too trivial?). Elaborating on this picture of a project being punctuated by a series of decisions of different types, the influence of the teacher will appear in the relative importance he attaches to each type. His value judgment in this respect will reflect his objectives for the project. It is this balance of values attaching to the frequency of student decisions, and type of decisions, that gives each project its individual character and reflects both the attainment and the aptitude of the student and the attitude of his teacher.

There is one further factor that requires mention when treating the project as a decision-chain model. It concerns the mode of work carried out by the student between significant points in the course of the project. If these significant points are the *major* decisions, the time between them can be said to be occupied in two modes. Chronologically the first is characterized by study on a *widening* front, where the aim is to accumulate relevant information, followed by activity on a *narrowing* front, during which the data gained is being 'put to work'. This aspect concerns us, because of the necessary balance that needs to be struck between the modes. The striking of the balance must be a matter for both teacher and student, and the manner of its achievement must affect the final assessment.

Lastly, we are concerned with the 'end-product'. This is the most tangible evidence we have, even if not *necessarily* the most important. What kind of end product might we expect? Almost invariably it will be a piece of written work which either stands alone or is related to some tangible artefact. This form of classification does not, however, go far enough, it merely distinguishes between 'thinking work' and 'constructional work'. We ought to go further and see the project as additionally requiring students to provide explanations based upon their own reading or experimental or constructional work and to criticize both ideas and products. All these factors, planning, explanation, criticism and construction should be taken into account when projects are assessed. At the same time we should bear in mind the degree of adventure involved, asking such questions as: has it been done before?; is it really new or just new to those looking at it?; is it merely a redevelopment of previous work and how new was the theme to the teachers concerned?

If we add these variables to those previously considered then we can discuss project definitions and project objectives more generally.

Most projects, however disparate they may appear at first sight, will fit this scheme. It may be going too far to project this 'complexity matrix' to a single verbal definition, but it can be attempted. If we describe a project as a teaching/learning activity which requires the student to determine one or more of the following, his strategy, his resources, his target; which presents a task which is not artificially compartmented nor idealized; which allows of a range of solutions rather than a unique answer; then we are on safe enough ground. If we further suggest that in project work the teacher crosses to the student's side of the fence separating the student from the answer, perhaps we are less secure. Still the point is worth making because it must affect the teachers part in assessment. Nevertheless, the matrix is still seen as being more useful than the condensed verbal definition, for it seems to support most graphically the earlier contention that a project was, if nothing else, an integrating activity.

At this point, having explored in some detail the kinds of activity that the term 'project work' may denote, we must use the details and classes so far discovered to elaborate *purposes* and *objectives*. The former is the answer to the question in 'why do I *employ* project work?'; the latter has to do with the skills and abilities that the activity is intended to develop in the student (and, let us again remind ourselves, in the teacher as well).

Table 1. Degrees of freedom in Project Work

| *'Variable', 'dimension' or 'degree of freedom'* | *'Scale', or extreme points of the spectrum* |
|---|---|
| Group size | Individual (rarely), to individual-plus-teacher, to individual-plus-teacher consultants and group-plus-teacher, to group-plus-teacher-plus-consultant |
| Spread of subject material involved | Two separate areas of a single subject, to the integration of several widely contrasting subjects |
| Nature of brief | *Narrow*, closely defining a recognizable target, to *wide*, where the choice of target is the onus of the student |
| Source of brief | Teacher provided, to selection from teacher-provided list, to student proposed |
| Balance of 'phases'<br>This again has a firm relationship to Nature and Source of brief | Emphasis on preliminary, or initiation, phase; to emphasis on course of project |
| *Types of decision required to be made by student, and frequency of these decisions* | *Strategy; information sources; information organization criteria; target validity* |
| Teacher influence | Relative value placed by teacher on the decision types described above. (The implication is that the teacher will take responsibility for certain types of decision, leaving other types to the student) |
| End-product characteristics | (i) 'thinking' or 'thinking + construction'<br>(ii) Description; criticism; explanation; production |
| Novelty of project | Novel to student, through novel to student and teacher, to 'totally novel' |

(Note: for "Nature of brief" and "Source of brief" — "This pair cross-refer")

Three broad purposes can be seen. It is convenient to divide them so, but it has to be recognized that these 'purpose bands' can overlap. Thus:

(a) Project work as a motivating element in teaching subjects already established in the curriculum. We imply here an alternative to didactic teaching, but do not necessarily have to go so far as describing that alternative as 'discovery method'.

(b) We may use project method as a form of 'professional simulation'. After some consideration, it may well be that this is the only real way to teach some subjects—of which a fairly obvious example is Design. Less directly, because we have taught the subject in traditional ways, may be the case of the physical sciences. In this latter instance, formal instruction is to some degree replaced by requiring the student to assume the role of the scientist by chipping away at his own knowledge boundary. In an educational sense, the fact that this boundary is far behind that of the contemporary is scarcely relevant, although the gap is not always that wide. Certainly, whatever the specific purpose, the development of attitudes is likely to be an important objective linked to this class of purpose.

(c) If (b) represented a set of purposes based on so-called vocational attitudes and abilities, this third group is connected with more general development. That is to say that the major *purpose* is to develop skills both in dexterity and intellect—and attitudes which are not the exclusive demand or preserve of a particular subject or profession. That is not to say that adherence to material derived from such a specific area is undesirable or impossible; it does, however, give freedom in meeting the natural interests of the student.

The general abilities just mentioned really require exemplification. We are talking, often enough, of facets of character and personality just as much as of academic worth. To give a few examples of such attributes: the confidence to take decisions; ability to generate and consider several possible answers to a problem, rather than the pursuit of the *first* idea; initiative and self-reliance. Perhaps this short list will go beyond indirectly the nature of the area under review, and forewarn us that, unlike more specific aims and objectives, assigning values and allocating level of award when assessing may be more than difficult, it may be inequitable and unrealistic. So far, a pattern of define: plan-expect: assess has been followed. The comment is worth making that there is a fourth phase and that is the use and interpretation of the assessment. In this area, it may be enough to describe the students' qualities, leaving assumption of value to those who require it.

In Figure 1 these purposes, and the development of purpose into more specific objectives have been laid down in diagrammatic form. Be it said at once that this chart applies to a particular part of the curriculum, namely creative technology.

It is not a self-contradiction to include class (c) objectives—since this is an example of how one area can develop general qualities—neither is the chart useful solely in technology teaching.

As an example of how purposes can vary, Figure 2 shows the chart modified to indicate priorities for three different cases:

(i) undergraduate students of technology, designing and making a public emergency service control system [diagram (a)];

(ii) VIth form girls studying the reasons behind vehicle design changes as part of a mixed-ability-and-subject general studies course [diagram (b)];

(iii) undergraduate girls undertaking a simple design task as part of a course in Education and Mathematics [diagram(c)].

It should follow, if Figure 2 indicates how a teacher balances his priorities in objectives, that this profile should influence—to some extent, but the idea of the syllable and the idea that order is important, for the name he hears is always /mama/ and never by any chance /amam/. We can scarcely talk about a system being involved as yet because there is no question of different noises standing for different things at this stage, but as soon as the baby recognizes a second word as being attached to a different thing, there is a language system in existence in his brain. The second word is most often /dada/ which becomes associated with the rather strange being who tends to come home at the end of the day and perhaps have a jolly five minutes with the baby at the point when mummy is out on her feet, having coped with the little angel for ten hours at a stretch. In order that the new word shall operate successfully it must be consistently distinguished from /mama/. The form of the word is very similar, the rhythm is the same, the loud parts of the syllables are the same, and the only feature that differentiates them is located in the /m/ and the /d/. Since the baby knows which word is which, his brain must have discovered some way of distinguishing /d/ from /m/, in other words it has fastened on to some acoustic cue which will do the job. Although /mama/ is made up to two syllables, the sound is continuous right through the /m/ and the vowel each time, so that there are two little swells of sound, but in /dada/ the sound is interrupted by a short silence, a kind of hiccough. The child's brain has only to pin its attention to this difference between the continuous and the interrupted sound and it will be able to tell infallibly when it hears /mama/ and when it hears /dada/. The child is now operating a language system, one which has not only two words attached to two things, but also three phonemes: /m/, /d/ and /a/. Now phoneme systems will only work as a whole and these three phonemes make a complete system, a mini-system if you like. There are only three pigeonholes and there is something to place in each of them. It is not a case of having forty pigeonholes all ready waiting to be used for different phonemes later on; the child must build the framework as he goes along and at present it consists of just three boxes.

Notice also that his brain has found acoustic cues which are only as complicated as the situation demands.

Let us follow our hypothetical baby a little further and imagine that the third word he recognizes consistently is a name for a grandparent, perhaps /nana/. To do this he must be able to distinguish not only /m/ and /d/ but also /m/ and /n/ and of course /d/ and /n/. The difference between the continuous and the interrupted sound will no longer do the whole job because both /m/ and /n/ are continuous, so some other way has to be found to separate these two sounds. It may be hard to believe but there is good sound evidence that even at this early age babies are capable of noticing differences in second formant transition.[†] When we first hear about this acoustic cue it seems to be an extremely subtle and sophisticated method of distinguishing between sounds, but we have to remember that if we use it as adults it is because we learned to do so as children. There is not much doubt that when the baby recognizes the difference between /mama/ and /nana/ he is relying on the transition cue. In doing so he has expanded his phoneme system by one and there are now four pigeonholes with something to go into each.

The next step might be the addition of a name for the other grand-parents, perhaps /baba/ and again the child's brain has a fresh problem. Up till now the interrupted sound always signalled /dada/ but here is a second interrupted sound which must be differentiated because it is attached to a different person. At this point we can see something of the economy of phoneme systems because this small group of two interrupted sounds can be effectively split by the use of the second formant transition cue which already differentiates the two continuous sounds, /m/ and /n/. The brain evolves only the cues that are needed to make the required distinctions and with the system in its present form three cues are enough: the softer-louder cue takes care of the vowel parts of the syllables; the continuous-interrupted cue puts the /m, n/ on one side and the /d, b/ on the other, and then the transition cue separates both /n/ from /m/ and /d/ from /b/. Once more the phoneme system is complete as it stands, with a framework of five pigeonholes for the five phonemes to be distinguished, and it happens that the job can be done with three acoustic cues.

It is important to keep clearly in mind the mechanism by which these developments come about. The first factor is that some person or some thing in the baby's small world takes on a particular interest for him, causing him for the time being to be specially attentive to the word which is associated with it. In order to be sure when this word is said, he has to be able to distinguish it reliably from the other words he already recognizes and his brain sets about the task of finding a cue which is effective. This will quite probably mean that a new phoneme has to be set up, very often by splitting an existing class, as in the case both of continuous sounds and of interrupted ones. So although the child's unconscious purpose is to learn a new word, because of the nature of the language system, he is busy forging for himself an ever expanding phoneme system. We can scarcely follow through step by step the expansion of the system up to the forty-member adult system of English and in any case there is great variation in the way this is done by individual children. The principle, however, is always that which has been illustrated: a phoneme system at every stage complete in itself and determined by the distinctions between words that have to be made. Not every new word recognized calls for a fresh phoneme; it may present existing phonemes in a new order, as is the case for every word learned by an adult, but from time to time a new group of sounds and a new cue become necessary. The child whom we left with the five phoneme system will find the need a little later to notice the hissing sounds which occur in English words; perhaps he gets rather interested in his *shoe*. This hissing sound is a continuous one like /m, n/ but of a very different character so he will pick out the hiss as a fresh kind of sound. But at first all hisses will be the same for him and will form just one class until some new word forces him to split up the hisses, to put a partition in the pigeonhole used for them and to realize that *shoe* and *sock* start off with different hisses, one low-pitched and the other high-pitched. By this kind of process the phoneme framework expands and expands as the child feels the pressure of interest in external things and his brain evolves the acoustic cues needed to make the additional distinctions. By the time the child is about five years old, he will have learned to recognize all the differences involved in the adult system of phonemes, that is in English the forty-odd classes of sound. He cannot yet of course produce in his own speech sounds which adequately embody all these distinctions, but he is now operating with the adult system because he uses it in the reception of speech. Again we have to remember that reception runs ahead of production, that is to say that during the period of language acquisition there is a time lag between the development of recognition and production. One often hears a mother say about her baby at a certain stage 'He understands everything you say to him' and she is implying that he cannot yet say all that he understands; she has noted the time lag between reception and production.

The ability to talk is developing at its own pace all this time, so we will now take a look at what is happening on this side. The baby wants to talk in order to influence events in the world around him and recognition stages are a step in this end. As soon as some progress has been made in speech reception he will try his hand, or his tongue rather, at wielding the magic himself. One might think that with all the practice he put in during the babbling stage this should not give him too much trouble, but in fact it does. The practice was generalized practice which was not linked to a language system and it is an interesting and vital fact that articulations which the baby produced readily in the earlier period cannot simply be called back and pressed into service for the purposes of the phoneme system. Differences in articulation must now be tailored systematically to the demands of the language and this is why prior recognition is so important. The child's aim is to reproduce in his own speech the acoustic cues his brain has evolved for taking in other people's.

In a general sense this is brought about through imitation, mainly of his mother's speech, which is also of course the source of his ability to recognize. Our own speech reaches us in a unique and private version so that when the child imitates there can never be anything like a perfect match between the sounds he hears from other people and the results of his attempts to imitate. What he can do, however, is to try to make sounds in which he detects the acoustic cues he has already learned. This accounts for the lag between reception and production; it takes time for the continually expanding framework of reception to exert its influence on his articulations. He begins with cues that are effective for the distinctions he needs to make and these, from the viewpoint of the complete adult system, are gross distinctions like that between a continuous and an interrupted sound or, at a later stage, between an interrupted and a hissing sound, without any discrimination among the various hissing sounds. When this type of cue is applied to the child's own speech it gives rise to all the childish pronunciations which parents and indeed all the rest of us find so delightful. For some time he will be content to form syllables with almost any kind of interruption, producing sequences like /pudi tat/ for *pussy cat* or /iku gogi/ for *little doggie*. As time goes on the child will be recognizing a wider and wider range of things and will do his best to reproduce them, getting in whatever cues he can; he will tackle things like /bano/ for *piano*, /dohin/ for *dolphin*, /budlozer/ for *bulldozer,* /cocker bisik/ for *chocolate biscuit* and so on. He is doing his best to embody in his own sounds the cues he uses in recognition but obviously what he produces is not all that easy for his listeners to decode. His best audience from every point of view is his mother and there is always a stage when she acts as his interpreter to the rest of the world; but he will not be satisfied for very long if there is only one person whose actions can be influenced by his speech so there is constant pressure on him to modify his pronunciation in order to make what he says easily understood by a wider circle of adults. He can do this by introducing progressively more of the cues his brain has evolved for speech reception. Some distinctions are more difficult for him to manage than others; he may well be halfway through his fifth year before he can articulate very presentable /th/ sounds or a /r/ sound like that of most of the adults around him. Some groups of consonants will give him trouble for quite a long time. For English children the distinction between the initial sounds of *chain* and *train* is a difficult one to achieve. It will probably not have struck you that they are at all alike but if you say the two words in succession, you will notice that the acoustic effect is remarkably similar, the first being just a little higher pitched than the second. Here again the child will have learned to recognize the distinction long before he can produce it and it is interesting that, even when he can pronounce the two sounds, he finds it hard to know when to use one and when to use the other. You may for instance hear a child at this stage say *treeks* for *cheeks, trin* for *chin* and *satrel* for *satchel.* Another confusion that occurs is between /tr/ and /tw/ and this is understandable since for a long time the child has probably been saying /w/ in place of /r/, *wed wabbit* and so on. When he at last succeeds in making the difference, he will still be in doubt when to use each of them and may come out with *trelve* for *twelve, trist* for *twist,* or even rather charmingly 'Trinkle, trinkle little star'.

While the child's pronunciation is shaped mainly by the pressure of the phoneme system, it is at the same time the result of imitation, in normal circumstances of his mother's speech. The phoneme system itself is derived from this model which is responsible also for the more detailed quality of the sounds produced, what is often referred to as the 'accent' of the speaker. In English this is very largely a matter of the quality of the vowel sounds, in which the language system allows a good deal more variation than in the consonants. In determining this aspect of a child's speech, the mother's accent is usually paramount even where it differs from that of most of the other adults who surround the child. A child of a Scottish mother, brought up from birth in London, say, is almost certain to speak with a Scottish accent to some degree. The same influence is strong, too, in deciding characteristics of rhythm and intonation, both the grammatical component of intonation and its use in the expression of emotion. Children begin very early to imitate the tunes of the mother's speech but just as the pronunciation of vowels and consonants is shaped by the need to be understood, so the use of tone and rhythm is modified so as to convey what is intended to a whole circle of adult listeners.

By the time a child is about five years old, then, he has built up by a process of expansion a phoneme system which coincides with that of the adult language around him, he has evolved a set of acoustic cues that enable him to recognize all the necessary distinctions when he is listening to speech, he has applied the knowledge of these cues to his own speech so as to make it intelligible, at least with some degree of good will, to those around him, he has learned to recognize and to produce the appropriate rhythm and intonation patterns and his pronunciation has taken on through imitation most of the features that will characterize his accent. Yet all this has been done by learning new words; one might almost say that these other things are a by-product, though an absolutely essential by-product, of his adding to his vocabulary. In conformity with the general principle, the additions are to his passive vocabulary first, though in these early stages of language acquisition we can be fairly sure that all words will pass from the passive to the active vocabulary. It will be well to consider at this point just what happens as the new words are learned.

For the small child, words are noises which stand for things or people and when he knows only a handful of words, they can stand for only a few items in his world. One of the interesting things that happens is that the area which one word covers for the child changes as time passes; one can say, if you like, that the meaning of the word expands and contracts. A very clear example of this is the word /dada/. When the baby first learns it, it refers to the one person who appears at somewhat lengthy intervals and is so named by mummy. Some weeks later, however, when the child is at the stage of being taken out in the streets by his mother, the meaning of this word expands to include almost any figure in trousers and perhaps a moustache or beard, no matter where or when he appears. The child will then hail loudly any such figure as 'Dada', not without embarrassment to mummy. The meaning of the word will contract again, however, when another word is added to the vocabulary, the word *man*, which is soon seen to refer to the general class and the word /dada/ reverts to its reference to one person only.

Because the world is so full of a number of things, even for a small child, and because he has to build up his store of words bit by bit, this kind of fluctuation in the area of reference of a word goes on continually. One small boy, for instance, learned the word *ladder*, which he pronounced incidentally /ladler/, when the house opposite to his own was being painted. But in a short space of time /ladler/ meant for him a ladder, anything at all propped against the side of a house, any shape such as the back of a garden seat with parallel members and slats across *and* any man in white overalls. Of course it was only a matter of time before the learning of a few additional words would reduce the reference of the word once again until it meant simply – a ladder. For another small boy, at one period, *rain* meant not only wet stuff that fell but also *a reason for not going out*. In perfectly fine weather at midday, when it was too hot to go into the garden, he would go to the door, hold out his hand and say 'Rain', not as a question but as a statement meaning 'we don't go out'.

This brings up another important aspect of the function of words in the early stage of language development. Just as a word can cover a wide area of reference, so it can also function as the equivalent of an adult sentence. This is particularly the case when the child gets to the stage of putting two words together, an important development which we shall be looking at in a moment. For example, when the child says 'Mummy coat' this may simply mean 'That's mummy's coat' but it may also mean 'Where is mummy's coat?' or again 'Mummy should put her coat on so that we can go out'. Even the single word at an earlier stage will have different functions in different situations. /mama/ may at one time mean 'The name of the person I can see is Mama' but on another occasion it may mean 'The hat I'm pointing to belongs to Mama' or it may be the equivalent of the expression 'Mama do it', which the child will use later on. While his language has no explicit grammar, he will use the words he knows with different functions so that adding to his vocabulary is something rather more than just adding to his stock of words. At the age of eighteen months he may be using no more than about twenty words in this way but even three months later the number may have risen to something like two hundred.

Up to this point whatever the child says is basically an imitation of what he hears, though he is making it serve a rather wider range of functions. At about the age of two a great step forward is taken when the child strings two words together, because when this happens his mini-language now has a grammar. Grammar is not to be thought of as the host of complicated rules which we were supposed to learn, not without tears, in our schooldays, rules which we were expected to adhere to when speaking or writing and which we were continually 'breaking'. Real grammar is concerned with what people do when they talk and not with what they *should* do, and it consists of the principles of structure and sequence which apply when any given language is used. As soon as the small child puts two words together in English, he develops a principle, that is effectively a syntax, which controls the order of the words. This is the period when he will use over and over again such expressions as 'Bye-bye Mummy', 'Bye-bye sock', 'Bye-bye boat' and 'All-gone milk', 'All-gone flakes', 'All-gone car', 'All-gone soap' and so on. In all of these the names of different things are combined with a kind of operator word to make what are really sentences in the child language, in which the operator word must come first and then the name. When this principle is established, any new words will appear first in the name class, having of course been learned through recognition. A few very familiar words make up the operators but as time goes on words may pass from the name class into this class. While the child limits his remarks to two-word sequences, he will keep to this basic construction, that is to this syntax.

This stage in language development is extremely interesting because it differs from everything that has gone before. Up to this point the child's sounds and words have been copied from the speech of his mother or of other adults, but here quite suddenly is a development which does not represent a pattern that has been copied. Adults do not spontaneously say things like 'All-gone milk', which do not form part of their language. It is true that mothers may sometimes be concerned about 'teaching the child baby-talk' or they may be reproached by others for doing so. But the boot is entirely on the other foot and it is the baby that teaches mummy baby-talk. When adults use such expressions, they are doing so in imitation of the baby who is now creating his own language and not simply repeating what he hears. This step forward in the use of language represents very much a development in thinking because it means that the child is already grasping the principle which lies behind the use of verbs as well as nouns. From this point onwards, new words learned will eventually fall into different classes because of the different ways in which they will function in the language.

Combinations of an operator word and a name will meet the child's needs for some time but before very long he will extend his technique to include strings of three or four words. Many of his remarks may begin to sound like adult sentences but he will still use only words essential to his meanings and in most cases will keep to his own kind of syntax, producing sequences like 'Where you are?' and 'Mummy biscuits got?' which show clearly that he is evolving for himself the technique of making up sentences and is not just copying strings of words heard from adults.

The ensuing period in the child's life sees what is actually the most spectacular achievement that the child makes in any direction. In the space of about two short years the majority of children progress from remarks like 'Bye-bye sock' to quite complicated sentences on the adult model, things like 'Mummy, I don't think this tractor's as strong as the one Daddy bought me last week'. We take all this as a matter of course and do not realize how miraculous the process is. The child gets hours and hours of practice, virtually all his waking moments, since he is continually surrounded by adult speech. What he does is to infer from the thousands of examples he hears the principles of grammar and syntax which are operating in his native language and it is this that constitutes the most remarkable part of his achievement. With nearly every child there comes a point where language itself becomes intensely interesting and this serves to make his practice still more concentrated. Adults seldom realize that the child who is at the 'Why?' 'What's that?' stage is expressing his curiosity about words rather than things. A mother who has had to reply to the question 'What's that?' by saying 'A bicycle' a hundred times over may be forgiven for thinking her son is passionately interested in bicycles, but the truth is rather that he is learning the word *bicycle* and has to have it repeated many times to make sure he has got it. The same thing holds

Figure 1.1: Successive Stages of Speech and Language Development

The average child does not exist. If he did, he would probably reach the successive stages of speech and language development within the periods suggested in this table.

good with regard to the form of sentences and phrases. The question 'Why?' is an excellent way of hitting the jackpot of variations on a construction. We may imagine the child wants to know why, whereas he is much more keen to check that in reply you can say 'Because it is not so-and-so' or 'Because it is too so-and-so' or 'Because it is not so-and-so' or 'Because it is too so-and-so' or 'Because I haven't so-and-so' and even if he turns up a few 'don't knows', it has been well worth while from his point of view.

Systematic observation of children's speech during this period of language development produces convincing evidence that the child's brain is formulating the principles of the grammar for itself. Just from hearing what adults say the English child will infer, for example, that if something took place in the past you put -*ed* on to the end of words in one particular class, that if you have more than one of a thing, you add -*s* to another class of words, that if some quality is more in one case than in another, you put -*er* on to the word which refers to this quality, and so on. Within a short time the child's brain is stocked with formulations of this kind which he then applies in his own speech. He will apply them quite generally and most of the time this will produce acceptable remarks but sometimes the words which he forms in this way by analogy will not correspond to the usage of the adult language. When he has discovered how to make verbs refer to the past by ending them in -*ed,* he will use forms like *bringed, stranded* and *teached* and similarly he will make plurals such as *mouses* and *scissorses* and comparative forms like *gooder* and *badder.* People are inclined to say that this is because he has not yet learned English grammar, but the reverse is the truth; he does it because he *has* learned English grammar, or rather has inferred its laws for himself since it is clear that he has not heard these forms used by adult speakers.

Examples of many different kinds of formation by analogy can be culled from children's speech, some affecting sentence construction and word formation as can be seen in the two following examples, both of which display a rather charming inventiveness. The first occurred in the speech of a small boy who was heard to exclaim, 'You never do that, never'd you?', thereby showing an essential grasp of a complicated routine for converting a statement with an auxiliary verb into a question. The second concerns a father who, hearing something of a fracas breaking out in another room between an older and a younger daughter, called out loudly 'Deborah, tell Elizabeth not to argue!' What was his surprise, and since he was a linguist his delight too, to hear a childish voice say in authoritative tones 'Elizabeth, don't arg me'. This is an interesting illustration of the child's ability to get the morpheme string appropriately arranged even when not too sure of the content of the words. In the natural course of events, as the child hears more and more adult speech, words like *standed, teached, mouses, gooder* and so on give way to the adult forms, sometimes with explicit help from the parents, and ultimately the child's speech conforms in usage with that of the adults among whom he lives.

The development of grammar and syntax, like that of the phoneme system, takes place through the learning of new words. All of them go first into the passive vocabulary but in the early stages the child needs above all words to use, so that they pass fairly rapidly into his active vocabulary. It often happens that towards the middle of the second year the child concentrates on enlarging his passive vocabulary, which grows very quickly, and comparatively few new words appear in his own speech. During this time a child will usually refuse to repeat a word which he is just learning to recognize; there has to be some time lag before he will even say it aloud, let alone use it spontaneously in his own speech. In the ensuing months there is quite likely to be a marked increase in the number of words he transfers to his active vocabulary.

The words which are entered in our brain dictionary fall into a number of different word classes and three of these, the prepositions, conjunctions and pronouns, have a fixed number of items. During the period of language acquisition we learn the complete list of entries in these classes just as we learn the entire list of bound† morphemes and all this material taken together determines the form of what we say as distinct from its content. It is part of the economy of language that the form is regulated by choosing from a finite and restricted number of different elements, while the content is determined by choice from an infinitely greater range of possibilities. Language acquisition would scarcely be a practical proposition were it not for this arrangement; when we learn our mother tongue, we are able to acquire the complete stock of information demanded by the form of a spoken message during the learning period and as our experience and our mental powers increase, we employ these forms to express an ever greater variety of content. Consequently the words which we add to our cortical dictionary throughout life fall into the remaining word classes, nouns, verbs, adjectives and adverbs. Of these the nouns are the most numerous class, with verbs next, with adjectives some way behind and adverbs fewer still. These proportions are reflected in the child's language development. He begins by amassing a comparatively large stock of nouns and only one or two verbs; then about the age of two he will generally enlarge his stock of verbs rather rapidly, though the number will never equal that of the nouns. At this stage he will know a few adjectives, perhaps an adverb or two and one or two interrogative words such as

*what* and *where.* It is obvious that mental development and
development go hand in hand and interact very much with each other.
child's grasp of the relations of things in the outside world and his ability
to carry out mental operations do a great deal to influence the order in
which some word classes grow. A child does not find it easy even to
understand the meaning of prepositions, for example, and he therefore
does not use them in an early stage of his language learning. At the age of
about two he may learn a few, such as *to, in* and *on,* but it will be a long
time before he can use words like *under, behind* and *before.* In a similar
way he will use the word *and* quite early, but he will be at the stage of
putting together complex sentences before he can handle *but, if* and
*though.* Up to the age of two or more, a child refers to himself by name
and in the third person and therefore pronouns do not appear in his speech
until he begins to refer to himself as *me* or *I,* other pronouns coming into
his vocabulary later still.

Individual children naturally develop in their own way and at their own
pace with respect to speech and language as they do with everything else
and the average child remains a figment of the statistical imagination. We
may say, as a rough guide to the rate at which vocabulary grows, however,
that at two years of age a child may be using about 200 different words;
at three this will have risen to about 1000, and at four to something like
2000. An estimate of adult active vocabulary is 4000–5000 words
and it may seem strange that the rest of one's life leads to no more than
a two-to-one increase. The point is, however, that the 2000 words the
child commands comprise the form words, the prepositions, conjunctions
and pronouns, and all the commonest nouns and verbs, without which
we should not be able to say anything at all, so the twofold increase
leaves a considerable margin for the less common words, the technical
and specialist vocabularies which characterize the speech of individual
adult speakers.

The task of learning our mother tongue, then, is one which we accom-
plish essentially in the first five years of life. We evolve for ourselves the
phoneme system, the acoustic cues for distinguishing sounds, the grammar
and the syntax, and we lay the foundations of our personal dictionary. All
this is derived from the sound of adult speech by which we are continually
surrounded and we copy, mainly from our mothers, our pronunciation,
intonation and rhythm. There may be some modifications in the last three
in the course of our subsequent experience, but it is extremely difficult to
make radical changes in our speech habits, as we all learn when we attempt
to acquire a foreign language. Because we devote such an enormous
amount of practice to the task, we are able to complete it painlessly and

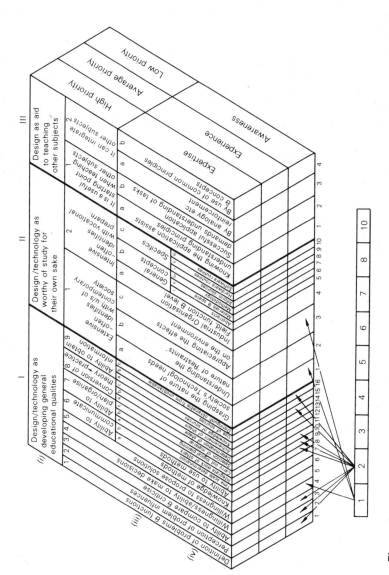

**Figure 1**

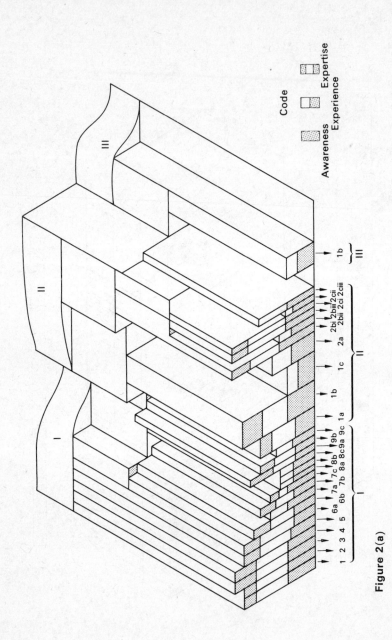

Figure 2(a)

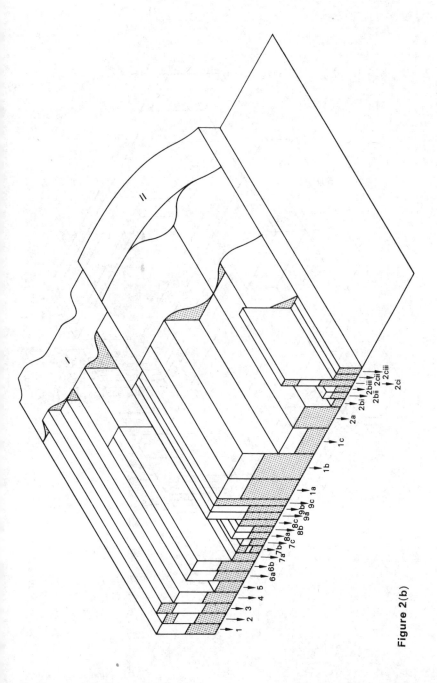

Figure 2(b)

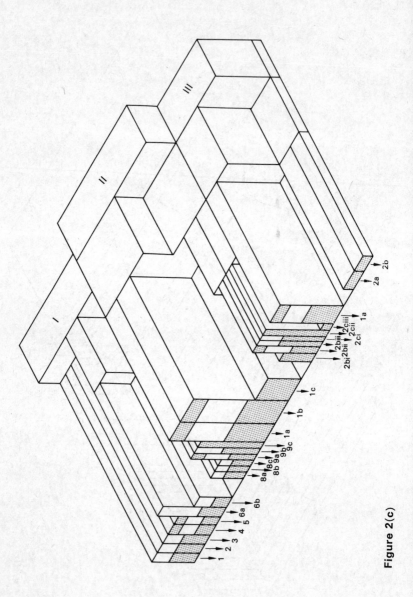

Figure 2(c)

probably not proportionately—the level of 'attainment' in each objective for each group. The degree of influence that does, or should, apply, is arguable. And as if this is not enough, the identity of those elements of the objective profile that—to put it crudely—carry marks, and those that serve to record student attributes only, is just as contentious. We are here at a transition point, passing between what we want to assess, and the ways in which we can assess it, meanwhile shooting the rapids represented by *scales* of assessment and reward.

Straightaway, we can lean on the analysis of schemes produced by Bloom and his colleagues. These are mentioned in other chapters, and need no further elaboration here. They do, however, deserve some comment in the context of the project, and there are three essential points worth making. The first is that, in cases where the project has a craft-based element the extrapolation into the psychomotor domain, produced by Sumner,[1] is of considerable help. The second point is one of reservation. A study of Figures 1 and 2 indicates that our objectives can be broken down into elements. While, in common with others, the author would not accept the Bloom 'scales' as they stand, the idea behind them is of great assistance; so much so that it has been possible to incorporate disciplinary distinctions into 'modified-Bloom' schemes. Now, if such schemes—whatever their source—can be applied to each *element* in turn, and we have found this to be possible, there is still a missing term. This omission is a large one, because—since a project is an integrating activity—the sum of the elements falls short of the attainment inherent in the overall project. Thus, on the one hand, a Bloom approach cannot cope with a total approach, while on the other hand the same approach can prove to be over-elaborate in respect of a single project element.

The former factor is dealt with later when discussing some actual project assessment schemes. The latter factor we have approached by providing a simplified scheme, broken down into just three levels. It is based on the premise that the elements of the project carry an expectancy that may not be either the highest possible, or even as high as that attainable *by* the student concerned—it all depends on priority of purpose, which leads both to budgeting of time and balancing of required attainment.

*Level I* corresponds to a general background grasp. In other words, we are attempting to generate an *awareness* of, say, the nature of the subject, or that part of the subject that we select for whatever reason, and we are satisfied if we get no further.

*Level II* goes beyond level I, as we are trying to relate the awareness and knowledge to specific cases. For instance, we may wish our students to be able to identify the restraints that apply when designing a river bridge, or to show how the design process developed in terms of the bridge, or to comment on current official policy in terms of power production. If level I represents a broad base, level II is exercising the mind by extending some of the base into, say, a commentary on selected situations. In other words, we go beyond the acquisition of knowledge and the generation of awareness to the point where those involved express an opinion in some way, albeit in their own terms. This does not mean that we hope the student will act like a professional, we merely wish to give him *experience* of a situation.

In *level III* we are positively encouraging the student to take on the role of a professional when confronted with, say, a technological situation. The clear implication is that this is the first step towards becoming a professional technologist, in this case, and that therefore we are expecting a measure of *expertise*.

While it is probably expecting too much to demonstrate a real correspondence between these broad levels and Bloom, Figure 3 shows a form

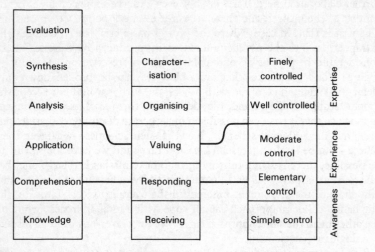

**Figure 3** The suggested cut-offs for the three levels of involvement

of cut-off where the three levels are cut across all of Bloom's three domains. To illustrate these in use, Figure 4 shows the three examples given earlier with the required levels superimposed.

To summarize this whole question of identification of purpose and objective, upon which the real business of assessment depends, let us say the following:

Firstly, one identifies the general purpose for adopting the project method;

Secondly, one breaks this basic purpose, together with its 'side-bands' (that stretch into the other types), down into elemental objectives;

Thirdly, one assigns teaching priorities in respect of each element;

Fourthly, one assigns to each element the degree of penetration hoped for;

Fifthly, one recognizes that this is an initial step intended to ensure good control and surveillance, and that

    (i) a fine-structured taxonomy of objectives may overwhelm any single element and therefore a coarser scheme is more appropriate;

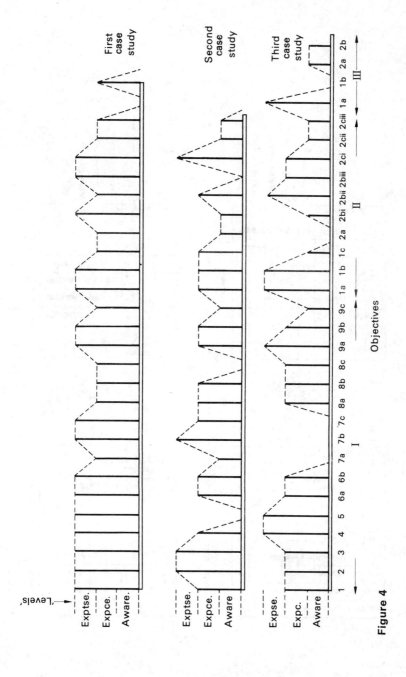

**Figure 4**

Simple movement
Elementary control
Moderate control
Well–controlled
Finely controlled

● Probable level required
▬ Probable range of level, required
□ Possible level, or range of levels

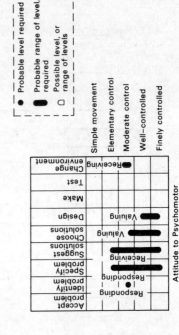

Psychomotor

Attitude to Psychomotor

Acquisition of knowledge
Comprehension
Application
Analysis
Synthesis
Evaluation

Cognitive (or mental dexterity)

Receiving
Responding
Valuing
Assimilating (organising)
Generating new values

Affective (or attitudes/values)

Accept problem
Identify problem
Specify problem
Suggest solutions
Choose solution
Design
Make
Test
Deliver
Change environment

**Figure 5**

(ii) obversely, adequate assessment of each element may still fail to do sufficient justice to the project as a whole.

As a last example before closing the chapter with a review of the assessment schemes available, there is a technique worth mentioning. It concerns in fact the examples in technology quoted earlier. An analysis has been reported elsewhere[2] of a complete technological project which results in an idealized model of a design/make/evaluate activity, consisting of a number of stages. Figure 5 indicates this, and shows an estimate of the levels that can reasonably be expected to apply to each stage in terms of Bloom's analysis. Since a project in this general area can be built up by linking stages together in various orders, this master diagram (i.e. Figure 5) can be used when preparing planning/control schemes such as those shown in Figures 3 and 4. A comparison of Figures 3, 4, and 5 shows that the connection is hardly a complete one, but it does at least provide some realistic basis. Figure 6 shows the result of this kind of preparation being applied to the other two projects (namely, a criticism of a design for a VIth form general studies course, and a limited design exercise for a 'non-practical' set of undergraduate mathematicians).

Let us now review the types of assessment available to us, in terms of schemes that have been used experimentally, or are now established more permanently. A warning must, however, be issued first. Circumstances do alter cases. Even where approaches to projects have been far enough proven to be regarded as standardized, the objectives must still lie in the hands of the teacher, since they guide the teacher's supervisory role (or should do). This being so, schemes of assessment have to be teacher-based. As was noted earlier, the best project-wreckers are those schemes developed for one method and purpose, and then mis-applied to others. This is to say that, ideally, the teacher prepares his own scheme; one that is firmly based on his own policy.

What general evidence is there available upon which to construct assessment? The list is formidable, but well worth giving, and it can be divided into two parts: student-provided, and teacher provided. The two parts provide direct parallels, as Table 2 below infers.

The importance of examining the course of the project as it proceeds, as well as retrospectively, has already been discussed. There are two areas to be considered—those of teacher action and of pupil activity. Let us take the teacher action first; set out below are the questions that the teacher is recommended to ask *before* launching the project (developed by the author as part of the inauguration of the Oxford Board's Advanced level course in Design, A83).

A checklist of questions (developed by M. Deere) for consideration by the project tutor provides a useful guide to the choice of a suitable project topic. It is stressed that the tutors' answers should be merely a guide to possible difficulties inherent in the problem and providing an example

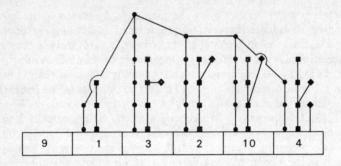

As carried out– mode no. 1

Alternative approach –mode no.2

• Cognitive

■ Affective

◆ Skill

◆ Indicates
a level of
attitude towards
a degree of skill

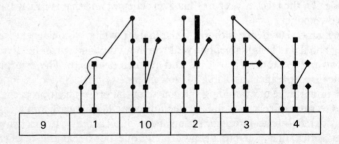

**Figure 6**

**Table 2.** Range of evidence available for project assessment

| Student | Teacher |
| --- | --- |
| S.1 His first intended target | T.1 Teachers choice of target |
| S.2 His justification for choosing it | T.2 As S.2 |
| S.3 Any changes in target | T.3 As S.3 |
| S.4 His reasons for these | T.4 As S.4 |
| S.5 The information that he gathers | — |
| S.6 His methods used to secure S.5 | T.6 Teacher comment on S.6 |
| S.7 His sources for S.5 | T.7 Teacher comment on S.7 |
| S.8 His own evaluation of S.5, 6, 7 | T.8 Teacher comment on S.8 |
| S.9 His record of his planning actions and his decisions | T.9 Teacher comment on S.9 and his own notes of S.14 |
| S.10 His final report | T.10 Teacher comment on S.10 |
| S.11 His final product if any | T.11 Teacher comment on S.11 |
| S.12 Any oral presentation of his work | T.12 Teacher comment on S.12 |
| S.13 His evaluation, on completion, of S.1 to S.11 inclusive | T.13 Teacher comment on S.13 |
| S.14 The continuing dialogue with his teacher | T.14 Teacher comments on his actions taken throughout the project |
| S.15 His response to question on completion from either teacher or a third party | T.15 Teacher overall evaluation of student doing project |
| | T.16 Teacher justification for T.5 to T.13 and T.15 |

of the minimal level of attainment rather than an indication of any required problem solution. The questions are:

1. What is the real problem that the student seeks to solve?
2. Is the problem novel to (a) the student?
   (b) the teacher?
   (c) absolutely?
3. What is the likely outcome (a) optimistically?
   (b) pessimistically?
4. What are the three most difficult problems—inherent in the project— that the student is likely to meet?
5. (i) what degree of challenge does the project present to the student?
   (ii) Is the student's interest in the chosen problem sufficient to sustain him through the project?
6. (i) In a general way, what stages do you expect the project to go through, and on what time-scale will they occur?
   (ii) If a group of students is involved, does the work-plan indicate individual responsibility and/or tasks for each member?
7. (i) Which of the following resources are likely to be available?
   (ii) Are these resources going to be adequate?
   (a) finance
   (b) materials

(c) equipment
(d) source material
(e) specialist advice.

8. Does the task give the student adequate opportunity to show achievement on each of the objectives?

In order to understand the nature of the project process it is helpful to classify the different activities which occur into a number of classes or stages, and to order these stages into their most likely order of appearance. This classification into stages is also generally adhered to when writing up or reporting the progress of the project after completion. However, it should be remembered that in the practical situation these stages overlap both in content and in timing.

The activities which are featured in each of these project stages are those given in Figures 5 and 8(d).

Set out below, on the other hand, are those questions to be asked frequently as the project proceeds in order to assess the teachers' own understanding of the work (developed by Miss W. A. Carter and the author during work done at Reading University in 1969)

Strategy

At what stage is the group working?
When are they likely to finish this stage?
Does this still allow them to finish the project as planned?
If not, is the overall objective to be cut back?
Are they still gathering information (scanning)?
If so, should they now stop, and begin to organize and decide upon it?
If they should continue to scan, should they continue to develop the same lines, or should they open up new ones?
If they have reached the focussing stage, is this premature?
What is the likely outcome of the focussing stage?
Is it going to be incomplete, satisfactory, or overdetailed?

Recording

Have the group adequately recorded:
the questions they asked (or experiments carried out)?
the answers that they received?
the ideas that they generated?
the decisions that they took?
the doubts or reservations that they had?

While both of these have the initial purpose of assisting the teacher 'parochially', it will be obvious that a more formal record will assist with ultimate assessment. Such a formal record can, indeed, be incorporated in pupil records. Figure 7 shows a most useful device, developed by the author in this case for undergraduate project work involving groups. Nevertheless, it is not confined to that level. In the section of the chart marked 1 the pupils are encouraged to draw up a rudimentary planning scheme in the form of a vertical bar chart schedule. The significant points on the bar chart are described in section 2 and the objective is described in section 3. As the project proceeds, this planning chart is replotted at intervals in section 1, expanding the details as necessary. Significant decisions are recorded in section 4, and each group member records his own action and

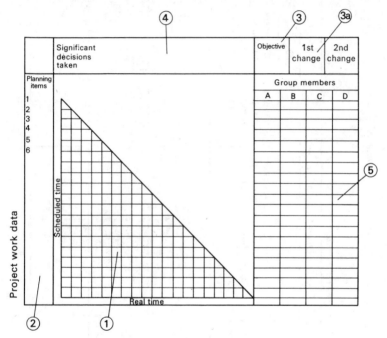

**Figure 7** Project control chart (Based on EMI 'Slip Chart')

responsibility at frequent intervals in section 5. The nature of the section 1 layout is such that failure to meet schedule times is recorded by a droop in the line connecting each event at each replotting. The reason for this can be related both to decisions taken, and to member-action, and if a retargetting is required, thus cutting back the complexity of the end-result, this is recorded in section 3a. In effect, Figure 7 serves three purposes: it enforces planning, it records action, and it presents much of the evidence required at final assessment. Its main shortcoming is that it omits much of the detail of corresponding teacher action, although the teacher would be encouraged to endorse the chart as frequently as may be required. Figure 8, however, shows the extent to which teacher action may be recorded. This is again

Group...................................................... Date......................................................

## Teacher Role Record Sheet

Please tick activities carried out in directing or assisting the group.

| | Obtaining Information | | | | | | | |
| --- | --- | --- | --- | --- | --- | --- | --- | --- |
| | *Facts etc.* | | | | *Sources* | | | |
| | *Emphasized facts previously learned* | *Suggested what relevant facts might be* | *Pursued facts on behalf of group* | *Gave specific information from own experience* | *Suggested books to read* | *Suggested contacts etc. outside school* | *Suggested contacts etc. within the school* | *Suggested experiments to carry out* |
| Please tick if carried out | | | | | | | | |
| Did this cause difficulty? | | | | | | | | |
| Should have been done, but wasn't | | | | | | | | |

Figure 8(a)

**Organizing the Group**

| | Allocating tasks and resources | | | | | Setting time scales: accelerating or extending stages of project | | | | | Deciding goals or subgoals | | | | |
|---|---|---|---|---|---|---|---|---|---|---|---|---|---|---|---|
| | (1) Made decision for group | (2) Giving alternatives for group to choose | (3) Making group decide | (4) Confirming group decision | (5) No Action | (1) Made decision for group | (2) Giving alternatives for group to choose | (3) Making group decide | (4) Confirming group decision | (5) No Action | (1) Made decision for group | (2) Giving alternatives for group to choose | (3) Making group decide | (4) Confirming group decision | (5) No Action |
| Tick action | | | | | | | | | | | | | | | |
| Tick the most desirable | | | | | | | | | | | | | | | |
| Tick most difficult action | | | | | | | | | | | | | | | |

**Figure 8(b)**

## Organizing Information

| | Summarized or correlated into information collected | Extended or amplified information | Explained or interpreted information | Corrected information | Rejected information |
|---|---|---|---|---|---|
| Please tick if carried out | | | | | |
| Did this cause difficulty | | | | | |
| Should have been done but wasn't | | | | | |

## Drawing Conclusions, or making decisions

| | Gave the group the correct conclusion or made the decision for them | Give list of possible conclusions or decisions and asked them to select | Forced group to come to own conclusion or make own decision | Confirmed Groups conclusion or decision | Took no action |
|---|---|---|---|---|---|
| Tick action carried out | | | | | |
| Tick the most desirable action | | | | | |
| Tick the most difficult action | | | | | |

**Figure 8(c)**

| Stage 1 | Stage 2 | Stage 3 | Stage4 | Stage5 | Stage 6 | Stage 7 | Stage 8 | Stage 9 | Stage 10 |
|---|---|---|---|---|---|---|---|---|---|
| Accept problem situation | Identify problem | Specify problem | Propose alternative outline solutions | Choose a solution | Detail design | Make and assemble | Test | Deliver device or system | Change environment |

$<$ Represents scanning phase  $>$ Represents focussing phase

Please indicate on the diagram at the end of each session the stage of the project in:

(1) The design line
(2) Focussing and scanning

e.g. If, at the end of the third lesson, the group has been collecting information for proposing alternative solutions to the problem set, you would indicate this by drawing a line as shown below.

(3) Represents the session and the line is drawn in the diverging part of the diagram to show that this is a scanning activity.

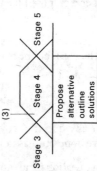

**Figure 8(d)**

125

part of the Carter/Deere work at Reading, and is included as a suggested basis for teacher record charts.

Moving to methods of final assessment, Figure 9 represents an interesting two-stage system. The form and questions are reasonably self-evident, and there are two observations that can be made. The first is that a minimum range of activities and/or decision types have to be made in order for the candidate to pass at all, and the second is that the teachers' own comments on each question have to relate to real evidence. There are problems. The first is that the real evidence just referred to is the candidate's report. This puts a great onus on the teacher to ensure that 'mark-worthy' material is recorded at the time. The second problem is that it is doubtful if form B can satisfactorily extend the form A 'Yes/No' technique. One would also query, whether *all* the degrees of freedom laid out in Table 1 are covered adequately. On the other hand, this technique does allow flexibility in discovering these factors by teacher–examiner–student negotiation, and in this particular case (an Advanced level course) this has been exploited in practice.

In addition to this 'binary' approach there are two other possibilities: the 'accumulated points' scheme, and the 'weighted scale' scheme. A simple and interesting form of the accumulated points scheme is practised by a school in the Midlands. Here the school looked for decisions made by the students in the course of their work, classified them into type, and then allocated marks to each type. For example, each decision based on information found in a text book might carry 4 points, while each action that directly sought information from an external source might carry 5. This is good in principle, but can be absurd in practice. For instance, four letters to suppliers ordering materials can carry far more reward that a single inspired idea deriving from a reconsideration of standard principles. This is the real danger, that flexibility can be lost. However, this need not be so, as we see from the questionnaire set out below.

### *Proposed Questionnaire and Marking Scheme for Project Technology*

1. Wherever possible, all questions should be assessed and a mark awarded.

2. Each question carries a maximum of 5 marks.
   If the work has been excellent, award 5 marks.

   | | |
   |---|---|
   | very good | 4 |
   | good | 3 |
   | fair | 2 |
   | poor | 1 |

   For any question covering an aspect of the work a candidate should have done but has not—0.

3. If a question is not applicable to the particular project being assessed, then the column alongside that question should be left blank.

**Figure 9(a)** The assessment of course work in engineering science

---

1. Two forms, A and B, will be provided. The forms will be completed by the teacher acting as the internal assessor, who will be asked to enter in the spaces provided appropriate references to the candidate's journal or reports in justification of the decisions made.

   Each candidate must reach a satisfactory standard in respect of the aspects of his work assessed in Form A (see example attached) in order to satisfy the examiners in his course work. The assessment of the aspects of his work dealt with in Form B will determine the actual mark to be allotted to the candidate for his course work.

---

**Figure 9(b)**

---

2. *Form A* (see the attached proforma for the proposed lay-out of the questionnaire)

   In addition to the details of the candidate and the instructions to the assessor, the Form will include the following questions. It will provide spaces for the journal or report references. The assessor will be required to answer YES or NO to each question.

   (i) (Each question is to be answered once for each experiment on the basis of the written evidence provided by the candidate's report)

   1. Has the candidate shown an understanding of the problems set?
   2. Has the candidate shown useful application to the task?
   3. Has the candidate made safe use of the apparatus involved?
   4. Has the candidate succeeded in making accurate observations within the limits of the apparatus used?
   5. Has the candidate made estimates of the tolerances and errors incurred where called for?
   6. Has the candidate checked doubtful observations where possible?
   7. Are the findings of the investigation consistent with the observations made?
   8. Is the final report both clear and complete?

   (ii) *Project*

   9. Did the candidate made a significant contribution to the work plan?
   10. Has the candidate used the work plan with intelligence?
   11. Has the candidate made use of and indicated relevant and independent sources of information available to him? (e.g. has he consulted books to which he was not directed?)
   12. Is the final report both clear and complete?

---

*(Sample lay-out of questionnaire)*
*Instructions to internal assessor*  For each experiment and for the project, answer each of the questions (these are given on the separate sheet) by entering YES or NO in the space provided. Enter also the appropriate references to the candidate's journal or report in the space provided.

Name of candidate: ...........................
Name of centre: ................................
.........................Centre No...............

**FORM A**

| QUESTIONS | EXPERIMENT NO. 1 | | EXPERIMENT NO. 2 | | EXPERIMENT NO. 3 | | EXPERIMENT NO. 4 | |
|---|---|---|---|---|---|---|---|---|
| | Yes/No | Report (or journal) reference | Yes/No | Report (or journal) reference | Yes/No | Report (or journal) reference | Yes/No | Report (or journal) reference |
| 1 | | | | | | | | |
| 2 | | | | | | | | |
| 3 | | | | | | | | |
| 4 | | | | | | | | |
| 5 | | | | | | | | |
| 6 | | | | | | | | |
| 7 | | | | | | | | |
| 8 | | | | | | | | |

| Project Questions | Yes/No | Report (or journal) reference | COMMENTS |
|---|---|---|---|
| 9 | | | |
| 10 | | | |
| 11 | | | |
| 12 | | | |

................................ (signed) ....................................... (date)

(Internal Assessor)

**Figure 9(c)**

**Figure 9(d)**

---

3. *Form B*

This Form will require answers of YES or NO to the questions listed below for each of the chosen experiments and project. Spaces will be included for reference to specific points in the journal and report, and other comments.

1. Has the candidate elicited any valid hypothesis from any set of observations?
2. Has the candidate shown mathematical ability in the formulation or moderation of hypotheses?
3. Has the candidate shown initiative in deciding the experimental procedures to be adopted?
4. Has the candidate shown initiative in devising or assembling experimental apparatus?
5. Has the candidate shown any understanding of the relative importance of the various experimental errors incurred in the course of this work?
6. Has the candidate discussed alternative approaches or solutions?
7. Did the candidate independently formulate the problem in a manner appropriate for its solution?
8. Does the candidate both show any recognition of any implicit assumptions (e.g. recognition of the limitations of physical laws) and assess their importance?
9. Has the candidate made a valid critique of his work?
10. Has the candidate been skilful or resourceful or thorough in the application of established design, craft or assembly procedures, or in the methodical (or statistical) handling of results?

*Note*: Form B, for which a sample is *not* provided, will follow the general pattern of Form A.

---

4. To obtain the final marks:
   (a) Multiply by 5 the total number of questions it was possible to assess, i.e. find the maximum number of marks it was possible for the candidate to obtain.
   (b) Add up the total number of marks awarded to the candidate.
   (c) Give the final mark as a percentage.

*Questionnaire*

1. Has the candidate understood the problem set and its purpose?
2. Has the candidate sought out all known data concerning the project?
3. Has the candidate considered the various ways in which his problem could have been solved?
4. Has the candidate given reasoned arguments for their rejection?
5. Has the candidate carried out any experiments or made any models to help the choice of approach to the problem?
6. Has the candidate carried out any tests to find out the limits within which the apparatus must function?
7. Has the candidate drawn up a suitable work plan to ensure that the work will be carried out in logical sequence?
8. Has the candidate submitted a plan that can be accepted with very little modification?

9. If modification of the work plan was necessary, just how successfully has the candidate been able to modify it?

10. Has the candidate shown simplicity of design or is his apparatus too complicated?

11. Does the design of the apparatus show a real understanding of the limits within which it must function?

12. Has the candidate made the correct choice of materials for this apparatus?

13. How original has the candidate been in the design of the apparatus?

14. How ingenious has the candidate been in the use of available materials, bits of equipment or apparatus?

15. Has the candidate shown any real initiative during the making of the apparatus?

16. Has the candidate shown persistence in overcoming problems arising as the work progressed?

17. Bearing in mind the known practical ability and previous practical experience of the candidate, is the apparatus well made?

18. Is the apparatus made accurately enough to enable it to function correctly within the limits required by the experiment?

19. Did the candidate thoroughly test his apparatus prior to actually using it for experimental purposes?

20. How skilful was the candidate in carrying out his experiments within the limits of the apparatus?

21. Has the candidate shown an understanding of the relative importance of any experimental errors?

22. Has the candidate checked doubtful observations where possible?

23. Has the candidate correctly evaluated the experimental results obtained?

24. Has the candidate appreciated the accuracy of the results?

25. Has the candidate been aware of any assumption he has made while obtaining his results?

26. Even although no solution was possible, how successful has the candidate been with the project?

27. Is the final report written in clear, simple English, and with an economy of words?

28. Are the diagrams, drawings, graphs, etc. well presented?

29. Is the discussion of the problems and their solution fully comprehensive?

30. Is the discussion and appraisal of the results well presented?

31. How clear are the conclusions reached?

32. Has the candidate shown in his conclusions a real understanding of the problem?

33. Has the candidate been aware of any problems that still remain to be overcome?

34. Has the candidate given any suggestions as to how these problems might be solved?

35. Has the candidate suggested any future experimental work using the apparatus that has been made?
36. Has the candidate been aware of or suggested any other line of investigation that may have come to light during the working period?
37. Has the candidate suggested any modification to the apparatus or its use?
38. Has the candidate made full use of his potential while doing his project work?
39. A maximum of 10 further marks may be awarded if it is felt that some important aspect of the candidate's work has not been covered or emphasized enough by the questionnaire.

*Analysis of Marking Schedule*
*Section 1.*     Planning.
Research     6 questions     30 marks  ⎫
Work Plan     3 questions     15 marks  ⎬ Total of 45 marks.

*Section* II     Execution.
Design     4 questions     20 marks  ⎫
Practical work 5 questions     25 marks  ⎬ Total of 80 marks.
Results     7 questions     35 marks  ⎭

*Section III*     Conclusions and Final Report.
Conclusions drawn 7 questions     35 marks  ⎫
Future prospects 6 questions     30 marks  ⎬ Total of 65 marks

*Section IV*     Additional marks awarded     Total of 10 marks.
    Maximum Possible Marks 200.

From the start, we see that this neither asks for teacher involvement to be declared, nor does it seek justification for teacher marking. Apart from this, it must be remembered that, like all good assessment schemes, it applies only to the work for which it was designed—this is given in the preamble in the form of objectives. To its credit, the scheme is flexible to the extent that certain objectives can be neglected without loss of mark-potential, although the degree to which this can be done is not stated. This apart, its scope is general enough—for a 'construct' based project. This can be seen from a comparison with Table 1. The example does, however, prompt two comments: might we not wish to *record* an aptitude without *necessarily* incorporating the grading given in the final score?; is there not a danger in this scheme of overmarking the report as an end in itself without allowing for other forms of communication? This *is* shown in the other example of this kind, set out below.

*Method of Assessment*
    The assessment should be first carried out by those who have supervised the work and again by an external moderator. The procedure should be as follows.

1. When the candidate has studied his problem and evolved a course of action, he should offer his notes and sketches relating to this for an internal assessment. A grading should then be awarded and the candidate advised what modifications to make, if any, to ensure that his plan is a workable one. The candidate should then continue with the project until completed.
2. The finalized notes, drawings and modifications should be examined and given a grading.
3. Any pieces of constructed experimental apparatus or tools should be examined and graded for ingenuity etc.
4. The finished project should be examined and graded.
5. The candidate should then be interviewed with his project, and all notes and drawings. Relevant questions should indicate the completeness of his notes. His demonstrations and answers to questions should indicate the extent to which he has understood all that has taken place and that his contribution to the project has been reasonable. This is important in the case of group projects.

*Gradings*

These should be based on the following list of questions under each heading and every question should be awarded points on this basis. 10 for excellent, 8 for good, 5 for reasonable and 2 for poor. This gives 150 possible marks. The questions are as follows:

1. (a) Does the initial plan show that the candidate fully appreciates the complexity of the question and the purpose of its solution?
   (b) How little modification of the plan was necessary?
2. (a) Are the drawings neatly executed and comprehensive?
   (b) Do the notes indicate that the candidate has shown clear logical thinking?
3. (a) How much ingenuity was shown in the experimental apparatus and special tools?
   (b) What degree of workmanship do they show?
4. (a) If the finished project is a practical one to what extent does it work, or if it is a written thesis is it clear and conclusive?
   (b) How complex is the design?
   (c) What is the standard of workmanship?
   (d) How long did it take to build?
5. (a) How convincing was the candidate's explanation of his procedure in solving the problem?
   (b) How much contribution does he appear to have made?
   (c) How good is the workmanship considering his previous practical experience? (Has he taken an O-level in craft or technical drawing for instance?)
   (d) What degree of confidence did he show in the demonstration and explanation of the function of his finished project?

(e) To what extent does the candidate appear to have benefited from his participation in the work?

However, there are things to cause concern. The spread of abilities tested is narrow, and the questions imply the preservation of one of the undesirable features mentioned earlier: a basic criterion based on professional performance. While this and other features give cause for disquiet, at least the *interpretation* can be flexible.

Before moving to broader-based assessments, a study of the 'points' system will suggest some principles to remember. Points systems are not necessarily less subjective than others; in fact, apparently rigid points systems can allow flexibility in interpretation. As a result, it can be argued, not only that too much detail is superfluous but that an assessment scheme of this kind could lead to a stereotyped approach inimical to the whole project method idea.

Figures 7 and 10 suggest the possibility of a compromise. Figure 10 is, in fact, the final assessment sheet attaching to Figure 7—in this sense the two schemes are complementary. The order of completion is as follows:

(i) supervisor scrutinises Figure 7 as it develops;

(ii) on this basis he completes Figure 10, using items I(a) to (e) to arrive at I(f). It will be noted that he completes this as a group award, making separate awards for each group member only where the individual is above or below the standard achieved by the group;

(iii) he then completes Sections II and III not so much as ends in themselves, but rather to provide information for the awarding panel to consider;

(iv) the awarding panel, consisting of all supervisors and some external assessors, interviews each group and moderates the project group awards before proceeding to grade each individual. At this time, the supervisor may well be asked to justify his completion of Figure 10 by reference to Figure 7. In any event Figure 7 serves as a basis for individual interview by the panel members. The main feature of Figure 10 is that rather than allocating points, the award is based on an above-or-below-par basis. The same is true for Figure 11, which is a development for use in an A-level course which places a high premium on project work. In this case the teacher indicates three things under several main headings:

Rating on a literal spectrum
His own involvement
His justification.

The actual weighting of the first five headings is allowed to 'float' from year to year—a necessary feature in a developmental scheme—while the last heading is included so as to allow 'non-markable' items to be duly considered.

There is one further question to be answered, and this concerns formal examinations. So far this chapter has tended to imply that these do not apply to project work, yet this is hardly true. In some shape or form, project work is part of the whole curriculum. If, as the writer believes, its

Title . . . . . . . . . . . . . . .

Team members : only tick if different to the Group assessment

| | Group as a whole | A | B | C | D | E |
|---|---|---|---|---|---|---|
| | | | | | | |

I. ACADEMIC

(a) *Comprehension*
Complete understanding of project as a whole
Good understanding, but incomplete in parts
Average
Rather poor or incomplete understanding
Substantial lack of understanding

(b) *Use of Theory* (Relates to other parts of the course)
Very intelligent and accurate use of theory
Application of theory much in evidence
Average
Limited or rather inaccurate use of theory
Neglect of theory

(c) *Information* (Relates to exploration *outside* the rest of the course)
Discovered all necessary information relative to the problem
Discovered a great deal of the necessary information but incomplete in parts
Average
Substantial gaps in information discovered
Almost complete lack of relevant information

**Figure 10(a)** Project Assessment Sheet

| | Group as a whole | A | B | C | D | E |
|---|---|---|---|---|---|---|
| | | | | | | |

I. (*Academic*)—continued

(d) *Commercial Awareness* (If you feel that this item does
not apply, please say so)
Consistent awareness of commercial exploitation
Evidence that there was a general awareness of
commercial exploitation, but some reservations
Average
Some lack of appreciation of commercial implications
Total disregard of commercial exploitation

(e) *Extrapolation and Forward Vision*
Consistent awareness of future possibilities of project
Team took account of future possibilities on occasion
Average
Did not really look far beyond the immediate objective
Totally disregarded future developments

(f) *General Academic Performance*

1st
2.1
2.2
3rd
Pass
Fail

**Figure 10(b)**

135

| | Group as a whole | A | B | C | D | E |
|---|---|---|---|---|---|---|
| | | | | | | |

II. GENERAL

(a) *Practical Acumen*
- Always able to apply theory in practical terms
- Showed marked practical flair and ability to improvise
- Average
- Considerable lack of ability to put theory into practice
- Unable to put theory into practice

(b) *Attention to Detail*
- Every aspect followed through in every detail
- Some areas skimped in terms of detail
- Average
- Most of the project shows rather poor attention to detail
- Bored by the details of the project

(c) *Ingenuity*
- Very ingenious
- Evidence of considerable enterprise
- Average
- Little enterprise shown
- No imagination

(d) *Initiative & Guidance*
- Team wholly able to stand on its own feet; very resourceful
- Unsought guidance necessary on occasion
- Average
- Team leans rather heavily on outside help
- Unable to make progress without considerable help

Figure 10(c)

| | Group as a whole | A | B | C | D | E |
|---|---|---|---|---|---|---|
| | | | | | | |

II. *(General)*—continued

(e) *Application*

Team devoted a considerable amount of their own time
Team showed marked evidence of enthusiasm for the project
Team regularly worked the hours timetabled
Evidence of lack of enthusiasm; slackness in attendance
Wholly disinterested in project

(f) *General Engineering 'common-sense' performance*

Excellent
Good
Average
Fair
Poor

III. MANAGERIAL

(a) *Planning*

Whole project well planned in advance:
Generally good, but faulty on occasion
Average
Planning rather rudimentary
Little evidence of any planning at all

(b) *Teamwork*

Good co-ordination between members of team
Generally good co-ordination, but some areas of disorganization
Average

**Figure 10(d)**

137

| | Group as a whole | A | B | C | D | E |
|---|---|---|---|---|---|---|
| III. (*Managerial*)—continued | | | | | | |
| Efforts of individuals rather unco-ordinated | | | | | | |
| Just a collection of individual, unrelated contributions | | | | | | |
| (c) *Records* | | | | | | |
| All decisions and results accurately recorded | | | | | | |
| Generally good, but with some noticeable gaps | | | | | | |
| Average | | | | | | |
| Records incomplete and sparse | | | | | | |
| Poor or non-existent | | | | | | |
| (d) *Report* (Please tick as many as apply, and add any further comments) | | | | | | |
| Well written and readable | | | | | | |
| Accurate | | | | | | |
| Logically presented | | | | | | |
| Well integrated | | | | | | |
| Well illustrated | | | | | | |
| Would give a complete picture of the project to any following team | | | | | | |
| (e) *General Performance in Organisation and Communications* | | | | | | |
| Excellent | | | | | | |
| Good | | | | | | |
| Average | | | | | | |
| Fair | | | | | | |
| Poor | | | | | | |

M.T.D. 10th June, 69.

**Figure 10(e)**

138

success or failure depends upon pre-identification of purpose—and thereby the laying down of criteria for assessment—then *that* process depends for its success on the selection of objectives that supplement or complement those of the whole curriculum. In the example just referred to as Figure 10, project work was connected to a course of teaching in 'project approaches and techniques', and this course was examined 'formally'. Now, while the questions are directed towards testing comprehension of routines, etc., if one wishes to see these routines incorporated in the project work that one sets up, they can be based on the student's own project task. In this way one can assess the student's general attitude and ability, and whether he can transfer lessons learnt in one situation to another, less familiar, area. Set out below is an example of such a question.

(*Sample*) *Question X:* 'Consider your own Final-year design project. Prepare a critical-path-diagram for the "as-developed" project, and also a similar diagram representing your views as to the "ideal" course of the project. Indicate both time allocation *and* the division of individual responsibility between group members.'

(*Sample*) *Question Y:* 'Prepare a detailed specification for the end-product of your current project. You are quite entitled to incorporate experience gained during the course of the project.'

In this same area—the measurement of 'transferability'—it is possible to use unfamiliar situations. Set out here is the style of question used by Carter and Deere to examine the effectiveness of project techniques.

*Sheet 1*

1. Christmas Day falls on a Monday. A large Christmas tree arrives on Saturday and is decorated. It soon becomes clear that it must be supported at some height, to keep it out of reach of a two-year-old.
2. The school Physics Laboratory has a compression testing machine and a local builder asks the school to test some samples of concrete.
3. A moon expedition needs to have some means of transport to enable its members to move around the moon's surface once they arrive.
4. A child has lost most of the use of one of its limbs and requires some device to overcome this handicap.
5. The Borough Engineer asks the school for the assistance of the sixth form in carrying out a traffic survey for his Department.
6. An ironmonger finds he spends much of his time counting out nuts and bolts to meet the varying requirements of his customers. He would like a machine, which he could pre-set, to do this while he is serving other customers.
7. The school Science Society has built a small rocket and the Chemistry Master would like to use this to test the energy liberated in Chemical Reactions.
8. A new town is planned around Newbury. It is required to install plant to meet the considerably increased power requirement which the new development will demand.

**A83 DESIGN** (Assessment form A)

Project Title: _____

**PROJECT ASSESSMENT**

**SCHOOL:**

**CANDIDATE  TUTOR:**

**RATING** Tick one box per row

| | A | B | C | D | E |
|---|---|---|---|---|---|

**TEACHER INVOLVEMENT**

*Candidate worked largely unaided* | *reasonable support & exchange of ideas* | *considerable assistance & provision of ideas necessary*

**JUSTIFICATION**
*Where appropriate refer to the report; the product; log book; notes, or sketches; tutor's impression; any other factors*

HOW WELL WAS TASK COMPREHENDED?
Consider scope of understanding; accuracy of information used; evaluation of completed task.

HOW SOUNDLY HAS THE CANDIDATE BASED HIS DECISIONS?
Consider: logic (where appropriate); range of options considered; criteria established.

HOW WELL HAS THE CANDIDATE FORMULATED AND CARRIED OUT RELEVANT TESTS OR EXPERIMENTS?

**Figure 11**

WHAT IS THE QUALITY OF
THE CANDIDATES REPORT ?
Consider : accuracy ;
completeness ; clarity ;
conviction ; use of diagrams.

| | | | | |
|---|---|---|---|---|

Consider candidates original level of skill & the resources available
{ CONSTRUCTIONAL SKILL/TECHNIQUE
{ GRAPHIC SKILL/TECHNIQUE

COMMENT ON THE FOLLOWING FEATURES OF THE CANDIDATE'S PROJECT WORK
Aesthetic sensitivity & judgment
Range & quality of ideas
Adventure & Novelty of

**Figure 11** (continued)

## Techniques of Assessment

### Sheet 2

I tackled this sheet (tick which is true)

| 1st | 2nd | 3rd | 4th | 5th |

Fill in the table below.
Put a tick in the appropriate box if you think that any of the actions below, labelled A to J, would help you to develop your chosen solutions to the technological situations listed 1 to 8 on sheet 1.

| Technological situation on Sheet 1 | 1 | 2 | 3 | 4 | 5 | 6 | 7 | 8 |
|---|---|---|---|---|---|---|---|---|
| A. List functions you want to carry out | | | | | | | | |
| B. Choose material to make it from ✓ | | | ` | | | | | |
| C. Find out how much money is available for project | | | | | | | | |
| D. Decide which skills are needed for different stages in development | | | | | | | | |
| E. Draw up a time-table before you begin | | | | | | | | |
| F. Go to a firm of Management Consultants | | | | | | | | |
| G. Draw a sketch of what you want to make | | | | | | | | |
| H. Decide if you have enough of the right type of manpower to carry it out | | | | | | | | |
| I. Buy necessary equipment | | | | | | | | |
| J. Go to the Library | | | | | | | | |

### Sheet 3

*Selecting the best solution from several suggested*

The Law states that tablets given on a doctor's prescription must be counted by a qualified pharmacist. He spends many hours doing this routine work, as it is essential he gives exactly the correct number. He would save a great deal of time if he had a machine which could be preset to count out the tablets.

The following machines A, B, C were suggested:

A
  (i) Does not always count exactly the correct number of tablets.
  (ii) Is easy to clean.
  (iii) Is expensive to produce.

B
  (i) Always counts the correct number of tablets.
  (ii) Is very difficult to clean.
  (iii) Is fairly expensive to produce.

C
 (i) Does not always count the correct number of tablets.
 (ii) Is very easy to clean.
(iii) Is very cheap to produce.

Which, if any, of these machines do you think would be the best to develop?

---

It was administered following a short, self-contained, project course. Although it is of the open-ended type, there is no reason why multiple-choice items should not achieve the same end. The last example, below, is of this kind. As part of an evaluative routine to check a major curriculum development exercise, it may well derive from the previous example—it certainly sets out to achieve the same end, albeit for a larger student population.

*Technological Problems*

1. You have 40 minutes to answer the questions in this folder. Please read each question carefully and study the example which is given.
2. There is plenty of time to complete all the questions.
3. The question is on the left-hand page and you should write your answer on the right-hand page.

ANSWER ALL QUESTIONS

NAME .......................................................

SCHOOL.....................................................

FORM .....................

*Question 1*
Before an article is made a number of factors have to be taken into account.

*Example*: In designing an overhead electricity cable you would look for a material which met the following conditions.

> as cheap as possible
> resistant to corrosion
> strong
> light in weight
> good conductor of electricity

The most important factor is the last one.
On the opposite page you will see a list of factors which might be important in the design of objects. In the case of the electricity cable the factors we have chosen are:

| A | C | D | F | K | | | Most important | K |

Now we would like you to choose the factors which are important in the design of:

(a) a 1 pint milk container for daily delivery
(b) a material suitable for surfacing a road
(c) a coin

## WHAT YOU HAVE TO DO
Fill in the letters in the boxes below and put the most important one in the circle at the end.

*Answer 1*

(a) Milk container

Most important

(b) Road material

Most important

(c) Coin

Most important

*Factors*

## A FACTOR MAY APPEAR IN MORE THAN ONE ANSWER.

A  low cost.
B  resistance to impact.
C  resistance to corrosion.
D  strength.
E  ease of cleaning.
F  lightness.
G  attractiveness.
H  ease of identification.
I  non-poisonous.
J  easily sterilised.
K  good electrical conductor.
L  bad electrical conductor.
M  dissolves in water.
N  does not dissolve in water.

*Question 2*

When you are faced with a problem to solve it is sensible to think of a number of different solutions. You can then choose one to try out.

*Example*: Problem: measure the speed of a model racing car.

Solutions: 1. Take a high speed cine film.
2. Use two photo-cells and a relay-operated clock.
3. Use a stopwatch and measured distance.
4. Fix a tape to car on which marks are made at regular time intervals.

## *WHAT YOU HAVE TO DO*

Below are three problems. Choose ONE and make your own list of solutions on the opposite page.

(a) Open a tin can without a proper opener.
(b) Leave a message at a friend's house when you do not have a pencil and paper.
(c) Count the number of people who pass a certain point in a busy high-street in one hour.

In conclusion, what can be said about the impact of assessment upon the project? First that the legitimate need to involve teachers in the development of objectives and criteria for project work means that they cannot be omitted from participating in the process of assessment. This participation must involve, however, a firm identification and comprehension of objectives by the teacher himself. Secondly, there is a danger that assessment in the context of national examinations will lead to the development of stereotyped and rigid approaches to project work in the interests of reliability. This must be resisted—validity is more significant than reliability. We cannot properly understand project work or come successfully to terms with its assessment unless we are willing to encourage and identify those other qualities, of value to the individual, which we do not intend to assess.

# 8 The Application of Statistics to Assessment

## R. B. Morrison

The word statistics is used in two senses. In one sense it is used to mean description of measurements, as in the case of a distribution of marks or scores for a test or the output figures for a factory. In its other sense it means an inferential method, which goes beyond pure description and attempts to discern a pattern in what appears at first sight to be a haphazard collection of data. It is a method for coping with an uncertain situation or a situation influenced by a number of variable factors. The language of statistics is not the language of certainty, for statistics cannot prove anything, but the language of probability.

The statistics needed for a meaningful treatment of marks and test scores requires little more competence in algebra and arithmetic than that achieved by most pupils before they leave school. The computations involved are simple and straightforward, although at times they can be long and tedious. The difficulty in appreciating statistics more often arises from a failure to understand the relevance and limitations of the particular techniques which have been evolved than from difficulties with the mathematics. Statistical method has aptly been described as a method for organizing data so as to bring out its full significance.

In assessment we require efficient ways of tabulating marks and scores to see what characteristics they have. We need to work out averages or mean values and indices of spread for the accumulated data. Individuals differ from each other, and the same individual varies also in ability and performance over a period of time. The same holds true for a group of individuals. The degree of uncertainty or error for a single measurement or set of measurements needs to be appreciated, and where possible calculated. Statistical methods are available for finding out if an observed difference between two measurements or sets of measurements is significant or more likely to be due to chance. The statistical technique of correlation shows to what degree various traits, abilities or skills go together or are associated with each other. In these and other ways, statistics provides a valuable tool in educational research and a means of approaching the problems of assessment in particular. In this chapter we shall be concerned with some of these applications.

The first methodical statistical investigation into assessment in this country was carried out by a team including Cyril Burt, C. E. Spearman and Godfrey Thomson and formed the basis of the now classic Hartog and Rhodes report of 1935. A fuller version was published later under the title of 'An Examination of Examinations'. Four types of error in the reliability of assessment were noted.

(a) Differences in the standard of marking between examiners, some being too lenient and others too severe.

(b) Differences in the spread of marks over the available mark scale, some bunching and others spreading out the marks too much.

(c) Differences in the ranking of candidates, many essays correlating by only 0·5.

(d) Random errors not included in the others.

This report did much to show that the marking of narrative or essay-type questions in written examinations was far from being reliable. It soon became apparent that some markers were inclined to be lenient, others severe. Some bunched their marks and others discriminated more over the available range of marks. Even in the matter of agreement on the rank order of candidates, much was left to be desired. This unreliability of the assessment procedures in use, especially in the assessment of essay work, has naturally led to concern.

If statistical methods have shown that all is not well in the field of assessment, perhaps the same method might suggest ways in which the situation could be improved. Might the application of statistical techniques assist in minimizing those errors due to lenient or severe marking, to differential spreading of the marks and the apparent failure of assessors to agree?

## The interpretation of mark distributions

The first statistical exercise after a test or examination is to produce a frequency distribution for the scores or marks obtained by the candidates. For small entries, such as the classroom test, this often takes the form of a distribution based upon individual marks within an appropriate range of marks. Thus an English composition marked out of 10 might give a frequency distribution similar to that shown in Table 1(a). For a large entry, probably marked on a percentage scale, the marks are usually grouped into appropriate classes with a frequency distribution similar to that shown in Table 1(b). This might be the kind of distribution for an assistant examiner with one of the examining boards.

If the test or examination were valid and the marking without error, the marks obtained by the candidates would faithfully reflect their abilities. The average or mean mark would then indicate the central tendency of ability

**Table 1.  Frequency Distribution of Marks**

| (a) Mark | frequency | (b) Class | frequency |
|---|---|---|---|
| 10 | 1 | 90–99 | 10 |
| 9 | 2 | 80–89 | 27 |
| 8 | 4 | 70–79 | 41 |
| 7 | 6 | 60–69 | 69 |
| 6 | 9 | 50–59 | 153 |
| 5 | 11 | 40–49 | 129 |
| 4 | 7 | 30–39 | 81 |
| 3 | 2 | 20–29 | 42 |
| 2 | 2 | 10–19 | 23 |
| 1 | 1 | 0– 9 | 5 |

| | | | |
|---|---|---|---|
| Entry = 45 | | Entry = 580 | |
| Mean (M) = 5·6 | | Mean (M) = 50·0 | |
| S.D. ($\sigma$) = 1·8 | | S.D. ($\sigma$) = 18·0 | |

for the group as a whole, whilst the spread or scatter of the marks would express the range of ability present in the entry. The calculation of a mean value ($M$) and an appropriate index of spread of the marks thus afford useful information concerning the behaviour of the group as a whole. The index of spread usually calculated is the standard deviation ($\sigma$). The reader is referred to standard texts for the methods available for calculating the mean and standard deviation for a distribution of marks. The values of these statistics for the two distributions of Table 1 are quoted below the appropriate distribution. For both these distributions, the mean value of the marks is located fairly centrally on the respective scales and the standard deviation is approximately one-sixth of the range of marks. This suggests in each case a fairly balanced heterogeneous group of candidates spread over the ability range. A higher mean value would have suggested a higher ability group, and a lower mean value a lower ability group. Similarly, if the standard deviation had been lower, i.e. the marks more bunched, this would have meant a more homogeneous ability group.

The conclusions of the previous paragraph are based on the assumptions previously stated, namely, that the test or examination is valid and the marking free from error. In practice this is not always the case. For standardized tests and the scoring of objective tests the assumptions are reasonable, but for essay-type examinations they are often not warranted. One cannot have a lenient or severe marker for objective tests, or one who is inclined to bunch marks, because the marking is completely objective. It is quite possible, however, to have this state of affairs with essay-type examinations and impression assessment, as Hartog and Rhodes *et al.* have found. Such errors may be serious where the marking does not conform to a reasonably specific mark scheme, or where no attempt is made to minimize them by scaling the marks.

Where leniency or severity, or differential spreading of the marks is suspected, it is important to scale the marks so that the subjective error of the marker is minimized. The process of scaling or standardization of marks is to ensure that the frequency distributions from various markers conform to an agreed standard, so that each candidate receives a mark which has been effectively corrected for any anomalies in the marking. In team marking the agreed distribution is usually that of the chief examiner and every care is taken to ensure that the team of examiners conforms. The agreed standardized scale, however, could equally be one to which all examiners, including the chief examiner, conformed.

## Scaling of marks

Scaling requires the adjustment of an examiner's raw marks to scaled marks such that the scaled distribution of marks will conform to an agreed mean $(M_s)$ and standard deviation $(\sigma_s)$. The basis of a common method for scaling marks is to ensure that the deviation of a raw mark $(X)$ from the mean $(M)$ expressed in standard deviation units $(\sigma)$ is the same as the deviation of the corresponding scaled mark $(X_s)$ from the scaled mean $(M_s)$, also expressed in standard deviation units $(\sigma_s)$. This may be expressed mathematically as:

$$\frac{X_s - M_s}{\sigma_s} = \frac{X - M}{\sigma}$$

or re-arranging

$$X_s = X \frac{\sigma_s}{\sigma} - \left[ \frac{\sigma_s}{\sigma} M - M_s \right].$$

As an example of scaling, we shall suppose that a chief examiner has marked a sample of scripts and obtained a mean and standard deviation of 40% and 15% respectively. This means that $M_s = 40\%$ and $\sigma_s = 15\%$. An assistant examiner is given the same scripts to mark and obtains a mean and standard deviation of 50% and 10% respectively, i.e. $M = 50\%$ and $\sigma = 10\%$. Taking the chief examiner's standard as the criterion, the assistant examiner has erred on the lenient side and has also bunched his marks. The assistant examiner's marks therefore need to be scaled using the scaling equation above. Substituting in this equation we obtain a scaling equation for the examiner, namely:

$$X_s = 1 \cdot 5X - 35.$$

It will be seen that the assistant examiner's raw mark corresponding to his mean of 50% becomes 40% when scaled, i.e. the mean for the chief examiner. The equation enables us to convert all his raw marks $(X)$ into equivalent scaled marks $(X_s)$. Thus a raw mark of 40% becomes 25%, a raw mark of 60% becomes 55% when scaled and so on. This scaling procedure adjusts both the mean and standard deviation to an agreed mean and standard deviation, thus correcting for both leniency or severity and bunching or excessive spreading of the marks, simultaneously. At the same time the scaling transformation is a linear transformation, which means that the basic shape of the original distribution of marks is unchanged. If the original distribution were basically skewed, it remains skewed after scaling. It should also be noted that *the rank order of the candidates is unaffected by the scaling process.* An analogous process is the conversion of degrees Centigrade to degrees Fahrenheit. Such a scaling does not alter the intrinsic degree of hotness or coldness of anything measured; it merely changes the label of one scale for that of the other.

Whilst it is often accepted that leniency or severity in marking needs to be corrected, the need for conformity in the spread of marks is not so readily appreciated. This need arises whenever equal weighting is required. The weighting of questions, or of individual components of an assessment, is not automatically guaranteed by assigning the same maximum to each question or component unless the assessor makes full use of the range of marks allocated. One who bunches the marks is working on a restricted range compared with one who spreads the marks excessively over the range. The effect of this is to reduce the weighting by the former and to increase the weighting by the latter. This differential weighting will have an adverse effect upon the candidates. Those candidates at the top end of the scale will be penalized by the former assessor and receive a bonus from the latter. Conversely, the candidates at the bottom end of the scale will receive a bonus from the former and be penalized by the latter.

The discussion above assumes that each marker has a similar sample of scripts to mark as that of each of his colleagues, or alternatively has been compared with a chief examiner using the same initial batch of scripts. This is important, for where markers have dissimilar samples to mark the observed differences between markers may well be genuine and reflect an actual difference between the performances of the groups of candidates. Unless one can be assured of these assumptions then scaling should not be carried out. Unfortunately, in this event, possible errors in marking may go undetected and uncorrected. It is therefore worth considering a marking procedure which either requires an agreement trial with the chief examiner beforehand, or one which, as far as possible, guarantees matched samples for each marker.

## The interpretation of grade distributions

In most assessment programmes the marks or scores are a means to an end, i.e. to ensure the candidates are distributed in a correct rank order of ability. The final measure is then usually stated in the form of a grade, each grade being related to the mark distribution according to suitably agreed criteria. Thus, it might be agreed that the top 5% of the candidates in *an average year* be deemed to have reached the standard of Grade A, the next 20% Grade B and so on. It should be noted that the grade specification needs to be based upon the performance expected in *an average year*. This then defines statistically the standards of the assessment and gives a clearer idea of the standards it is desired to maintain. It also allows for possible variations in the ability of the entry from year to year. A slavish application of a grade specification every year would not do this. In a 'good' year, some candidates worthy of Grade A would not get this grade, and in a 'poor' year more would get this grade than was justified.

The grade specification acts as an initial guideline or yardstick. The candidates at the grade boundaries then need to have their performances carefully scrutinized to decide whether their initial grade should stand or be adjusted. A large examining board would probably find little variability in the entry from year to year and the grade percentages would not vary by more than a few per cent. A small college or school group, however, is likely to vary much more and a more detailed scrutiny would be required.

Grading is not always based upon a previously obtained mark distribution. In the case of impression marking the grade is often allocated directly, usually on a 5-point scale. The choice of a suitable scale for assessment depends to a large extent upon the kind of precision the assessment may be expected to achieve. A percentage scale for assessment in mathematics may be reasonable whereas it would not be so for assessing English compositions. The criterion here is whether a difference of 1% in the mark is meaningful. Distinction should be made between direct marking on a percentage (100 point) scale and the conversion of marks, say out of 20, to percentages. Such a conversion retains the 20-point scale because only 20 corresponding percentages would be represented. The conversion has not made the assessment any more precise.

There are other cases where marking out of 20, out of 10 or out of any other maximum mark may be inappropriate. This arises where the scale interval cannot be regarded as linear. If a student-teacher is assessed on teaching practice on a 5-point scale by marking out of 5, it is implied that the difference in ability as between 4 and 5 is the same as that between 2 and 3. A better approach might be to use a 5-point scale based upon grades from A to E, where the grades are defined in a similar way to that already outlined, i.e. Grade A is the standard of performance we might expect 5% of the entry to reach in an average year, Grade B 20% and so on. Such a 5-point scale is certainly not linear, and the use of letters in such cases prevents the temptation to think it is!

The use of grades, as distinct from marks, does not prevent the possibility of leniency or severity or a differential spreading of grades similar to that found in marking. The grade specification for an average year, however, does provide a suitable yardstick against which an assessor's grade distribution may be measured. Some departure from this yardstick must be expected due to the variability from entry to entry, but a significant departure requires investigation. If the departure is of the kind that might be expected statistically once every four years, then it is likely to be acceptable, but if the departure might be expected once every hundred years, there is justification for thinking that grading error is involved.

## Profile assessment*

An overall assessment is usually made up of a number of individual assessment components each contributing to the final result. Each component may be measuring a different skill and be differently weighted from the others. Further, some components may be measured directly in terms of marks based upon a marking scheme, whilst others may be stated in terms of letter grades based upon impression or an agreed grade specification for an average year. Assuming the marks and grades to have been scaled where necessary to minimize possible errors, on what basis is the final assessment to be arrived at?

It should be stated at this point that the practice of adding marks, even when scaled, is often a dubious practice. In the first place, measures of *different* things should not be added. No one would add the speedometer reading of one's car to the oil pressure reading and imagine one had come up with a result which was in any way meaningful. In education, however, we frequently add mathematics marks to art marks to cookery marks and

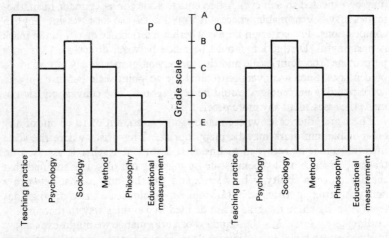

**Figure 1** Assessment Profiles

so on and proclaim the total as being in some sort of way a measure of 'overall ability'. We even award prizes on this basis! Unless component marks are highly correlated, suggesting the assessment of a common ability the component marks should not be added. Secondly, the adding of marks obscures relevant information on performance and masks real differences between candidates. Figure 1 shows in diagrammatic form the performances of two student-teachers in terms of what is known as a profile assessment, where each basic component is clearly delineated.

A close inspection of these profiles shows that, apart from teaching practice and educational measurement, the two students have obtained precisely

* For further discussion of Profiles see Chapter 12.

the same grades for the remaining components. Further, their performances on teaching practice and educational measurement are exactly reversed. If some kind of averaging were carried out, both students would be likely to have the same total mark or average. Viewed as a meaningful measure, the same total or average would suggest that both students are of equal merit. But are they? If the purpose of the assessment is to determine the ability of students as potentially competent and practical teachers, then they are not equally able. P is clearly better on this criterion than Q. This is simply an illustrative example of how an assessment profile provides more relevant information, just as medical diagnosis requires profiles for a patient and not the sum or average of his temperature, blood pressure, etc. We really should try to resist the temptation when presented with figures always to add them; there are other interesting things to do with them!

If the profile in terms of grades for a mixed assessment programme is a preferable form for stating a candidate's performance, two problems arise. First, how may marks be converted to equivalent grades? Secondly, how may the component grades in the profile be combined (not added) to give a basis for final awards?

## Conversion of marks to grades

We shall suppose that those components assessed by grades have been scaled where necessary on a 5-point scale where the percentage of candidates in each grade conforms to the statistical expectancy for an average year or entry. Let the grade specification be:

Grade: A B C D E
% in Grade: 5 20 50 20 5

Those components which have been marked now need to be scaled to the specified grades. This requires finding appropriate partition points for the frequency distribution of marks such that between these points the specified percentage of candidates will be found. In the case of a simple distribution of marks such as that of Table 1(a), the grade specification of percentages applied to the entry of 45, requires the following numbers of candidates in each grade: A (2·25), B (9·00), C (22·50), D (9·00) and E (2·25). As fractions of candidates are not possible, we need to round off these numbers keeping in mind that a reasonable departure from the specification is permissible. A close approximation to the specification would result if those candidates with marks of 9 and 10 (3) were initially given Grade A, those with marks 7 and 8 (10) Grade B, those with marks 5 and 6 (20) Grade C, those with marks 3 and 4 (9) Grade D and finally those with marks 1 and 2 (3) Grade E. This initial division needs to be amended in the light of a scrutiny of borderline cases as mentioned earlier.

In the case of a large entry, the partition points need to be found from a cumulative frequency distribution or ogive for the marks. We shall consider the distribution of Table 1(b) as an example to illustrate the procedure.

The limits of the classes into which the marks have been grouped are represented by the mid-points between them, thus 49·5 is the upper limit for the class 40–49, and so on. Further, 129 + 81 + 42 + 23 + 5 = 280 candidates have marks which are less than 49·5. A similar cumulative number of candidates may be found which expresses the number of candidates below the upper limit of any particular class. Converting such numbers into percentages by multiplying by 100 and dividing by the total entry of 580, we obtain the percentage cumulative frequency distribution given in graphical form in Figure 2. This graph may be used to obtain the desired partition points for converting marks into grades.

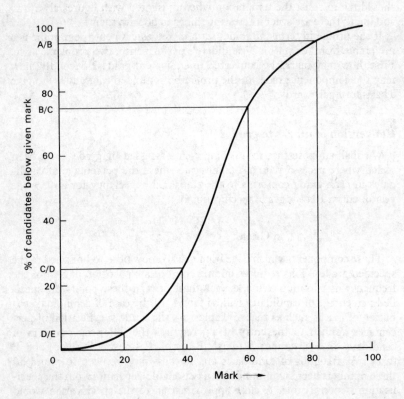

**Figure 2** Conversion of marks to grades

If Grade A is to contain 5% of the candidates, then 95% must fall below this grade. The partition point on the mark scale of the graph corresponding to the Grade A/B boundary at 95% is found to be at 82. Seventy-five per cent of candidates fall below the Grade B/C boundary, the corresponding partition point being at 60. In a similar way the Grade C/D and Grade D/E boundaries yield partition points of 39% and 20% respectively. The conversion of marks into grades may be summarized by a Mark Range–Grade Table:

| Mark range | Grade |
|---|---|
| 82% and above | A |
| 60%–81% | B |
| 39%–59% | C |
| 20%–38% | D |
| 19% and below | E |

The procedure described here does not require the original mark distribution to be scaled first, and unlike some procedures it does not depend on the distribution being normal. Further, the procedure is applicable to any grading system once the grade specification in use is known.

## Grade combination

Because grades rarely correspond to a linear scale, it is quite invalid to assign numbers to them so as to be able to perform available mathematical techniques unless the non-linearity is taken into account. The common practice of assigning the numbers 1 to 5 to a 5-point non-linear scale is quite wrong. Certain appropriate conversions from grades to equivalent numbers are available, but most depend upon the assumption that the underlying distribution is normal, which is rarely the case. But even where an appropriate conversion can be applied, the gain in mathematical power is often less than the loss in educational significance. This being so, how may we retain the advantages of a grade profile and combine the grades to provide a final overall grade?

We might consider this in relation to the student-teacher profile mentioned earlier. Let us suppose that the final grades are to be in terms of Distinction, Merit and Pass. We shall further suppose that the teaching practice component is to have more 'weight' than the other components. These requirements may be met by a specified set of combination rules. Thus, to qualify for a distinction, a student must have a Grade A on teaching practice together with at least two Grade As and three Grade Bs on the other components. The 'weighting' of teaching practice is achieved by making a more stringent requirement for this component than for the others. To qualify for merit, we might specify at least Grade B on teaching practice together with at least three Grade Bs and two Grade Cs elsewhere in the assessment profile, and so on. The appropriate combination rules need to be worked out in relation to (a) the grade specification for the components, and (b) the final grade or award specification. It will be clear that if the grade specification is a generous one for the components, more stringent combination rules will be required to satisfy a less generous final grade specification and vice versa.

## Validity

The research of Hartog and Rhodes and of those who followed concentrated almost entirely upon the unreliability of many assessment procedures, i.e. the failure to achieve a desirable level of agreement and consistency between examiners. Few appeared to question the validity of the assessment, i.e. whether it was measuring what it was intended to measure. It was noticed again and again that examiners could not agree always on the mark to be given to a particular essay-type question, but few queried if the question was worth asking in the first place. It is quite possible to envisage a highly reliable assessment procedure, but this does not automatically guarantee that the procedure is assessing those course objectives it is considered desirable to assess. There would be an improvement in inter-marker reliability for English compositions if the markers confined their marks to spelling, punctuation, use of capital letters, i.e. the pure mechanics of composition. In this event no one would pretend that we are validly measuring the ability to write compositions, for many of the important facets of writing have been excluded. Quite often there has to be a compromise between reliability and validity. In the last resort, however, assessment is primarily concerned with validity.

There are many ways of looking at validity, and only a few are discussed here. The accuracy with which a test measures what it is intended to measure is known as empirical validity. It refers to the relationship between test scores or examination marks and a criterion which specifies what the assessment is designed to measure. As statistics cannot generate educational ideas, the required specification becomes a matter for educationalists to formulate. Statistics can only help in the appraisal of already formulated ideas. Content validity is concerned with how well the assessment samples the content area of a course. Concurrent validity involves the relation between test scores and an accepted criterion of the ability the test is designed to measure. In this case the criterion is less a specification than an experienced judgment, such as teacher estimates. A difficulty here is that teacher estimates are not always reliable.

Generally speaking, validation requires wherever possible a specific definition of the achievement to be measured. It has been stated that operational definitions are the only unambiguous definitions in that they define in terms of recognizable behaviours. No method of assessment validation is completely empirical and we must accept a strong subjective element. The problem is often one of getting agreement between assessors on what the appropriate operational definitions should be. As P. E. Vernon has stated:

> The practical understanding of an individual is still an art rather than a science, though it may be greatly assisted by scientific tests and guided by the results of objective experiments and statistical studies.

This chapter has tried to outline some of the ways in which statistical studies have assisted in the continuing improvement of assessment approach and practice.

# Problems of Assessment

# 9 Course Work and Continuous Assessment

## Trevor J. Rogers

The use made of external examinations in secondary education, however such use is viewed, is a matter of serious concern to every teacher.

Generally speaking, external examinations are used to provide information about the pupils, information that may be used by teachers and others to decide the suitability of the pupil for a subsequent course, either at school or at an establishment of higher education; information that may determine whether the pupil is an acceptable entrant to certain professions; information that may be used by employers for recruitment and in allocating the individual to a role in industry or commerce.

The degree of importance attached to such information and its well-nigh universal and unquestioned acceptance, may be recognized by the pupils themselves and become not only an incentive to learning of a certain kind, but an indication to them of what society regards as their most important characteristics.

When teachers in turn become too impressed with the importance of examination results, then the temptation to distort the teaching in order to obtain satisfying results becomes evident. This is the root cause of the dichotomy that undoubtedly existed, and to a certain extent still exists, between examinations and education. The development of examinations has been such that, despite the stirring and high-sounding claims of educationalists, the history of our secondary education in this century is, in no small measure, the history of certain examinations. The restrictive influences of these external examinations on the development of the curriculum in the secondary stage is not our present concern; but the high regard paid to examination results and the general belief that these results provide irrefutable and complete evidence of a young person's level of academic attainment and, indeed, of his potential, must arouse deep concern regarding the nature of such examining. The necessity then of a careful consideration of conventional methods of examining techniques is a matter of prime importance, particularly to teachers for whom the welfare and future prospects of their pupils matter. Let the following quotation remind us what we seek to improve.

> The examination itself in its modern guise, fits in well with the rational and impersonal ethos nurtured by bureaucracy and industrialization. The candidate often becomes a number rather than a name; he is given the same set of questions permitting the same varieties of choice as his companions up and down the country. . . . The marking is impersonally assessed by remote figures whose prerogative extends only to the facts in the shape of answers placed before them and who judge in accordance with rationally assessed pre-arranged criteria of relevance and correctness. In some examinations, elaborate 'scaling' devices produce the pre-determined percentages of distinctions, passes, etc. Examination administration, we are assured by an expert, is an 'exceedingly complicated technical problem'.[1]

To restrict the measurement of the pupil's attainment to the consideration of evidence consisting solely of a written script or scripts, completed in stipulated periods of time on certain dates, is insufficient data to presume to deduce results of such consequential importance to the individual. The direction of development in recent years has lain in augmenting rather than replacing conventional techniques although the nature and function of end-of-course written examinations have been improved immensely. P. J. Kelly lists the following abilities that were assessed by written examinations in the exercise with which he was concerned:

recall of facts;
recall of principles;
use of numerical data;
construction of hypotheses;
assessment of hypotheses;
design of experiments;
coherent communication.[2]

However, restricting the measurement of pupils' abilities to the use of a single technique may well impoverish the value of the result. If the view of what constitutes attainment in any area of the curriculum is set down, then the need for multiple measuring instruments becomes obvious. Kelly's list suggests that the outcomes of courses of instruction consist of more than the ability to recall and use information, but rather involve the acquisition of a range of abilities or skills and the development of certain behaviours. There are outcomes of teaching other than cognitive development, as for example

development of disciplined working habits,
acquisition of study skills, e.g. use of reference books,
establishment of interests likely to be permanent,
development of aesthetic taste,

social sensitivity,
inculcation of a social attitude, etc.

The development of matching forms of assessment has however, been slow and research into such techniques has not yet produced clearly defined, universally accepted forms. The difficulties, as Eggleston and Kerr suggest in their book *Studies in Assessment*,[3] are formidable but this must not deter those who wish to undertake such work. The publication of Schools Council Examinations Bulletin No. 1 gave forthright official encouragement to the provision by the proposed regional examining boards of not only external examinations on syllabuses produced by the boards, but also of external moderation for the assessment of pupils undertaken by schools (or groups of schools) on syllabuses prepared by the teachers in those schools. Thus was provided the way to demonstrate that curriculum and examinations are two sides of the same coin and that it is only when they operate together that the goals of education can be adequately and satisfactorily reached. When the teacher is involved with curriculum development, the link between educating and examining is strengthened and the tasks become complementary. Opportunities for teachers to control examinations have integrated examinations more realistically and usefully with the teaching in the schools.

In this role, the first task of the teachers, individually, in local groups or in the subject panels of regional boards, is to state, in precise terms, the objectives of their studies, whether these be an innovation in the curriculum or a traditional subject discipline. Logically, the next step is to plan learning experiences appropriate for attaining these objectives. Such experiences will vary with the kind of objective aimed at and must be put together to form some kind of coherent programme or syllabus. Next it is obviously necessary to check how far the learning experiences have actually produced the desired results in terms of the stated aims. This evaluation process will identify the strengths and weaknesses of the plans conceived to attain the objectives. As a result of evaluation, it is possible to note in what respects the curriculum is effective and in what respects it needs improvement. Thus the ideal of 'diagnostic teaching' will be close to fulfilment because of the 'feedback' that this sequence would provide. The better the system works, the greater the value of the feedback and the closer is the ideal to being achieved.

It must be clearly understood, however, that the measurement involved in curriculum evaluation is not confined to an examination or assessment of pupil performance. It is usual to regard assessment leading to the gradings of pupils as a terminal decision whatever techniques are used; evaluation on the other hand is 'a constant probing for the best way to move forward'.[4] Thus curriculum evaluation, as Eggleston brings out in Chapter 15, involves a different approach to that required for individual pupil assessment. Nevertheless, the value to the teacher when he controls the examination, spreads widely over his professional role. Such control facilitates curriculum development, it helps in curriculum evaluation, it avoids the divorce between examinations and curriculum, and through mode 3 (see Chapter 14) it secures for the teachers the right to determine both the objectives of their teaching and the kind of course which, in their circumstances, enables them to realize most effectively these objectives and to take a major part in evaluating the work of their pupils.

It is natural, therefore, that the desire to augment the assessment techniques should point in the direction of the involvement of teachers in assessment; the fear that the curriculum is determined by the completely independent and external examination is thus allayed to the benefit of the development of the former and the enrichment of the latter. It also points to the development of assessment on a continuous basis. This is in line with current educational thinking which places great emphasis upon the individual pupil and designs procedures and practices in order to recognize and take advantage of individual differences.

A comparable procedure to continuous educational assessment is to be found in the study of control systems. A missile, for example, which 'homes' on the target does not, necessarily, move along the path initially planned for it. Its course is constantly modified in accordance with 'feedback' information it provides its controllers. The missile's programme, in turn, receives information which makes it take compensatory movements. A similar process can be recognized in the sequence of learning experiences provided to bring about a pupil's attainment of the knowledge, skills and abilities his course intended he should acquire. The objectives must be clearly recognized by the teacher and by continuous evaluation of the pupil's progress, the teacher is provided with the feedback information which is necessary for individual adjustment. This technique of continuous assessment is not as simple as at first appears. Although allusion to this technique has tended to become very popular with teachers, the procedure still lacks the rigour and definition which will make it nationally acceptable and give it equal status with more conventional techniques usually applied as end-of-course procedures. The late Dr Stephen Wiseman's 'off the cuff' comments on this method made at the University of London University Entrance and School Examinations Council's seventh annual conference, indicate that the method does not necessarily remedy all the weaknesses of measurement by examinations:

What about continuous assessment as a means of examination? I think it is an enormously useful and powerful way of assessment for certain purposes and for certain purposes only. What worries me is the tendency for people to climb on the band wagon and to regard continuous assessment as solving everybody's problem in every subject. This is nonsense. There are certain aspects of subjects, certain objectives which you are aiming at in your teaching, for which continuous assessment is contra-indicated. If you want to measure factual knowledge. It is fashionable nowadays to play down factual knowledge and to say that the important things are attitudes and things of this sort—so they are—but so is factual knowledge. You cannot have an educated person who does not know anything, and therefore you have got to have a certain amount of knowledge and in order to test that you do not need continuous assessment. When you come to the development of aesthetic attitudes and the development of skills, then continuous assessment comes into its own. I would, therefore, say two things: first—continuous assessment should be used when it is clear that it is going to be an advantage to do so; do not think that it can be applied everywhere. Secondly, remember that if you take it on, you are really giving yourself an enormous amount of work to do; the teacher involvement in terms of hours and labour is very high indeed. It is worth it, provided you do it in the areas where you need to.[5]

Professor J. T. Allanson makes much the same point very cogently when he says

The most reliable indicator of ripeness in pears and cheeses is still a well-informed thumb and it would be silly to ignore the extent to which good teachers have been able to make valid distinctions between good and bad educational practices using intuition without the support of precise definitions, analysis and measurement. But a great deal of discussion about assessment has at best been vague and at worst been rubbish because there has been no attempt to specify or to measure.[6]

One cannot afford to ignore the very real problems that face teachers involved in continuous assessment. Apart from the need for rigorous thinking about what is being done and why, there is the possibility of conflict arising between the teacher's two roles of teacher and assessor. This could change for the worse the atmosphere of the classroom. The very real benefits, however, that can result from continuous teacher assessment, which have been indicated earlier in this chapter, make certain that its use will extend in the future. It is, therefore, imperative that teachers concern themselves with its problems and procedures. It is worth making the point, moreover, that the teacher, by virtue of his position, is the only person able to conduct such assessment.

Critical appraisal of the continuous involvement of the teacher in assessment has not been aided by the confusion in the use of terminology and by different interpretations placed upon the same words by different individuals and organizations. 'Continuous assessment' is in reality an umbrella descriptive term and is not a technique of assessment. It is often, however, used in this latter sense. 'Internal assessment' is often used as if it were synonymous with 'continuous assessment'. It may, indeed, often be so but it is not necessary that it should be. Finally, 'course work' is sometimes used as if it was the same as 'continuous assessment'. This is by no means always the case; in certain circumstances course work can perfectly well be assessed on a single occasion by an external agency. It is hoped that the remainder of this chapter, which will deal in turn with course work and continuous assessment, will clarify the situation and perhaps lead to a more careful use of terms, thus avoiding misunderstanding and misapprehension.

## The assesment of course work

Many teachers believe that a realistic measure of attainment is possible when such an assessment is based on the pupil's work performed during the normal period of his course. Such a procedure could well reinforce the consideration of the pupil's responses made on a particular occasion towards the end of his course in reply to stimuli in the form of 'questions' set by an examiner who can only imagine the nature of the pupil's reaction to the course followed. Until that specific occasion, the only item common to both examiner and pupil was the examination syllabus. If the objectives to such a syllabus had been stated in the most useful form for teaching and assessing, that is, in terms which specified the kind of behaviour it was expected the pupil would acquire during the course and the content or area of study in which this behaviour would operate, then the written test and the assessment of course work could only be complementary.

There are obviously many subjects in which the examination of course work is essential if these subjects are not to be restricted by the requirements of external examinations. Art is an obvious example. The need to send to the external examiner art work undertaken in examination time, initially tends to restrict art to a two-dimensional means of expression, whereas an assessment of course work would encourage the growth of three-dimensional work and allow complete freedom as to the size of the work. Pupils in the 'craft' subjects (woodwork, metal work, needlework), all subjects covered by the title 'education through the use of materials', obviously benefit from the freedom enjoyed by having their assessments based, to a large extent, on the quality of their course work.

This range of subjects can be extended with some value to include housecraft, music and science. In housecraft the teacher is able to record the continuous development of the pupil in practical work. Similarly, the acquisition of laboratory skills in science can be continuously assessed. Music, by its nature, presents a number of problems as an examination subject. As an art form concerned with the creation and presentation of sound in an ordered way, it demands practical and live expression. This involves performance and a certain measure of practical ability, as well as corporate activity. Music takes place in time. This presents difficulties as songs and pieces studied, and possibly performed, over a period of time cannot be kept in the repertoire at concert standard, since new works have to be learnt. It is not always desirable or practical, even today, to record pieces learnt by pupils for presentation at an end-of-course examination. The examination in music should act as a stimulant to all kinds of practical music and allow pupils to find pleasure in their own music making. 'Technical' drawing is another area where work completed by candidates during their courses would indicate certain abilities better than an end-of-course examination, although the latter could be used with advantage to test the ability to visualize three-dimensional objects from drawings on one plane and vice versa. Indeed, in most subjects of the curriculum teachers who have had experience of being involved with assessment now advocate the consideration of course work (or of a project) as complementary to the end-of-course examination.

The first problem in connection with internal assessment of this kind is the dilemma that faces the teacher as to what guidance he should give the pupil if the completed work might be used as evidence of attainment. Let it be clearly understood that the involvement of the teacher in assessing attainment must in no way diminish the quality and extent of his teaching. The teacher is not expected to withdraw from his role of extending his pupils. The teacher will know how much actual help he has given the pupil in the completion of any piece of work. This fact alone determines that the teacher must at least be 'consulted' at the moderating stages, but this role must not restrict the teacher's duty to teach in any way whatsoever.

The second problem concerns the nature of the moderation. (This is discussed more fully in Chapter 11.) When a school enters a candidate for an external examination, this act invites comparability of the standards of attainment at that school with the standards of pupils at a similar stage in other schools. The achievement of such comparability is the desired end product of moderation. Naturally, examining boards regard their responsibility in this respect most seriously, since a lack of thoroughness and justice will not only call in question their own standards, but that of the examination as a whole. Indeed, boards could at present be accused of having interfered unduly with educational progress in order to make the application of comparability easier. The selection of 'set books' is an example of this. To ask questions on one play and one of two novels will ensure that the responses at least refer to the same few texts. This may make comparability of standards easier but the pupil's education is thereby unnecessarily cramped. The introduction of an element of course work assessment, with the corollary that this will have to include a degree of internal or teacher assessment, increases the difficulty of equating standards in any subject. The variety of the work contributes to such difficulty but a restriction of learning experiences in order to ease the problem cannot be accepted any longer; educational considerations must have priority over examination devices. Ways must, therefore, be sought to establish comparability of standards and such methods must be seen to be of such a nature that their quality and justice will ensure universal acceptance. It is a bitter disappointment, therefore, that little or no assistance from the normal sources of research has been forthcoming in this respect. Eggleston and Kerr's *Studies in Assessment*[3] have described exercises in this kind of work and the Schools Council Examination Bulletins series have indicated other activities in this field. But in the main, the work can only be described as that of enthusiastic teachers, convinced of the value of this development, groping forward, striving towards satisfactory means of moderation and Eggleston's and Kerr's studies apart, largely unassisted by systematic educational research.

The prime necessity that there should be concrete evidence of the pupil/candidate's work available for moderation is possible in most, but not in all, cases where course work is involved. Housecraft and music, for example, involve transitory activities so that the assessment cannot be deferred until the end of the course or to a set-piece examination. Indeed, the acquisition of practical skills in the science laboratory or a pupil's progress in the acquisition of craft skills, would undoubtedly be more valid if based on frequent if not continuous observations during the course rather than on an appraisal of a set of completed artifacts. This element of teacher assessment made during the course, with the teacher as sole arbiter, added to the fact that the amount of help given by the teacher to any individual pupil is known only to the teacher, is one of the sources of doubt regarding the justice of comparability in this area.

It is obvious that teachers must discuss this problem of comparability with each other so that instances where the teacher has been the sole arbiter of standards are shared with his colleagues. Local groups of subject teachers must, therefore, be encouraged and facilities of all kinds for meetings provided. At this stage teachers will see evidence of course work for themselves; they will discuss comparability with one another and define standards for themselves. This development of group discussion is a recent growth and in harmony with curriculum development underlines an ever growing need for teacher centres:

P. J. Kelly states:
. . . However it was at the local level that participation (by teachers) was seen to be most significant. . . . Teachers . . . met once or twice a term. They dealt with various aspects of the work of the trials, including the examinations. . . . An understanding of the objectives and techniques of the examination was acquired by the teachers . . . in a very short time. The examination incorporated a much greater range of innovation than had ever been included in any previous A level Biology examination. Yet it is not an exaggeration to claim it was absorbed into the professional practice of the trial teachers within a year.[2]

To suggest that agreement on standards of course work in this way is easy and smooth would be most misleading. Additional aids in the preparation of a common set of criteria, 'practice' assessment and discussions of differences or full scale 'Agreement Trials' as devised by the West Yorkshire and Lindsey Regional Examinations Board, are required. These Agreement Trials are fully explained in Schools Council Examinations Bulletin No. 5.

Another difficulty in course work assessment is the question of what part of the period of the pupil's course is to provide the necessary evidence for moderation. If the secondary stage is regarded as being normally of five years' duration, should all the work be taken from the final year? As the Ordinary level examination usually takes place later in the school year than CSE, it may be more practical for a GCE board than for a CSE board to state:

A single assessment at the end of a course can only give a measure of the final attainments of the candidates, but with continuous assessment the rate of progress of the students inevitably comes into the grading. Whether this is desirable depends on the subject, the qualities being assessed and the uses to which the assessment results are put. The JMB has ruled that schools must assess candidates on the basis of the standard reached by the end of the course and the five samples of work sent, for a sample of the students only, to the moderator are required 'to show a varied range of work and to reflect the standard achieved by the end of the course'.[5]

It was in 1963 that the Joint Matriculation Board initiated its experiment in the school assessment of course work in English Language with the approval of the SSEC and the financial support of the DES. The experiment (which it should be mentioned preceded the introduction of CSE and gave a much needed boost to the standing of course work by showing that moderation of such work on a substantial scale is a practical proposition) was described thus:

(a) To devise and follow methods of training groups of pupils in the use and understanding of English, the teaching not being specifically directed towards preparing them for O level examination papers in English Language as at present constituted: and

(b) To devise means of making school assessments which can be endorsed by the Board as indicating that by the end of their Upper-fifth form course pupils have achieved not less than O level pass standard in their writing and understanding of English.[7]

The contrast between this and the quotation from Bantock's book on page 158 is most significant.

The difficulties attendant upon the use of an assessment of course work as a basis for grading candidates and the resulting problems of comparability, have been lucidly described in the reports of the Joint Matriculation Board on the experimental scheme (JMB Occasional Publication Nos 22, 26 and 31). The first interim report by Hewitt and Gordon (OP 22) emphasizes the early difficulties, but the justification for pursuing the work is amply demonstrated by J. A. Petch in the second interim report (OP 26). The third report (OP 31) shows the extension of the scheme which carries 'course work assessment' to its logical conclusion in that the scheme makes provision for the award of Ordinary Level passes in English Language without the evidence of formal examinations of any kind.

The North Western CSE board has a similar arrangement for the submission of a 'Folio of Writing' to assess the candidate's ability in the writing of continuous language. In this case, however, it is suggested that the work should be that carried out in the autumn and spring terms of the fifth year but that work from the previous summer term of the fourth year might be included. Work undertaken prior to that term should only be included in exceptional circumstances. It is clear, therefore, that course work assessment can be so arranged that the standard of attainment at the culmination of the course is what matters.

The problem of whether the work is solely that of the candidate still lingers. Some work might have been completed by the pupil at home with the possible assistance of other people. The JMB rules that some of the pieces submitted for assessment must have been carried out in class. What then of the teacher's help? It might be argued that the teacher invariably stimulates and guides the work. The North Western CSE Board has defined 'usual teacher guidance' as follows:

> What constitutes the usual guidance depends on the teacher and will vary with different types of work. No matter what stimuli are used—books, films, TV, radio, records, theatre, painting, music, visits—or how the teacher treats these; no matter how much discussion of the subject takes place, led by the teacher; the sole criterion is, 'Did the candidate write this himself?'[8]

The experience of a number of CSE boards as well as that of the JMB, would suggest that a satisfactory general pattern for the moderation of course work can be established along the following lines:

(a) meetings during the year of teachers on a local basis to discuss samples of work and to try to reach mutually agreed definitions of standards;

(b) assessment of the candidates' work by their own teachers;

(c) exhibition of the work or of samples of the work on the same local basis and involving the same teachers. A moderator or assessor of the Board may be present at these meetings which provide opportunities for teachers to see standards as it were in action. The 'order of merit' is invariably left as decided by the teacher and comparability of standards is achieved by an adjustment of 'grades' or 'marks' or whatever unit of measurement is used;

(d) samples from each local group are sent to the chief moderator (assessor) for the Board to ensure 'regional' equality.

This system appears to work well in practice but it is regrettable that teachers achieve competence in assessing and moderating only through experience; there is little evidence of inservice training except that which is provided by the boards themselves. University Departments of Education and the Schools Council could also help in evaluating the validity and reliability of the system and, by building up the expertise of the teaching profession as a whole, ensure its general acceptability both inside and outside the profession.

## Continuous assessment

The basic argument for continuous assessment arises out of the rather fragmentary nature of much of our present day assessment. Assessment is in one sense an analytic process. In order to evaluate each individual pupil as objectively as possible, it is necessary to break down the pupil's total performance or total behaviour pattern in relation to a particular course of study. This task is performed through a precise statement of objectives which sets down the abilities, skills and behaviour expected of pupils at the end of courses as a result of having followed them. The flaw in this approach is that it implies that the whole person is comprised of isolated reactions. We know, however, that no single aspect of a pupil's behaviour can be understood without reference to the total behaviour pattern, that is, without reference to the whole person. A way of redressing the balance is through continuous assessment carried out by the pupil's own teacher who is in a unique position to see the pupil as a whole person as well as to help with the assessment of his progress analytically. Continuous assessment thus implies consideration of the teacher's image of the pupil as a person and it will include analytic processes which help towards this end.

It is recognized that tests are not precise instruments of measurement. For the sake of validity it may be argued that the process of assessing a pupil's progress should be continuous. In this sense written tests, oral questioning and discussions, projects, reports, classwork, homework, etc. are all considered as assessment measures. Therefore records need to be kept. This is not something dramatically new. It simply involves a consciousness on the part of the teacher that there is a need for a constant feedback from the pupil; it draws attention at the end of the course to the weaknesses of any one test or group of tests and to the point that guidance in teaching requires constant 'feedback' if the teaching is to realize its optimum value. Continuous assessment in one sense, therefore, simply means gaining more and better information about the pupil and using this as the course develops. It also implies that the teacher's focus is shifted from the class as a single entity and directed towards developing the full potential of each individual to his/her fullest level of human worth.

A CSE examining board which has undertaken valuable pioneering work in the adoption of continuous assessment is the West Yorkshire and Lindsey Regional Examinations Board, which refers to the process as follows:

It is essential, at the outset, to establish what is meant by continuous assessment. As a term of art it is more susceptible to description than to definition:

(a) It represents continuing awareness, by the teacher, of the development and knowledge of his pupils; it is a process which extends over a period of time: the gradual build-up of a cumulative judgment about performance.

(b) A teacher making use of continuous assessment is looking for signs which show the growth of thinking processes and the development of those varying abilities towards which the teaching is aimed; he is more concerned with signposts than with the whole itinerary.

(c) An end of course examination will test achievement at one point of time within the limits of the test; under continuous assessment there is knowledge not only of this achievement but also of progression towards it: not merely of where he has got to but also of how he got there.[9]

This board has also taken a leading part in the development of mode 3 methods of examining and in its advice on the preparation of such a submission it not only stresses the importance of precise objectives and how these are to be realized but also 'detail of the criteria by which judgments are to be made on the work done by pupils'.

The board's guidance continues:

Freedom must be reserved to the teacher to decide how he will evaluate performance. The method chosen (how) will obviously vary according to the criteria (what he is looking for); each, however, must be appropriate to the other. It would, for example, be somewhat incongruous to attempt a judgment on mathematical precision by means of an oral examination. The Board of course must require that evidence be forthcoming in corroboration of the cumulative judgment of the teacher. Judgments will be based on evidence; both the judgments and the evidence on which they are based will be built up over a period of time. This is the true meaning of cumulative. The keeping of records thus becomes an essential; the particular kind of record cannot be a haphazard choice—in any scheme which is planned with the care and balance appropriate to continuous assessment, the record MUST be related to the declared aims and objectives. Put another way: those records which are adequate for assessment are those which are necessary for good teaching. This is recognized by the Board; it appreciates the process of thought involved in a maturing judgment and therefore subscribes to the view that a system which over administers, which prescribes records that are unduly precise (unless this is spelled out in the aims and objectives) and seeks to quantify at all stages, may well destroy the substance of what it sets out to achieve. This keeping of records is not merely the duty of the school; it applies equally to the Inter-school Assessor following each visit. It is therefore vital that all Inter-school Assessors, before setting foot in any school, make quite certain that they have absorbed the inmost meaning of what has been written above; it is not sufficient to have read the words and nothing more.[9]

The keeping of records of each pupil does not of itself imply a continuous assessment but without such records continuous assessment, particularly in a situation requiring external moderation, is virtually impossible.

There is no doubt that as a method of providing teachers with information of the teaching/learning relationship for each pupil, continuous assessment is extremely valuable. Indeed, all good teachers follow this procedure, with a varying amount of record keeping. So valuable is this kind of assessment on educational grounds that it is natural that teachers should desire its adoption as a method of measuring attainment within the context of an external nationally recognized examination. There is an inherent danger, however, in the adoption of continuous assessment for such purposes. In viewing the 'whole pupil', it is possible that the teacher will include the personal characteristics and 'qualities' of the pupil. The term 'quality' in this context should be considered together with the terms 'objectives' and 'outcomes'. 'Objectives' are what the teacher aims to achieve when planning his course; 'outcomes' are the actual achievements as measured through assessment; 'qualities' connote broader 'outcomes' such as growth of intellectual pursuits, growth of interest, sensitivity, co-operation with peers in group work, and other acceptable attitudes. It may be unfair to imply to such phrases as 'cumulative judgment', 'signs which show growth of thinking processes', 'not only achievement but also of progression towards it' used by the West Yorkshire and Lindsey Board, that the personal qualities of the pupil are involved but they may well be so.

It is impossible indeed to consider continuous assessment without discussing the assessment of certain attributes of personality which do not fall within the area of cognitive skills. (See Chapters 6 and 10.) Where qualities such as perseverance, consistency of effort and the like are concerned, it is obvious that only the teacher is in a position to make judgments. It is equally obvious that very severe difficulties are involved in relation to moderation if these qualities are to be assessed in an examination, indeed it is arguable whether moderation in any acceptable objective sense is possible. This does not mean, however, that these attributes ought not to be assessed within the context of 'external' examination as part of an overall pattern of assessment, but it does mean that the very greatest care will have to be taken by those who are proposing to undertake it. It does also mean that these qualities or attributes should be rewarded only in so far as they affect attainment. As the East Midlands Board warns:

> The teacher may be influenced too much by his attitude to the child, e.g. the pupil's characteristics, such as effort, industry and perseverance, may be rewarded too generously.[10]

The subjective nature of the assessment, far from lessening the demands made upon the assessors, if anything increases them. The need for a clear statement of what is being undertaken, careful planning and a detailed record of what has been done, remain paramount. Such assessment is, moreover, something which is best undertaken within a school on a departmental rather than an individual basis.

This chapter has drawn attention to some of the problems as well as to the advantages of continuous assessment and the use of course work. It has not of itself established the rigour and definition that is desirable, but hopefully it has contributed to it. Such rigour can ultimately only come from practice and experience. Whether continuous assessment is designed for internal classroom use or in an external examination, the basic requirements, as this chapter has endeavoured to underline, remain the same, *viz*:

(1) Careful consideration of objectives, both in a partial and in a total sense. Over-emphasis upon the score obtained in yesterday's test, however well designed it may have been, is as undesirable as over-emphasis upon last term's overall performance. As always, balance is all important.

(2) Knowledge of and, ideally, ability to construct assessment appropriate for the achievement of the objectives.

(3) Careful planning. The more closely the assessment and the teaching are knit together, the more imperative it is that detailed planning takes place. If this is not done then there will inevitably be distortion.

(4) The maintenance of detailed records. This is as much for the teachers' benefit as for that of any outside agency. Very little research appears to have been done in this area, although the current Swindon scheme of pupil record cards is interesting in this respect.

In summary, teachers making use of continuous assessment in any organized framework, require commitment, experience and assistance. The first two cannot be provided for them, they will instead emerge from the environment in which the teachers work and from their willingness to devote time and effort, often in adverse circumstances, to the realization of their aims. Assistance in the form of inservice training can, however, be provided. As this chapter, and indeed the whole book, has suggested such provision is at the present time inadequate. The need to increase and reinforce training through the use of all available agencies, remains crucial if improvements are to take place. One of the results of such training should be to secure greater objectivity and detachment on the part of teachers in relation to the assessment of their own pupils. If this occurs, then the benefits of continuous assessment can be obtained without the attendant disadvantages.

In the context of external examinations, moderation is all important. Hale, in Chapter 11, has described the major methods in current use and these are all exemplified in practice among the GCE and CSE examining boards. This range is well illustrated for example in the approaches adopted by the following CSE boards: the East Midlands (the achievement of a substantial measure of preliminary agreement upon descriptions of attainment or analysis of attitudes through precisely stated objectives, well constructed periodic classroom tests and maintenance of proper records), the West Yorkshire and Lindsey (additional emphasis upon consensus of teachers' opinions) and the North Western (effort to establish the use of scaling). Whatever the method used, whether it be completely statistical or involve the establishment of a consensus judgment through the use of groups of teachers, it depends in the last resort upon the knowledge, hard work and experience of the teaching profession.

Improvements in the expertise 'at the grass roots' should show themselves in greater willingness to discuss and set down objectives, in the improvement of the quality of teacher-made tests and school records, and in a desire to participate in a more formal sense in the process of pupil assessment. This can only result in an easing of the problems at the national level and make it more likely that a wider range of assessment procedures will be used and that teachers will not only be more involved, but that their involvement will be more significant in relation to the results awarded to their own pupils. In such development, continuous assessment has a contribution to make. As Eggleston says 'Potentially this method of assessment has a most valuable part to play. The advantages of applying test situations—not necessarily formal tests over a period of two years— removes many of the disadvantages of the "one-shot examination" for the following reasons:

(1) behaviours can be sampled more thoroughly;
(2) variations of performance can be distributed about a mean value;
(3) the factual content of the syllabus becomes less demanding, thus giving greater freedom of choice of subject matter;
(4) the teacher is made aware of the effectiveness of his teaching;
(5) teaching will be related to a comprehensive array of objectives with greater facility than is possible with examinations of limited duration.'[10]

That it will provide a more valid assessment goes without saying. Only the teaching profession can, however, turn this potential into a reality.

## References

[1] G. H. Bantock, *Education in an Industrial Society*. (London, Faber, 1963) p. 70.
[2] P. J. Kelly, 'Re-appraisal of Examinations'. *Journal of Curriculum Studies*, 3 (1971), No. 2 (London, Collins).
[3] J. F. Eggleston and J. F. Kerr, *Studies in Assessment* (London, English Universities Press, 1969).
[4] F. T. Wilhelms, *The Curriculum*, edited by R. Hooper (Edinburgh, Oliver & Boyd, 1971), p. 325.
[5] University of London University Entrance and Schools Examinations Council (1970), Conference Report No. 3, p. 51.
[6] J. T. Allanson—Paper on Continuous Assessment submitted for discussion at the Schools Council, October 1970.
[7] Joint Matriculation Board (1965), Occasional Publication No. 22, p. 1.
[8] North Western Secondary School Examinations Board, 'Guidance to Teachers on "Folio of Writing" in English'.
[9] West Yorkshire and Lindsey Regional Examinations Board—An information leaflet for schools on continuous assessment.
[10] East Midland Regional Examinations Board—Paper submitted to Second Examinations Committee of the Schools Council, October 1970.
[11] J. F. Eggleston, *A Critical Review of Assessment Procedures in Secondary School Science*. (Research Unit for Assessment and Curriculum Studies, University of Leicester, 1965), p. 55.

Permission to reproduce quotations in this chapter has been granted by the individuals, publishers and examining boards concerned.

# 10 The Assessment of Attitudes

## J. C. Mathews

**Three types of educational outcomes**

Education produces, or is intended to produce, changes in children. Teachers bear the heavy responsibility of guiding, influencing and encouraging those changes and—to a large extent—determining what those changes should be. If a child is unchanged at the end of an educational process, or is changed in such a way that it is harmful to himself or his fellows, then the process has been useless or worse than useless. It seems self-evident, therefore, that a teacher should be able to describe those changes, observe them, and—in the widest sense of the word—*assess* them, so that he may account for his stewardship of the children's present and future welfare.

'The education of the whole child' and such-like aims sound very fine and are unlikely to be denied, but when it comes down to actually describing the changes which education engenders a more precise description is required. Inevitably, the search for precision is an analytical one; that is we seek to divide the total and very complex behaviour of children into its parts and to describe each separately. There is nothing new in this; it is a function of the social and physical sciences and of most human activity. The main divisions of the outcomes of education are thinking, feeling and doing (in technical terms the cognitive, affective and psychomotor domains). It must be said at the outset that any analysis of human behaviour into categories such as those three does violence to the whole. Rarely, if ever, can a single behaviour be said to be solely thinking, or feeling, or doing. Educational outcomes inevitably contain elements of all three. Nevertheless, it is apparent that we can often say that one of the three predominates and a separate description of it may aid its understanding. Some examples may help to make the point.

An acceptable educational objective may be that a pupil should be able to write a coherent piece of prose in order to review critically a literary work. To do so he will certainly have to exercise considerable cognitive ability: he must be able to remember, to comprehend, to analyse, to apply concepts and rules, and finally arrange his thoughts in such a way that his essay is a communication intelligible to others. At the same time, a small degree of physical competence is necessary in actually reading and writing, without which no communication would be possible. But, in addition, the pupil must have been *predisposed* to undertake the necessary study: his *feelings* with regard to the study of literature must have been such that he was willing not only to read literature but to *respond* to it: at the very least he must have been willing to *co-operate* with his teachers or be *motivated* to study on his own: he may even have *enjoyed* it and be sufficiently interested to *wish* to pursue similar studies without being coerced or bribed into doing so: it is possible that he had a favourable *attitude* to the study of literature. The words in italics in the last sentence refer to types of behaviour which we recognize as different in kind from purely cognitive and physical behaviour and it is these words and others like them which are in constant use in describing educational objectives and outcomes. Collectively they are called *affective* behaviours.* In an actual test situation in which a pupil has to demonstrate his ability to write a critical review of a literary work measurements which are likely to be made will be predominantly in the cognitive domain with a smaller, but essential, physical element. It may be suspected that the pupil is favourably disposed to the study of literature, but it is by no means certain and it would be rash to suppose that skill in such exercises necessarily reflects any particular attitude to literature. Much the same could be said for the solution of a mathematical problem: the skills taught and tested are mainly cognitive. Even the most cursory analysis of examinations and assessment in general reveals that testing for the attainment of cognitive objectives is pre-eminent.

Before expanding the last point, a further example will indicate the interaction of the three types of behaviour. An unexceptional educational objective might be that every pupil should be able to swim a hundred metres at some stage of his schooling. The outcome is easily tested (if not easily taught!) and the observed behaviour is entirely physical. But surely the teaching and the testing must have cognitive and affective elements. There are rules to be learned and applied; there are safety regulations and codes of behaviour which must be accepted; there must be will-power and satisfaction in achievement. The whole behaviour is compounded of all three domains, but the physical predominates. It is tempting to dwell on similar psychomotor objectives, which some think—with good reason—to be neglected in our schools; but it is necessary to return to the main theme of this chapter.

The reason for the pre-eminence of teaching for cognitive objectives and testing for cognitive outcomes is not hard to find. It is traditional: schools

* The term 'attitudes' is loosely used and is capable of many different interpretations. For the purpose of the discussion in this section it is given its widest meaning to include all educational objectives and outcomes other than those which are strictly cognitive and physical.

as we know them have grown from academic roots. The education and even the training of teachers is largely of the mind. Above all, nearly the whole of our assessment procedures have been directed to cognitive outcomes; partly because they are most readily defined and agreed, and partly because they are most easily assessed. Not as readily or as easily as we may have supposed in the past—much of this book will testify to that—but we are much more willing and much more competent to measure the ability to solve, for example, a mathematical problem than we are to test for attitudes towards mathematics and other affective objectives.

## Affective outcomes of education

The almost total absence of assessment of attitudes in the *outcome* of education is all the more remarkable when one contrasts the emphasis given to it in statements about the *aims* and *objectives* of education. Despite the strong academic bias of our schools there has been, from the earliest times, a constant declaration of affective objectives. In the schools of the last century teachers, parents and even pupils proclaimed objectives such as character development, training for leadership, training to serve, and so on. Nowadays such objectives are more implicit than explicit and the proclamations sound a new note:

'Developing moral sensibility'[1]
'Developing aesthetic sensibility'[1]
'In the middle years there will be particular emphasis upon the development of learning skills and of *favourable attitudes*'[2]
'The need for more people with scientific training and with a *critical attitude of mind* has become a matter of national concern'.[3]

(author's italics)

'. . . to respond to challenges which require physical skill and mental alertness and through this *confidence* is gained leading to *satisfaction*, *self respect*, and *poise*'[4] (author's italics)

And from a recent study into the importance which Sixth Form Students attached to the objectives of their courses, a high rating was given to:

'Encourage you to be independent'
'Help you to develop your character and personality'
'Give you experience of taking responsibility'.

(In passing, it is interesting to note that the students rated less highly the objective: 'Help you to develop a questioning attitude'.)

All the above quotations could more appropriately be called general aims rather than objectives. Nevertheless, they reflect the *intention* of curriculum innovators, teachers, and pupils, to use schools as a means of attaining affective objectives.

What are the affective attainments arising from those intentions? It is not easy to get answers to that question. There are those who deny the propriety of even specifying affective objectives. There are those who are prepared to specify affective objectives but are not prepared to assess attainment of them. There are those who are prepared to do both but the latter only under the seal of confidence, and unknown to the pupil. But should not we teachers be held accountable for what we do and for what we say that we hope to do? And accountability is not possible without some form of assessment.

The foregoing pages are intended to indicate the nature of the educational outcomes loosely called 'attitudes' and to give a glimpse of some moral, philosophical and psychological implications of the debate in which teachers must be engaged with regard to them. Unless we are prepared to accept purely cognitive and physical functions of education we cannot avoid this debate. For the rest of this section it will be assumed that education *is* concerned with the attitudes of children and, necessarily, with attempts to assess whether certain attitudes have been attained. Hence, the following pages discuss attempts to describe, observe and measure attitudes.

## What are attitudes?

The progress which has been made in recent years in the assessment of cognitive attainment has arisen as much from clear statements and systematic classification of cognitive abilities as from changes in assessment techniques. The classification systems of Bloom[6] and Gagné,[7] while by no means universally accepted, have at least given rise to a more precise use of terms and a more disciplined analysis of attainment in the cognitive domain. As a result, communication between examiners has been improved, so that now we at least understand what each other is talking about, even if we agree to differ. Furthermore, the classifications referred to above have laid bare the limitations and deficiencies of traditional forms of assessment.

So, if we are to assess affective attainment, the first step is to describe attainment in operational terms. This will mean the provision of statements about specific behaviour which can at least be observed if not accurately measured. The more specific the statement the more likely is it to be observable and measurable.

Affective aims such as, 'A humanities course should lead to . . . an imaginative sympathy with subjective human experience'[8] are laudable, but how do you know whether your pupils have attained 'imaginative sympathy'? Whereas a related attainment such as, voluntarily helps at a community centre for old people, is capable of verification. Operational statements of this type are now commonplace in the cognitive domain and could well lead to greater precision both in statements of objectives and assessment of attainment. A tentative start has been made in the affective domain and some examples will be given later.

At this point, however, attention must be drawn to the dangers inherent in the move to greater precision. If precision of definition and reliability of assessment are to be the sole criteria of what is to be taught, the curriculum of our schools could become limited to a very small area of human experience and behaviour. As always, the conflict between general, ideal aims and specific, measurable attainment is likely to be resolved by compromise. Meanwhile, the move towards operational descriptions of affective objectives and attainment is a healthy one: it will at least make educators face reality and the need to substantiate their more extravagant claims.

## The classification of 'attitudes'

Reference has already been made to analysis as a principal method of increasing our understanding. But analysis alone leads to fragmentation of what is observed and, if left at that, to a chaotic mixture of little pieces: a list of affective objectives arranged at random is likely to be unmanageable. Analysis must be followed by that equally useful tool, classification; the grouping of the separate entities into categories so that within each category is to be found things with a predominant, common feature. In the cognitive domain the work of Bloom is a typical example in which attainment is classified into six main categories (p. xvi). Furthermore, the groups are arranged in a particular order according to a basic principle, which in the Bloom classification is that of increasing complexity of mental operations. A classification so arranged is called a taxonomy. The validity of such taxonomies may be judged on several grounds: can the various categories be distinguished by those whose job it will be to teach and assess? Is the classification logical and can the principle on which it is based (e.g. complexity) be recognized and applied (again, by teachers and assessors)? And is it at variance with other accepted studies of human behaviour, philosophy and psychology, for example?

Given those qualifications, a taxonomy of affective behaviour could be useful, if only to give a focus to the search for a better understanding of what educators are trying to do. Krathwohl and others have constructed such a taxonomy, and—despite some obvious and admitted defects—it can be used as a framework against which statements of affective objectives and the methods of their assessment can be matched. It is intended as a basis for reference rather than a system to be slavishly followed.

The principle on which affective attainment is classified in Krathwohl's taxonomy is the degree to which a pupil accepts and adopts an educational experience. Five levels of acceptance are suggested:

(1) receiving or attending;
(2) responding;
(3) valuing;
(4) organization of values;
(5) characterization.

The last three are concerned with adoption of values: rising to the situation (level 5) in which an individual has adopted a particular set of values as the permanent characteristic of his way of living. The deliberate inculcation of a value or set of values in the young smacks of indoctrination. While in some areas, such as the valuing of objective truth this might be acceptable, on the whole it is not something which is readily acceptable in education in Britain. It follows that deliberate attempts to dispose children to accept an educational experience at level 3 or higher and, moreover, to use assessment procedures to find out the degree of acceptance are not likely to gain general approval, so the discussion in this section will be limited to the first two levels, receiving and responding.

The principle used in this taxonomy for classifying and arranging the affective outcome of education is called *internalization*. The main categories range from simply receiving an educational experience (1) to the complete acceptance of a way of life (5). Each main category can be divided into sub-levels, using the principle of internalization, and levels 1 and 2 yield the following:

*Level 1—Reception of an Educational Experience*

1.1. *Awareness*—the lowest level—the pupil is simply conscious of the educational activity.

1.2. *Willingness* to receive—the pupil is not only aware that something is going on, he is willing to submit to it without coercion.

1.3. *Controlled or Selected* attention—the pupil is not only willing to give his attention, he discriminates between the various experiences and exercises preference of one over the other.

*Level 2—Responding to an Educational Experience*

2.1 *Acquiescence in Responding*—the pupil not only pays attention, he agrees to respond to it; perhaps unwillingly and without seeing the need to do so and, perhaps, because he will be punished if he does not do so. He is obedient and compliant, but not self-motivated.

2.2. *Willingness to Respond*—the pupil is prepared to respond voluntarily. This is a state of co-operation and above that of mere obedience.

2.3. *Satisfaction in Responding*—the pupil responds even more positively. There is now an emotional element, although at a very low level, but at least the pupil likes what he is doing.

What is important in any classification is that it should work; it should be possible for observers to allocate, with substantial agreement amongst themselves, their actual observations into the appropriate categories in the classification. If this cannot be done, the classification is no more than a useless mental exercise.

An example of how such a classification might be done is given below.

AN EXAMPLE OF VARIOUS LEVELS OF AN AFFECTIVE OBJECTIVE

One general aim in a science course* might be 'to develop satisfactory attitudes to safety regulations in the laboratory'. A typical statement of an

* See also Chapter 6 for further references to the assessment of 'attitudes' in relation to science courses.

educational aim in the affective domain, but lacking precision, giving little indication of what 'satisfactory' means, and giving no guidance on appropriate behaviour which could be observed and assessed and thus give some indication as to whether the objective had been attained. It is in this translation from general aims to specific behaviours that a classification of objectives such as Krathwohl's can help. One possible translation of the general aim could be as follows:

*Level 1.1.* The pupil is aware that there are such things as safety regulations.

*Level 1.2.* He is willing to be told about them.

*Level 1.3.* He exercises controlled attention—he may accept the importance of fire hazards but be indifferent to others and still not respond to any of them; but to have controlled attention implies that he at least knows what some of the regulations are.

*Level 2.1.* He obeys safety regulations when reminded of them and because he may get into trouble if he does not.

*Level 2.2.* He complies willingly with safety regulations and would observe them even if he were not under supervision.

*Level 2.3.* He much prefers working in a laboratory in which safety regulations are scrupulously observed than in one in which regulations are absent or not observed.

Affective behaviour below level 2 is really not worth very much by itself, since there is no response to the situation; nevertheless, willingness to receive is a prerequisite of responding and all teachers will have had experience of classes and individual pupils who simply 'did not want to know'. Strictly speaking, an attitude cannot be said to have been adopted until a pupil has 'internalized' the experience at least at level 2.2; merely receiving and acquiescing under duress cannot be said to be an attainment of an attitude, although the lower levels may be said to be the start of an interest or an appreciation. Notice, too, that both cognitive and physical behaviour may be an essential part of the affective attainment: controlled attention is not possible unless some knowledge and understanding have been acquired and response implies a physical manifestation of the inward decision to respond.

Space does not allow a more complete exposition of the Krathwohl taxonomy nor of further examples of its application. Readers may like to try exercises similar to that above in their own areas of teaching. What do you mean, for example, when you claim to teach for 'an *appreciation* of literature', 'a *liking* for music', '*sensitivity* towards other people', '*valuing* of objective evidence', 'a *concern* for the environment'?

## The observation of 'Attitudes'

So much for the description and categorization of attitudes; but that is only the first step. The purpose of this book is to discuss assessment and, before assessment, must come observation. In the physical domain attainment normally has a clear visual manifestation. In the cognitive domain, although it may be difficult or impossible to know what actual mental processes are taking place, we do have many sophisticated tests which allow pupils to manifest their cognitive achievements; but the manifestation of affective attainment is a much less predictable outcome. How *do* you observe 'a satisfaction in listening to music' or 'a respect for the feelings of others'?

Sometimes there may be clear manifestation of an attitude. A pupil who gets out one novel of Sir Walter Scott each week from the library and reads it from cover to cover (a rare bird nowadays!) could well be said to have reached at least the level of 'satisfaction of response' (2.3) to Scott's novels. A child who goes to Church each week when his parents do not and finally studies for Holy Orders could well have an attitude to religion at least at the 'commitment to a value' level (3.3). Someone who takes a partly-solved mathematical problem from the class to complete at home without being told to do so could be said to display *persistence*, another often proclaimed affective objective. Someone who repeatedly argues with you in class may have 'adopted a critical attitude' and finds satisfaction in doing so.

But to return to some of the other more subtle and more emotional categories of 'attitudes; there is sometimes no manifestation other than an inward one to the pupil himself. Satisfactions, preferences, willingness, do not always display themselves and, conversely, an apparent display of these attitudes can sometimes hide a very different real attitude within the pupil, leaving the observer completely deceived. So, before discussing *how* attitudes can be observed and assessed, consideration must be given to *who* should observe and assess.

For the assessment of educational attainment there are principally three possible agencies: external agencies, such as examining boards, the teachers of the pupils, and the pupils themselves. In assessment of cognitive ability the first has been the main agency, the second is being increasingly used, but the third not at all. If reliable, valid assessment of attitudes is to be accomplished, this emphasis may have to be reversed. In other words, if we really wish to know what our pupils think of various educational experiences and the degree to which they accept them and find satisfaction in them, we might have to ask them and rely on what *they* tell us rather than what others, teachers and examiners, tell us. This is not to say that teachers cannot assess certain attitudes in their pupils, or that objective tests do not exist for doing so; the point is that we are unlikely to get anything like a complete assessment unless we rely, to some extent, on self-assessment. In the conventional examining sense, the foregoing suggestion may appear revolutionary, but if the problem of assessment of attitudes is to be taken seriously rather than be paid mere lip-service, it is a suggestion which must be faced; and the first question which it raises is what techniques are available for external, teacher, or self assessment of attitudes and is there any place for such techniques in assessment procedures, particularly those which, like public examinations, are externally administered largely for the purpose of certification and career advancement.

## The techniques of attitude assessment

There is nothing new in attempts to assess people's attitudes. The Gallup poll and other similar polls do so regularly in the political sphere; marketing research and advertising research employ complex techniques to assess consumer attitudes. But is there a place for those or similar techniques in education? Most of the techniques use either the structured interview or various forms of written questionnaire. The following review of techniques is by no means exhaustive.

THE OPEN-ENDED INTERVIEW

In this the interviewer has one or two general aims and tends to conduct the interview 'off the cuff'. The respondent is allowed free-response and is in control of what goes on almost as much as the interviewer is. If either the interviewer or respondent wants to follow a new line, they are at liberty to do so. The interview is 'played by ear' not 'from a score'. There are advantages in this technique: questions, responses and attitudes are revealed, which the interviewer had not previously considered. The informality can lead to mutual trust and hence a truthful response.

In one sense much of a teacher's work is a protracted, informal, open-ended interview. Talking with pupils in and out of class builds up an informal opinion of each one—his likes, dislikes, enthusiasms, and prejudices —in fact a goodly part of the whole personality. On the basis of this informal contact teachers are often prepared to venture an assessment of certain of their pupils' attitudes and this assessment can be of great value, primarily in guidance for the pupil himself and secondly in guidance for those with whom the pupil is, or will be, in contact. If, for example, a music teacher wishes to assess whether or not his pupils find more satisfaction in playing the recorder than in listening to Bach's fugues, it should not be a difficult matter to find out by this informal, conversational method. But there are snags. An open-ended interview results in one person's assessment of one other person's attitudes. This may or may not correlate highly with another interviewer's assessment: the interviewers may ask different questions and hence assess different things; they may have different standards for judging the answers and who is to say which one is right? Moreover if they knew the respondent beforehand, they may subconsciously slant both their questions and their interpretation of the answers to match their preconceived judgment of the respondent's attitudes. The assessment could be strongly subjective and its validity and reliability in doubt.

THE STRUCTURED INTERVIEW

In the structured interview or, as it is sometimes called, the interview schedule, some of the objections are met by prescribing the exact wording and sequence of all the questions so that the interviewer simply reads out the questions and records the answer. In this way all the respondents are subjected to the same test and, if the interview has been carefully structured so that each question elicits only one or two points (rather like a structured examination question, Chapter 2), it is easier to standardize the test and agree about relative performances of the respondents. A further aid to standardization of the test and processing of the results is to limit the freedom of the respondent by allowing only a choice from a small number of predetermined answers, rather like a multiple-choice question. For example:

If you had a choice of the following activities this evening which would you prefer?
(A) Reading
(B) Painting
(C) Going to a musical concert
(D) Doing an experiment in science
(E) Watching Sport
(F) Taking part in sport
(G) None of these

This is a crude question and would have to be followed by others if information of any value was to accrue, and, herein lies one of the difficulties of the structured interview. One must pre-determine the course of the interview and all the subsequent questions. During the interview it may become obvious that more productive questions could have been asked or better responses suggested. In other words, the first use of an interview schedule must be like the pre-testing of an objective test and the outcome used to produce a more refined test. This is all very well for an organization geared to such procedures, but what of the classroom teacher; it is just as difficult for him to construct an interview schedule as it would be to construct an objective test.

WRITTEN TESTS OF ATTITUDES

These abound. Almost all of them, however, are of the structured, fixed response type and the product of much research and validation. They are not the sort of thing a teacher would wish to construct or *could* construct without training and a good deal of time and effort. Some can be purchased for research purposes—for example, those of the National Foundation for Educational Research[10] but it is doubtful whether much exists which could help the teacher in the assessment of his own pupils. The main reason is that tests are likely to be specific for one particular purpose and a teacher seeking a test which fits *his* course, and the affective objectives related to it, is not likely to find one which matches.

Space does not allow a full account of all the techniques of the professional attitude measurers. Readers who wish to pursue the matter further will find plenty of reading,[11] particularly in the field of educational research.

The Thurstone scale technique is to list a large number of statements about a particular topic, ranging from enthusiasm and strong commitment to it, through indifference, to strong rejection of it at the other end of the scale. Respondents are then asked to tick those statements with which they agree. Other tests are of the *forced choice* type in which respondents are asked whether they agree or disagree with each of a list of statements or if more refinement is required, whether they strongly agree, probably agree, probably disagree, or strongly disagree. Examples of other variations of items in attitude tests include:

(1) Complete the following sentence with one of the lettered responses: I would prefer ............ attention paid to safety regulations in our school laboratories than is paid at present.
A a lot more
B a little more
C a little less
D a lot less

(Note that in this example that the pupil is not allowed to hedge his bets by having a don't know category.)

(2) Indicate your attitude to the music of each of the composers listed below in one of the following ways:
A I like his music and listen to it whenever I have the chance
B I like his music but I do not listen to it very often
C I do not like his music
D I have never heard his music

1 Beethoven
2 Maxwell Davies
3 Tom Paxton etc.

These types of test resemble the structured and fixed response interview, but they can be administered on a large scale and do not demand so great an expenditure of resources. They could, if it were thought appropriate, be administered in a way similar to large-scale objective testing which is increasingly being used by examining boards.

DIRECT OBSERVATION

Both the interview and questionnaire technique depend on what *the respondent says* are his attitudes, and these statements may or may not accord with his real attitudes. To return to the example of the safety regulations in the laboratory: a pupil may *say* that he has a high regard for them, but direct observation by his teacher may reveal that *in practice* he disregards them. A pupil may say that he likes investigations and projects, but his teacher may observe that he does not display the necessary persistence to finish either in the face of difficulties. And although it may be possible to adopt a certain behaviour for a particular occasion, it is unlikely that such pretence could be kept up over a long period. So the teacher is in a strong position for assessing the manifestation of some attitudes and acting as a check on the outcome of more formal methods of assessment. But *should* the teacher do so? Should formal assessment of affective attainment take place? Is it taking place? And how can it be done if the answers to those questions is 'Yes'?


## Present and future assessment of attitudes

The answers to those three questions depends largely on decisions about the purpose of the assessment. The purpose of much of the assessment of cognitive ability is to discriminate between candidates and so to use the results to select for employment or further education; whether this is right or wrong is the subject of much debate, but the fact remains. The assessment of attitudes depends very largely on the co-operation of the respondents and on honest replies from them; and, if such assessment were to have any significant weight in selection procedures, or if pupils were to be subjected to penalties or criticism as a result of it, it is too much to expect that they would willingly give answers which would put them at a disadvantage. So, to the question 'Will the assessment of attitudes play a large part in discriminatory examination systems as we know them?', the author's answer would be 'Most unlikely', if not a flat 'No'. However, this does not exclude a small element of assessment of 'attitudes' which can be assessed by direct observation of students' behaviour by the teacher and there have already been some moves in that direction, of which the following are two examples.

In the Nuffield A-level Chemistry Examination* the practical work is assessed internally by teachers, the assessment counting 15% of the whole examination. In arriving at the objectives of the practical assessment, the teachers themselves were consulted and as a result, attitudes to practical work were included, the weighting being one-fifth of the practical assessment, that is 3% of the whole examination. Teachers are left with a good deal of freedom on how they arrive at this assessment, but observation of such qualities as willing co-operation with normal laboratory procedures, persistence in pursuing a practical problem even when difficulties arise, and enthusiasm for practical work as a worthwhile scientific pursuit, were suggested. Marks for this and the attainment of other objectives of practical work are entered on a pupil's record card and submitted to the examining board at the end of the course. The total mark may be subjected to a moderating procedure by the examining board, but the order of merit is not changed.

In the Schools Council Integrated Science Project† a 20% weighting is given to internal assessment by teachers, including the following objectives:

* According to the 1972 regulations of the University of London School Examinations Department.
† O-level Examination 1973 (Associated Examining Board). Reproduced by permission of the Schools Council Integrated Science Project.

'to show perseverance in designing and performing simple experiments and in other learning activities';
'being sceptical about suggested patterns, yet willing to search for and test for patterns';
'being concerned for the application of scientific knowledge within the community'.

The quoted objectives all fall within the affective domain and they constitute 40% of the teacher assessment, 8% of the whole examination.

It is perhaps a little early to judge the outcome of these and other assessments of 'attitudes' in public examinations. Nevertheless, such attempts should be welcomed; the objectives are explicit, where formerly they have been implicit; and the assessment is open and has a basis in principle, whereas other assessments of attitudes are confidential and based on ill-defined and variable principles. It should be noted that both the examples of assessment which have been quoted are teacher operated and it seems likely, at least for some time to come, that attempts at the assessment of attitudes will remain so rather than in the form of externally operated, written attitude tests. Provided that there are suitable safeguards to prevent injustice to individual candidates and for moderation between one teacher's marks and another's, there seems no reason why the first, tentative steps in assessment should not be extended to other subjects.

Both the assessments referred to form part of discriminatory examinations as defined above and the problems attending the assessment of attitudes for this purpose have already been mentioned. But that is only one purpose for assessment; there are two others which many think to be equally, if not more, important. First, the diagnostic assessment which the teacher uses in his day-to-day teaching to assess the progress of each of his pupils in order to *guide their future progress*; and, second, the assessment which is necessary to guide and evaluate the introduction of a new course, or curriculum, or style of teaching.

In the first of these two areas of assessment the purpose is to help the pupil, not to make statements about his merit relative to others. In these circumstances reliable and valid assessments of attitudes are more likely to be achieved. The co-operation of pupils will be more readily given and a greater range of assessment techniques will be acceptable. In the second, the same arguments apply. The co-operation of pupils is essential and usually readily given in any curricular innovation; the pupils' willingness to accept and enthusiasm for such innovation is every bit as important as the teacher's. Provided that it does not interfere too much with normal teaching, there is every reason for assessing pupils' attitudes frequently and rigorously during the design of a new course. In the latter, one is concerned with the attitudes of the *group* rather than those of the individual and in many instances anonymity of the replies can be preserved.

In this section the author is aware that he has raised more problems than he has given solutions. This is not a matter which is subject to facile solutions; the dangers of indoctrination, unfair treatment of pupils and a change in teacher/pupil relationships come immediately to mind. But at least let us be honest in this business; let us not make claims for educational objectives which are incapable of verification, and if we do assess attitudes let the assessment have some known and commonly accepted basis.

## References

[1] Schools Council, *16–19 Growth and Response* (Working Paper 45) (London, Evans/Methuen, 1972), p. 58.

[2] Schools Council, *Education in the Middle Years* (Working Paper 42) (London, Evans/Methuen, 1972), p. 42.

[3] Nuffield Chemistry, *Introduction and Guide* (London, Longmans/Penguin, 1966), p. 1.

[4] Schools Council, *Physical Education 8–13* (Working Paper 37) (London, Evans/Methuen, 1971), p. 13.

[5] Schools Council, *Sixth Form Survey*, Vol. 1 (Books for Schools Ltd, 1970), p. 122.

[6] *Taxonomy of Educational Objectives*, edited by B. S. Bloom. Handbook I. 'The Cognitive Domain' (London, Longmans, 1956).

[7] R. M. Gagné, *The Conditions of Learning* (New York, Holt, Rinehart & Winston, 1970).

[8] L. Stenhouse, 'The Humanities Curriculum', in *The Curriculum* edited by R. Hooper (Edinburgh, Oliver & Boyd, 1971).

[9] D. R. Krathwohl *et al.*, *Taxonomy of Educational Objectives*, Handbook II (London, Longmans, 1964).

[10] *NFER Test Catalogue*, National Foundation for Educational Research.

[11] J. D. Nisbet and N. J. Entwistle, *Educational Research Methods* (University of London Press, 1970).

# 11 Moderation

## D. E. Hale

Assessment must be meaningful if it is to serve a useful purpose. The recording of a mark in a record book or upon a certificate has little real meaning if it cannot be associated with degrees of achievement upon specified objectives within particular courses of study. This implies a need for comparison. The basis for such comparison may be another individual, another class, another school or, in the case of a national examination, nationally defined standards. Moderation provides a vehicle whereby such comparisons can be made in practice. In so doing conformity is achieved out of diversity. Put in another way, moderation is the process whereby the work of different pupils in different schools, assessed by different people upon different patterns of assessment, is brought into relationship with standards which are more widely based. Moderation must, therefore, of necessity follow assessment whenever common standards are to be applied to the work of more pupils than have been assessed by a single individual. Its scope and range can thus vary greatly.

The teacher in the classroom is required on many occasions to make judgments about his pupils. Such judgments not only help him to judge individual or class progress but also to evaluate the courses of study being undertaken. In recent years the impact of CSE and the development of Teachers' Centres, to name but two factors, have greatly reduced the isolation of teachers. This has enabled them to modify their own judgments in the light of the experience of others. Such modification is the essence of moderation which is not a process that can be undertaken by individuals working on their own. There are basically five possible methods of equating standards whether between examining boards, between schools and/or between different groups in the same schools. These are as follows:

(a) standard prescribed method of assessment;
(b) re-marking;
(c) assessment by groups;
(d) inspection;
(e) statistical moderation.

The method used does not, however, affect the basic principles underlying moderation nor the basic requirements for successful moderation. This chapter will look primarily at these requirements rather than describe the methods themselves in any detail. Specifically no reference will be made to actual statistical methods in current use; the reader who wishes to obtain further detail here could with advantage look at the procedures currently practised for mode 1 by the Yorkshire Regional Examinations Board and the work currently being undertaken by the Joint Matriculation Board in relation to the moderation of internal assessment of practical work in Science. Of the remaining four methods, (c) (assessment by groups) will receive rather more attention than the other three. This is felt to be appropriate in a practical handbook for teachers since it is the method which most comprehensively involves the teacher. The implications of the development of a system of moderation by consensus are, moreover, considerable in terms of the role of the teacher as assessor. Methods (a) (standard prescribed) and (d) (inspection) are extensively used at the present time by all GCE boards and most CSE boards; the former mainly for written work and the latter for orals, practicals and course work of all kinds. Method (b) (re-marking) is also quite commonly used, where sampling of initially marked work is involved for example with projects.

Consideration of the basic requirements for moderation necessitates going back to the beginning. This means first of all asking what basic information an assessor should have in his possession before he starts work. This is as follows:

(1) the objectives of the course of study from which the work comes;

(2) the skills which the course is intended to develop and the content to be covered—the syllabus;

(3) the pattern of assessment adopted to ensure that mastery of these skills can be demonstrated;

(4) the weighting of the various parts of the course as exemplified in the assessment. This may on occasions involve a detailed mark scheme.

This basic information is necessary whether the assessor subsequently moderates or not. Better informed assessors can only improve the quality of moderation and the facility with which it can be carried out. Moderation is essentially an exercise in communication and anything which improves the quality of the message can only be for the good. These four dimensions are all discussed in the book, indeed they are central to it, the first two primarily in the Introduction, the third throughout and the last mainly in Chapters 8, 12 and 14. Unfortunately, as the Introduction suggests, the definition of objectives is not something which teachers on the whole find easy to undertake. It is nevertheless, imperative that they make the attempt since such definition provides the possibility of making significant improvements to both assessment and moderation.

The information suggested above having been provided, the assessor starts his task. This requires the work of certain pupils to be marked or graded. Four things can happen:

(1) the marking or assessment will conform to the required standards whatever they may be;

(2) the marking or assessment will be consistently severe in relation to the required standards;

(3) the marking or assessment will be consistently lenient in relation to the required standards;

(4) the marking or assessment will bear no consistent relationship to the required standards.

The words marking and assessment have both been used since there is a growing tendency to work in grades rather than marks from the first stage of assessment. Of these four possibilities only the fourth is unsatisfactory for moderation purposes. Consistency of initial marking or assessment is absolutely vital to moderation. Such consistency will normally show itself in a reliable order of merit or rank order for the work assessed. At this stage it is worth noting that the work being assessed may be extremely varied. According to the subject and the pattern of assessment adopted it could consist of:

(1) written questions of all kinds;
(2) practical work;
(3) aural and oral work;
(4) projects or individual studies.

Part of it could also be submitted as course work or require continuous assessment. With consistency so necessary for satisfactory moderation it is essential that the procedures adopted are able to identify inconsistency in order that appropriate action can be taken. Within the moderation methods suggested earlier there are two extreme approaches embodied, although neither is as clear-cut in reality as the description which follows would suggest. These in their turn result in different ways of identifying the inconsistent and of making use of the information obtained. In the first approach the maximum influence is exerted upon those who assess before they commence their work in order to ensure that they are like minded and that this is reflected in their assessment. They thus start to moderate as they assess. The second one moves from an individual judgment (normally but not necessarily that of the pupil's own teacher) without the intrusion of any external influence such as a marking scheme to a consensus moderation involving a group of individual teachers. The two stages of assessment and moderation are thus undertaken separately. This first approach is epitomized by the elaborate and careful procedures adopted by the GCE boards. Here, those marking the work will be required before the examination takes place to study carefully a draft scheme of marking in conjunction with the actual question paper(s). At a standardization meeting held a few days after the examination has been completed they will all be required to mark the same small sample of work, often specially selected to illustrate likely difficulties. Following a discussion of this marking and a detailed scrutiny of the mark scheme a final version of the latter is agreed upon and this has to be followed by all examiners throughout their marking. The rigidity or otherwise of the scheme will, of course, vary with the subject. A check upon examiners' work is undertaken by means of sample scripts sent to a chief or senior assistant examiner on two or three occasions throughout the marking period. At the final stages of moderation a great deal of statistical information is available to those undertaking the moderation and it is upon this evidence and that of the actual marking which has been scrutinized that adjustments are made to those examiners who are felt to be severe or lenient. The inconsistent marker, if he emerges, will have all his 'scripts' re-marked and will equally certainly not be employed in the future.

The above description is inevitably a précis of the full procedures and the reader who requires further detail should consult *JMB/GCE The Work of the Joint Matriculation Board* by R. Christopher (October 1969), Occasional Publication No. 29. A disadvantage of these procedures is that they are rather lacking in flexibility and as such are particularly appropriate for large scale external examinations. They also in the main identify the inconsistent marker as the work proceeds rather than before it starts. The information gained is thus used to identify areas for remedial action rather than to determine the actual organization of the subsequent moderation. Little use is made of it either for training purposes and this makes it unsatisfactory for a system of consensus moderation involving large numbers of teachers.

The second approach is the one most closely associated with consensus moderation. Here, differences are deliberately identified in advance as part and parcel of a procedure designed to provide information about individual assessors in order that this can be utilized in the process of moderation itself. The device most commonly used for this purpose is known as an agreement trial. Its purpose is to identify three qualities all of which are essential for moderation whatever method may be used, namely:

(I) Discrimination
(II) Standards
(III) Conformity.

As Schools Council Examinations Bulletin No. 5, which describes an agreement trial in full explains* 'The purpose of an agreement trial is to see whether each moderator is sufficiently discriminating, conforming and moderate. He is discriminating if his range of marks is not much narrower than those of his fellows: the opposite of a discriminating moderator is an unduly timid one who awards too few good and bad and too many mediocre grades. A moderator conforms if his awards correlate well with those of his fellows. He is moderate if he is neither much more severe nor much more lenient than his colleagues.'

In an agreement trial we thus move beyond the rather negative identification of inconsistency as inimical to moderation to a more positive identification of qualities essential for moderation. Hitherto its use has been

* This quotation and the two tables which follow are reproduced from Schools Council Examinations Bulletin No. 5 (HMSO, 1965) by permission of the Schools Council and the Controller of Her Majesty's Stationery Office.

confined for moderation purposes almost exclusively to a number of CSE boards. There is no reason, however, why it should not be used more widely as part of the training given to teachers undertaking assessment and moderation whether it involves their own pupils or those from other schools.

It is usual to conduct an agreement trial upon the work of twenty candidates (pupils) arranged in five random blocks and it is convenient for the trial to be undertaken by a group of about twelve teachers. This number is suggested by the writer because he has found from experience that it ensures that all will be able to participate fully in the discussion which is an essential preliminary to the trial itself. In the example which follows every teacher participating in the trial is required to grade the work of each of the twenty candidates upon a 1 to 6 scale which corresponds to the five grades of CSE (1–5) and to the ungraded category (6). The gradings decided upon

**Table 1**

| Name of Candidate | | Grades awarded by moderators a–l | | | | | | | | | | | | |
|---|---|---|---|---|---|---|---|---|---|---|---|---|---|---|
| | | a | b | c | d | e | f | g | h | i | j | k | l | Average |
| | A | 4 | 4 | 4 | 3 | 4 | 4 | 3 | 1 | 4 | 4 | 4 | 4 | 4 |
| | B | 2 | 2 | 2 | 2 | 3 | 2 | 1 | 1 | 2 | 2 | 2 | 2 | 2 |
| | C | 6 | 5 | 5 | 5 | 5 | 5 | 5 | 5 | 5 | 5 | 5 | 5 | 5 |
| | D | 2 | 1 | 1 | 2 | 2 | 3 | 3 | 2 | 2 | 3 | 2 | 3 | 2 |
| Total | | 14 | 12 | 12 | 12 | 14 | 14 | 12 | 9 | 13 | 14 | 13 | 14 | 13 |
| Range | | 4 | 4 | 4 | 3 | 3 | 3 | 4 | 4 | 3 | 3 | 3 | 3 | 3 |
| | E | 3 | 3 | 3 | 4 | 3 | 5 | 3 | 3 | 3 | 3 | 3 | 3 | 3 |
| | F | 1 | 1 | 1 | 1 | 1 | 1 | 1 | 1 | 1 | 1 | 1 | 1 | 1 |
| | G | 5 | 6 | 6 | 6 | 5 | 5 | 6 | 6 | 6 | 6 | 6 | 6 | 6 |
| | H | 3 | 4 | 4 | 4 | 3 | 4 | 3 | 4 | 4 | 2 | 4 | 4 | 4 |
| Total | | 12 | 14 | 14 | 15 | 12 | 15 | 13 | 14 | 14 | 12 | 14 | 14 | 14 |
| Range | | 4 | 5 | 5 | 5 | 4 | 4 | 5 | 5 | 5 | 5 | 5 | 5 | 5 |
| | I | 2 | 2 | 2 | 2 | 4 | 3 | 2 | 3 | 3 | 3 | 3 | 3 | 3 |
| | J | 2 | 1 | 2 | 1 | 3 | 2 | 2 | 2 | 2 | 2 | 2 | 2 | 2 |
| | K | 5 | 5 | 5 | 6 | 5 | 5 | 5 | 6 | 5 | 5 | 5 | 4 | 5 |
| | L | 1 | 2 | 2 | 1 | 2 | 2 | 2 | 3 | 2 | 2 | 3 | 2 | 2 |
| Total | | 10 | 10 | 11 | 10 | 14 | 12 | 11 | 14 | 12 | 12 | 13 | 11 | 12 |
| Range | | 4 | 4 | 3 | 5 | 3 | 3 | 3 | 4 | 3 | 3 | 3 | 2 | 3 |
| | M | 4 | 2 | 3 | 4 | 3 | 4 | 5 | 5 | 5 | 4 | 5 | 4 | 4 |
| | N | 4 | 3 | 4 | 4 | 4 | 5 | 4 | 4 | 4 | 4 | 4 | 4 | 4 |
| | O | 5 | 4 | 4 | 3 | 4 | 3 | 4 | 4 | 4 | 5 | 4 | 4 | 4 |
| | P | 5 | 6 | 5 | 5 | 5 | 5 | 5 | 5 | 5 | 5 | 5 | 5 | 5 |
| Total | | 18 | 15 | 16 | 16 | 16 | 17 | 18 | 18 | 18 | 18 | 18 | 18 | 17 |
| Range | | 1 | 4 | 2 | 2 | 2 | 2 | 1 | 1 | 1 | 1 | 1 | 1 | 1 |
| | Q | 1 | 2 | 1 | 1 | 1 | 1 | 1 | 1 | 1 | 1 | 2 | 1 | 1 |
| | R | 1 | 1 | 2 | 1 | 1 | 2 | 1 | 1 | 1 | 1 | 1 | 1 | 1 |
| | S | 3 | 3 | 2 | 3 | 3 | 2 | 2 | 3 | 3 | 3 | 3 | 3 | 3 |
| | T | 2 | 1 | 2 | 1 | 2 | 2 | 1 | 2 | 2 | 2 | 2 | 2 | 2 |
| Total | | 7 | 7 | 7 | 6 | 7 | 7 | 5 | 7 | 7 | 7 | 8 | 7 | 7 |
| Range | | 2 | 2 | 1 | 2 | 2 | 1 | 1 | 2 | 2 | 2 | 2 | 2 | 2 |
| Grand Total | | 61 | 58 | 60 | 59 | 63 | 65 | 59 | 62 | 64 | 63 | 66 | 64 | 63 |
| Sum of Ranges | | 15 | 19 | 15 | 17 | 14 | 13 | 14 | 16 | 14 | 14 | 14 | 13 | 14 |

*Reproduced from Schools Council Examinations Bulletin No. 5*
In this example all the moderators are both discriminating and moderate (i.e. none of their sum of ranges is less than half the average sum of ranges, and all the grand totals fall within a central range of 10 of the average grand total).

by all the assessors for each of the candidates are then written out as a table.

From this information the following is calculated:

(1) the average grade for each candidate;
(2) the grade total and the grade range for each sub-group for each assessor.

This detail is used in its turn to complete the grand total of the grades awarded by each assessor. The grade ranges are then summed and averages worked out for both grade totals and sum of ranges. An example of a completed table is given below as Table 1.

The mathematics involved in these calculations are minimal and they probably take longer to describe than to do.

From this table it is possible to test the discrimination and standards (i.e. the severity and leniency) of the assessors. An assessor is timid if his sum of ranges is less than half the average sum of ranges; he is unduly severe or lenient if his grand total lies outside a central range of 10 points (i.e. five points either side) of the average grand total.

To measure conformity another table is completed upon which are entered the differences between the grades awarded to each candidate by each of the assessors and the average of all assessors' grades for every candidate. These differences are then totalled for each sub-group for each assessor and a sum of ranges for each assessor is also recorded. An example of this second table is given below as Table 2.

For this total sample of twenty candidates an assessor would not conform if the sum of his ranges for all five sub-groups exceeded 12.

All the information is now available upon which to base decisions about the use of individuals in the subsequent moderation. One method commonly used is to allow all those who in the trial meet the requirement in each of the tests for discrimination, standards and conformity to act as individual moderators. Experience has shown that where there is failure to meet all the requirements the one commonly not achieved is 'standards'—that is to say there is severity or leniency in the marking. Fortunately, it is relatively easy to overcome this by 'pairing' the most severe assessor with the most lenient assessor to work as a team. This 'pairing' can then be continued by using the next most severe assessor with the next most lenient assessor and so on until all who have fallen outside the acceptable ten point range in this text have been catered for.

For some moderation purposes it has been maintained that two heads are always better than one and the 'pairing' procedure has been extended to include all members taking part in a group moderation regardless of whether they met the trial requirements or not. This procedure is particularly convenient where work is brought to a consortium of subject teachers for moderation. It means, since it is accepted that a teacher cannot moderate the work of his own school when he has been involved in the initial assessment, that teachers from two other schools will be involved in the

**Table 2**

| Name of Candidate | Differences between the grades awarded by each moderator a–l and the average of all moderators' grades for each candidate | | | | | | | | | | | |
|---|---|---|---|---|---|---|---|---|---|---|---|---|
| | a | b | c | d | e | f | g | h | i | j | k | l |
| A | 0 | 0 | 0 | −1 | 0 | 0 | −1 | −3 | 0 | 0 | 0 | 0 |
| B | 0 | 0 | 0 | 0 | 1 | 0 | −1 | −1 | 0 | 0 | 0 | 0 |
| C | 1 | 0 | 0 | 0 | 0 | 0 | 0 | 0 | 0 | 0 | 0 | 0 |
| D | 0 | −1 | −1 | 0 | 0 | 1 | 1 | 0 | 0 | 1 | 0 | 1 |
| Range | 1 | 1 | 1 | 1 | 1 | 1 | 2 | 3 | 0 | 1 | 0 | 1 |
| E | 0 | 0 | 0 | 1 | 0 | 2 | 0 | 0 | 0 | 0 | 0 | 0 |
| F | 0 | 0 | 0 | 0 | 0 | 0 | 0 | 0 | 0 | 0 | 0 | 0 |
| G | −1 | 0 | 0 | 0 | −1 | −1 | 0 | 0 | 0 | 0 | 0 | 0 |
| H | −1 | 0 | 0 | 0 | −1 | 0 | −1 | 0 | 0 | −2 | 0 | 0 |
| Range | 1 | 0 | 0 | 1 | 1 | 3 | 1 | 0 | 0 | 2 | 0 | 0 |
| I | −1 | −1 | −1 | −1 | 1 | 0 | −1 | 0 | 0 | 0 | 0 | 0 |
| J | 0 | −1 | 0 | −1 | 1 | 0 | 0 | 0 | 0 | 0 | 0 | 0 |
| K | 0 | 0 | 0 | 1 | 0 | 0 | 0 | 1 | 0 | 0 | 0 | −1 |
| L | −1 | 0 | 0 | −1 | 0 | 0 | 0 | 1 | 0 | 0 | 1 | 0 |
| Range | 1 | 1 | 1 | 2 | 1 | 0 | 1 | 1 | 0 | 0 | 1 | 1 |
| M | 0 | −2 | −1 | 0 | −1 | 0 | 1 | 1 | 1 | 0 | 1 | 0 |
| N | 0 | −1 | 0 | 0 | 0 | 1 | 0 | 0 | 0 | 0 | 0 | 0 |
| O | 1 | 0 | 0 | −1 | 0 | −1 | 0 | 0 | 0 | 1 | 0 | 1 |
| P | 0 | 1 | 0 | 0 | 0 | 0 | 0 | 0 | 0 | 0 | 0 | 0 |
| Range | 1 | 3 | 1 | 1 | 1 | 2 | 1 | 1 | 1 | 1 | 1 | 1 |
| Q | 0 | 1 | 0 | 0 | 0 | 0 | 0 | 0 | 0 | 0 | 1 | 0 |
| R | 0 | 0 | 1 | 0 | 0 | 1 | 0 | 0 | 0 | 0 | 0 | 0 |
| S | 0 | 0 | −1 | 0 | 0 | −1 | −1 | 0 | 0 | 0 | 0 | 0 |
| T | 0 | −1 | 0 | −1 | 0 | 0 | −1 | 0 | 0 | 0 | 0 | 0 |
| Range | 0 | 2 | 2 | 1 | 0 | 2 | 1 | 0 | 0 | 0 | 1 | 0 |
| Sum of Ranges | 4 | 7 | 5 | 6 | 4 | 8 | 6 | 5 | 1 | 4 | 3 | 3 |

*Reproduced from Schools Council Examinations Bulletin No. 5*
In this example all the moderators conform (i.e. none of the sum of ranges exceeds 12).

moderation and that when group moderation has been completed teachers from three schools will have contributed to it.

Whatever method is used for the appointment of moderators the need for them to understand clearly the objectives of the courses which they are asked to moderate cannot be over stressed. This in its turn places the onus fairly and squarely upon all who prepare syllabuses and patterns of assessment to discuss and state clearly their objectives. This is as important for a mode 1 syllabus set by an examining board as it is for a mode 3 syllabus developed by a school.

Although it is usual to think of moderation as the stage that follows initial marking, it must be clearly understood that effective moderation cannot be isolated in this way. Unless the elements of an assessment take fully into account the objectives of the course and provide opportunities for candidates to demonstrate their mastery of these, then both initial marking and subsequent moderation will not reflect the real achievements of the candidates. This applies to whatever form of assessment is being used whether written, oral, practical or project. It also applies to any mark scheme or guidance provided by those undertaking the assessment. The perfect question, properly designed to test a clearly stated skill, will not achieve its purpose unless those answering it receive a proper return for doing what they have been asked to do.

It is clear that all work included for assessment should be capable of being moderated. This does not, however, mean that on one set day those undertaking the work must, or indeed ought to, see all the constituent parts. Often it will be necessary to moderate elements separately and in different places. Practical work in handicraft, for example, is best moderated by visits to schools whilst the written work in the same subject can be moderated outside the school by a group meeting of teachers. A roast dinner prepared as a practical test in Home Economics in March cannot be taken for moderation at a group meeting in May. The question then arises as to whom is the best person to undertake the moderation of this kind of work—work which will certainly increase as assessment more clearly reflects defined objectives and aims to assess relevant skills. The answer to this will, of course, depend to a great extent upon the type of assessment proposed. A set-piece practical or oral is capable of external assessment and moderation. Continuous assessment of say a range of defined practical skills can only be carried out by the teacher who actually teaches those being assessed. Clearly, the latter approach is likely to be the more valid but it is not without its difficulties as both Park and Whittaker indicate in Chapters 5 & 6. Experience has, moreover, shown that teacher moderation even when conducted on a sampling basis is extremely time consuming and requires the provision of training facilities hitherto conspicuous by their absence. The conduct of an oral test, for example, is a most demanding professional task and very few examining boards or other bodies provide anything in the way of training for it.

This raises the whole question of what kind of training facilities examining boards ought to provide in order to enable teachers to become better assessors and hence better moderators. Any such training must, of course, include explanations of a board's procedures, but it must also deal with general principles and describe the various techniques available. Opportunities must be given for discussion of course objectives and of weightings appropriate to the assessment of the elements that make up each course. The training must also be practical and involve the use of examples of work from previous examinations which it has been agreed reflect particular grade levels. This is often thought to be easy for written work and yet so often essential information is not provided. It does not really matter whether a suggested grade I piece of written work has been awarded a mark at all or whether, if there is a mark, it is 70 or 50; what does matter is that there should be a clear indication of the mastery of the particular objectives appropriate to the grade awarded and that from this information discussion should be stimulated. For practical work it is often more difficult to produce material for use at training courses, although wherever possible, this should be attempted. The use of photographs of pieces of practical work sometimes provides a suitable substitute for the work itself and these can illustrate the particular skills upon which the grade awards were based. Oral tests can be taped. Additional meaning can be given to such tapes if the teacher involved in the actual tests is present and can explain the ways in which he provided candidates with opportunities to demonstrate their skills. Such are a few examples of the kind of material which is necessary for training in moderation procedures.

Reference has been made to a number of moderation techniques which can be applied to various elements being assessed in a subject. Naturally, not all the techniques can be applied to all the situations which require moderation, particularly as the variety of the material produced for assessment increases. Reference must also be made to several situations which now arise outside the widely accepted area of subject moderation. Two interesting developments in particular require consideration in some detail. First, the moderation of continuous assessment (for a more detailed discussion of continuous assessment see Chapter 9), where it forms not a part, as was the case with the practicals mentioned earlier, but the whole of the assessment; and second there is the use of a board's examinations as a moderating instrument upon the teachers' assessments of their candidates in the same subject.

Where assessment is being undertaken exclusively on a continuous basis the problems would be substantially reduced if moderators were able to visit the schools concerned very frequently and were able on these occasions to discuss the progress of each pupil in great detail. This obviously is not possible, since it is unlikely that teacher moderators would be able to visit a school more than three times during the period of continuous assessment and that even then they would only be able to sample the work of candidates. The availability of suitably qualified external moderators in sufficient numbers is also extremely unlikely even if one wished to employ them. In such circumstances the teacher involved in both the teaching and in the initial assessment of such a course has two special duties as far as the moderators are concerned:

(1) to show that the course itself provides adequate opportunities for the pupils following it to master the skills previously defined, and

(2) to produce for them selected work undertaken by his pupils which they can moderate and upon which they can agree standards with him.

Great care must be taken to ensure that the moderators have an adequate but not excessive amount of work to moderate. The teacher must also be particularly careful to ensure that the selected work, whilst only a part of the whole, is also representative of the whole.

It will often also be necessary, for example where projects are involved, for the teacher to be able to indicate to the moderators why he has awarded a certain grade or a certain mark to a piece of work: this he must do by illustrating how each candidate has in that piece of work demonstrated his mastery of particular skills. Another essential feature of continuous assessment is that it should provide a continual up-dating of each pupil's attainment. This should present no insoluble problem as far as moderation is concerned, provided that the teachers of the course and the moderators are aware of the basis upon which the assessment is being conducted. Briefly, the point to be underlined here is that continuous assessment gives very special opportunities for candidates' mastery of skills to be recorded as they are achieved. It has in this way a great advantage over the single external examination taken on a set date. It must not, however, be forgotten that with continuous assessment, as with any other form of assessment, CSE and GCE examining boards have a clear duty to record attainment at the end of a course. The moderation must, therefore, be designed to take account of this.

The importance of a teacher's own assessment of his candidates in subject based examinations has already been indicated. A variety of interesting situations can arise when teachers are asked to recommend grades in advance of the actual assessment for each of their candidates. Most CSE boards ask for such recommendations, but the use made of them varies. A number of boards for example, use these initial grades, given before any formal examination by the board has taken place, as a yardstick against which discussion of any subsequent examination assessments take place. A smaller number of boards have accepted these teacher recommended grades as CSE grades upon which the examinations of the board are used only as moderating instruments. Where the differences between the teacher recommended grades and the board's monitoring instrument fall within acceptable limits, the teacher's recommended grades stand. In other cases discussions about the differences take place between the board's moderators and the school and the discrepancies are resolved either by agreement upon overall adjustments or by agreed statistical procedures.

The possibility of examining boards providing tests to monitor schools' recommended grades has very interesting possibilities. The scheme outlined above is designed to apply to mode 1 assessments, but it is possible to conceive the use of tests to monitor areas of mode 3 assessment. The vital point, however, whether the monitoring procedures are to be applied to mode 1 or mode 3 assessments, is that both the teacher's assessment and the monitoring test shall be concerned with the achievement of similar objectives at the various grade levels. Other problems, that of weighting for example, could arise but these can be resolved comparatively simply if one can be certain of one thing—agreement upon objectives.

Care has been taken in this chapter not to isolate the moderation procedures of any particular examining board and to describe them in detail. Rather an attempt has been made to illustrate a variety of possibilities for moderation in practice and to draw attention to certain underlying principles. In the past examining boards, while obviously employing a number of different approaches to moderation, have tended to make particular use of one method. This has been much truer of the GCE boards than of the CSE boards. This possibility is now no longer a realistic one. As assessment becomes more concerned to reflect stated objectives and the techniques used are designed to test the mastery of defined skills, so the moderation procedures used will have to vary to take account of what is being assessed. More complex patterns of assessment require more flexible moderation procedures. The greater involvement of the teacher in assessment will be paralleled in moderation. The need for training in the principles and practice of moderation will be as great as the need for it in relation to techniques of assessment. The responsibilities of a moderator are considerable, the demands made upon his time are substantial, but the rewards in terms of the increased quality and professionalism that such experience can bring to an individual's teaching make it a worthwhile one and one that active teachers ought to be willing to undertake.

# 12 The Presentation of Results

## G. M. Forrest

It is strange and unfortunate, that despite the efforts of teachers of mathematics, despite the existence of enlightened syllabuses (especially those of the type called 'modern' mathematics) and despite the interest there is in examinations, the prestige of the percentage is so high. One example of this is to be seen in the use made of percentages each year when thousands of school reports are prepared. A second way in which the prestige and power of the percentage is shown is when a pass percentage mark is decreed before an examination is completed by the candidates. Students are told that they must obtain '33% of the marks in order to pass'. External school examinations do not operate in this way; neither should internal examinations.

There are major differences between the two school examination systems which are intended for candidates who have completed five years of secondary schooling. In 1951 the General Certificate of Education was introduced at two levels. The Ordinary level of the GCE is a pass/fail examination; the standard of a pass corresponds to the 'credit' standard of the School Certificate which it replaced. Despite the efforts of the GCE examining boards the grades awarded at Ordinary level are unofficial. In July 1971 the Governing Council of the Schools Council decided not to accept proposals which would have removed the pass/fail concept and would have allowed boards to record a candidate's grades on his certificate.* It is the practice, however, to inform schools of the unofficial grades awarded to candidates. Grade 1 is the highest of the six passing grades; there are three failing grades. This system is used by six of the eight GCE boards. The University of London School Examinations Council reports candidates' results in terms of five grades only; the Southern Universities Joint Board reports results in the form of percentage marks. The first candidates were entered for the Certificate of Secondary Education in 1965. By 1970 there were over one million subject entries compared with about $2\frac{1}{4}$ million subject entries in GCE Ordinary level. From the start the examination differed from GCE in that it was not a pass/fail examination and that grades were recorded on certificates. Grade 1 is defined as being of such a standard that the candidate 'might reasonably have secured a pass in the

* At its meeting on 5 July 1973, however, the Governing Council of the Schools Council agreed to make a formal recommendation to the Secretary of State for Education and Science that these should be official grading of the results of GCE Ordinary level examinations.

O-level of the GCE examination'[1] had he been following a course of study leading to that examination. Grade 1 in CSE corresponds therefore to a pass in GCE, that is, to the unofficial grades 1 to 6. A second reference point has been fixed for the CSE; grade 4 is awarded to 'a 16-year-old pupil of average ability who has applied himself to a course of study regarded by teachers of the subject as appropriate to his age, ability and aptitude' (*op. cit*). Approximately equal numbers of candidates are placed in grades 2 and 3. Until 1971 grade 5 was recorded on a certificate only if the candidate had been awarded at least one grade 4 or better grade in one of his other subjects. From 1972 grade 5 was recognized in its own right and is recorded irrespective of a candidate's performance in other subjects. Performances below grade 5 are ungraded.

At the Advanced level of the GCE there are five passing grades which are recorded on certificates. The present system results from a report[2] issued in 1960 on the GCE Advanced level and its effect upon the type of work being attempted in sixth forms. The top grade, grade A, accounts for approximately 10% of the Advanced level entries in a subject; grade B accounts for about 15%, grade C 10%, grade D 15% and grade E 20%. Ordinary level passes are awarded to those candidates below the pass standard and they comprise about 20% of the entry. The remaining 10% of candidates are given a failing grade. In large subjects with normal entries the above proportions of grades are likely to be awarded. Where, however, the entry is small in number (or is atypical), boards have the power, which is exercised, to depart from these norms. A proposal from the Schools Council that a new 20 point grading scheme be introduced was rejected by the Secretary of State for Education and Science in August 1972.

In summary then Ordinary level is a pass/fail ungraded examination with one reference point (the pass/fail point) whereas CSE has two reference points (grades 1 and 4) with grades recorded upon certificates. Advanced level GCE is a pass/fail examination in which grades are recorded upon certificates.

Most of the problems which an examining board faces stem from the fact that it is dealing with thousands of candidates in the same subject and that therefore dozens or even hundreds of examiners are involved. Much of the effort must be concentrated on ensuring that a candidate is not at an advantage (or disadvantage) simply because his script has been marked by a particular examiner. Marking schemes are drawn up and agreed by the examiners. While the marking is progressing checks are made by the chief examiner to see if individual examiners are interpreting the mark scheme in the agreed way. Despite this it may be necessary, when all candidates' scripts have been marked, for adjustments to be made to the marking of scripts by particular examiners; in an extreme case the scripts from a particular examiner may have to be re-marked. Because of the importance of the pass/fail point at Ordinary level great care must be taken to ensure that no candidate is failed unjustly. All the GCE boards have some form of review of scripts in this critical area. At CSE the two reference grades attract particular attention and most boards make special arrangements for the review of candidates' work at the grade 2/grade 1 and grade 5/grade 4 borderlines. At Advanced level all GCE boards review scripts at the E/O borderline and in addition some boards do so at higher points.

It must not be thought that because a classroom teacher is dealing with comparatively few candidates he has no problems. General measurement problems are the same for him as they are for an examining board. There are, nevertheless, certain problems which stem from the fact that a teacher is working in relative isolation in his school and that it is therefore normally extremely difficult for him to be aware of the kind of 'absolute' standards to which examining boards attempt to conform.

In the discussion which follows it is assumed that the objectives of the teaching course have been clearly and completely defined, that the teaching syllabus has been satisfactorily set down and that the assessment techniques to be used are appropriate. Each component of the resulting assessment (practical work, course work, objective test, essay questions etc.) will result in the provision of a mark for each pupil.\* Somehow or other it is necessary to combine these marks so that the complete set of combined marks validly expresses the relationships between individual pupils' performances over the year. It may be asked 'Why not add the marks for each pupil and transform the resulting totals into an order of merit?' This can be done provided care is taken with those candidates who achieve the same total mark. Consider the following set of ten marks:

| | |
|---|---|
| 135 | 125 |
| 133 | 123 |
| 128 | 123 |
| 128 | 119 |
| 128 | 117 |

It may be seen that three pupils achieve the same total of 128 marks and that two tie at 123 marks. These marks can be ranked in different ways, for example:

| *Mark* | Ranking A | Ranking B | Ranking C |
|---|---|---|---|
| 135 | 1 | 1 | 1 |
| 133 | 2 | 2 | 2 |
| 128 | 3= | 3= | 4= |
| 128 | 3= | 3= | 4= |
| 128 | 3= | 3= | 4= |
| 125 | 4 | 6 | 6 |
| 123 | 5= | 7= | $7\frac{1}{2}$= |
| 123 | 5= | 7= | $7\frac{1}{2}$= |
| 119 | 6 | 9 | 9 |
| 117 | 7 | 10 | 10 |

\* It could result directly on the provision of a grade for each component. The discussion here is, however, being conducted in relation to marks from which grades may be subsequently derived.

At first glance there seems little difference between the three sets of rankings. It may be seen, however, that in Ranking A the last pupil is ranked 7 when there are in fact ten pupils. This is obviously misleading although the individual involved might not be displeased! This difficulty is overcome with Ranking B but here, as in Ranking A, the three candidates obtaining 128 marks are all given a rank of 3 which places them closer to the pupil above them than to the one below them. Ranking C removes this anomaly by treating the ranks as 'scores' in order to give each pupil the average rank of the three ranks involved. Thus the ranks of the third, fourth and fifth candidates are averaged $\left( \dfrac{3 + 4 + 5}{3} \right)$ which results in a rank of 4.

A similar thing is done with the two candidates achieving a mark of 123. These are the seventh and eighth candidates; their average rank is therefore $7\frac{1}{2}$. If rankings are to be meaningful, then the method used to produce Ranking C must be used. The price paid for greater meaning is that a pupil, as here, may receive a rather strange rank such as $7\frac{1}{2}$.

The adding together of the marks from the different components in the above example raises an interesting issue for any teacher. This is the problem of 'weighting'. The term 'weighting' is used in different senses. Weighting between examination papers is frequently thought of in terms of the number of marks allocated to them, so that two papers each marked out of, say, 50 marks are said to be 'equally' weighted. A teacher may consider weighting within a subject to be dependent upon the emphasis placed on one section of a syllabus compared with another. A course of instruction (whether based on an examination syllabus or not) may be weighted in terms of the preferences and prejudices (sometimes unconscious) of the teacher for or against certain topics. The weighting between examination papers may also be expressed in terms of the times allowed for their completion. We will use the term in a statistical sense so that it refers to the influence which the distribution of one set of marks has when one pupil's mark from it is added to his mark from a different distribution of marks.

It may be thought that if two sets of marks have the same average (or mean) or have been marked out of the same total, then marks are equivalent from one set to the other. Although on occasion this may be so, it will largely be a matter of chance because equal means do *not* ensure that equal weight is attached to the sets of marks. (The total number of marks out of which papers are marked is irrelevant in this connection.) The statistic which is normally used to describe the scatter, and thus to determine the weight which is attached to a set of marks, is the standard deviation.

The standard deviation is usually denoted by $\sigma$ (the Greek letter sigma). The standard deviation is described as the square root of the mean (average) of the squares of the deviations from the mean of the set of marks. In terms of a formula this is

$$\sigma = \sqrt{\frac{\Sigma(X - M)^2}{N}}$$

where $\sigma$ is the standard deviation
$X$ is any mark
$M$ is the mean of all marks
$N$ is the number of marks
$\Sigma$ is the capital letter sigma in the Greek alphabet and denotes summation, i.e. $\Sigma X$ is the sum of all $X$'s.

A simple example should help the reader to understand the calculation. Ten pupils gain the following marks:

15, 12, 10, 9, 8, 7, 7, 6, 4 and 2

These marks add to 80 so that their mean (or average) equals 8

$$\left( \text{Mean} = \frac{\Sigma X}{N} \right).$$

The marks are listed so that for each mark its deviation from the mean can be shown:

| Marks $X$ | Deviations $d = X-M$ | Squared deviations $(X-M)^2$ |
|:---:|:---:|:---:|
| 15 | +7 | 49 |
| 12 | +4 | 16 |
| 10 | +2 | 4 |
| 9 | +1 | 1 |
| 8 | 0 | 0 |
| 7 | −1 | 1 |
| 7 | −1 | 1 |
| 6 | −2 | 4 |
| 4 | −4 | 16 |
| 2 | −6 | 36 |
| $\Sigma X = 80$ | $\Sigma d = 0$ | $\Sigma(X-M)^2 = 128$ |

It will be seen that marks which are greater than the mean have positive deviations while those which are smaller than the mean have negative deviations. The deviations always cancel out so that the sum is 0. It will be seen also that the squared deviations are all positive and that their sum is 128 (i.e. $\Sigma d^2 = \Sigma(X-M)^2 = 128$).

It is now possible to calculate $\sigma$:

$$\sigma = \sqrt{\frac{\Sigma(X-M)^2}{N}}$$

$$= \sqrt{\frac{128}{10}}$$

$$= \sqrt{12 \cdot 8}$$

$$= \quad 3 \cdot 58.$$

*Problems of Assessment*

There are other methods for computing the standard deviation for a set of marks when the data are arranged in a form different from that given above. The reader is referred to the book listed in the suggestions for further reading (McIntosh, 1967) where details of the methods together with worked examples will be found.

The effect of two sets of marks having different standard deviations when marks from one set are added to those of the other may be seen in the following example. A group of fifteen pupils take two tests. The marks for each test, the total marks and the resulting rank positions are as follows:

| Pupil | Test I | Test II | Total | Rank |
|-------|--------|---------|-------|------|
| A | 86 | 86 | 172 | 1 |
| B | 76 | 88 | 164 | 2 |
| C | 74 | 72 | 146 | 7 |
| D | 70 | 85 | 155 | 4 |
| E | 72 | 65 | 137 | 9 |
| F | 66 | 67 | 133 | 12 |
| G | 79 | 71 | 150 | 6 |
| H | 80 | 80 | 160 | 3 |
| J | 71 | 65 | 136 | 10 |
| K | 73 | 71 | 144 | 8 |
| L | 76 | 52 | 128 | 13 |
| M | 76 | 59 | 135 | 11 |
| N | 67 | 52 | 119 | 14 |
| P | 65 | 49 | 114 | 15 |
| Q | 84 | 68 | 152 | 5 |

Two pupils obtained the same mark in each test (pupils A and H). Several marks appear in both lists. The means and standard deviations are as follows:

|  | Test I | Test II |
|--|--------|---------|
| Mean | 74·33 | 68·67 |
| Standard deviation | 6·0 | 12·0 |

Although Test II has a lower mean score, its standard deviation is twice that of Test I indicating that the spread or scatter of the marks is greater in Test II. A crude indication of this may be gained from an inspection of the range of marks in each distribution. In Test I the marks range from 65 to 86, whereas in Test II the range is from 49 to 88.

If the marks for Test I were 'stretched' so that the standard deviation was 12·0 then the weighting between the two tests would be equal and therefore the advantage of a high mark in Test II (or of a low mark in Test I) would be compensated. When transformed to a standard deviation of 12·0 but still with the the same mean* the marks for Test I become as follows

* The transformed marks have been rounded to integers; the mean of the fifteen marks is 74.67.

202

(the method whereby this is done need not be of concern at this point):

| Pupil | Test I ($\sigma = 12 \cdot 0$) | Test II | Total | Rank |
|---|---|---|---|---|
| A | 98 | 86 | 184 | 1 |
| B | 78 | 88 | 166 | $2\frac{1}{2} =$ |
| C | 74 | 72 | 146 | 7 |
| D | 66 | 85 | 151 | 6 |
| E | 70 | 65 | 135 | 10 |
| F | 58 | 67 | 125 | 13 |
| G | 84 | 71 | 155 | 5 |
| H | 86 | 80 | 166 | $2\frac{1}{2} =$ |
| J | 68 | 65 | 133 | 11 |
| K | 72 | 71 | 143 | 8 |
| L | 78 | 52 | 130 | 12 |
| M | 78 | 59 | 137 | 9 |
| N | 60 | 52 | 112 | 14 |
| P | 56 | 49 | 105 | 15 |
| Q | 94 | 68 | 162 | 4 |

It will be seen that the totals for all pupils except one are now different and that the rank order is different. This difference results from the extra weighting which has been given to the marks from Test I. Pupil D who was fourth now drops to sixth place; pupils B and H are now tied. All pupils except the top pair and bottom pair change position. It will thus be seen that the effect of changing the weighting of Test I is considerable.

Morrison in Chapter 8 introduced the idea of reporting candidates' performances in the form of profiles. An example will now be given to show what must be done in order to produce profiles for a class of pupils in an internal examination. Suppose that there are 32 pupils and that the examination has three components which are to have equal weight. To achieve the desired weighting each component will have to be scaled to the same standard deviation. The choice of standard deviation (and mean) is arbitrary; a mean of 60 and a standard deviation of 12 will result in scaled scores which will have a sufficient range for practical purposes. The table on page 204 gives the raw marks and scaled scores for the three components. The scaled scores were obtained by using the formula given in Chapter 8 (page 149).

$$X_s = \frac{\sigma_s}{\sigma} X - \left[ \frac{\sigma_s}{\sigma} M - M_s \right]$$

where $X_s$ is the scaled score corresponding to a raw mark of $X$,
$\quad \sigma_s$ is the standard deviation of the scaled scores,
$\quad \sigma$ is the standard deviation of the raw marks,
$\quad M$ is the mean of the raw marks,
$\quad M_s$ is the mean of the scaled scores.

We wish to scale to a mean of 60 and standard deviation of 12 so that

$$M_s = 60$$
$$\text{and } \sigma_s = 12.$$

The formula becomes

$$X_s = \frac{12}{\sigma}X - \left[\frac{12}{\sigma}M - 60\right].$$

The means and standard deviations of the raw marks for the three components are:

|  | Component A | Component B | Component C |
|---|---|---|---|
| Mean | 66·88 | 53·03 | 59·59 |
| Standard deviation | 13·31 | 10·61 | 17·52. |

In terms of what is required it may be seen that the mean of C is about right although that of A is too high and that of B is too low. The standard deviation in C is much too high; it is too low in B and a little high in A.

| Candidate number | Component A | | Component B | | Component C | |
|---|---|---|---|---|---|---|
| | Raw | Scaled | Raw | Scaled | Raw | Scaled |
| 1 | 91 | 82 | 69 | 78 | 89 | 80 |
| 2 | 51 | 46 | 50 | 57 | 69 | 66 |
| 3 | 60 | 54 | 51 | 58 | 79 | 73 |
| 4 | 52 | 47 | 44 | 50 | 68 | 66 |
| 5 | 62 | 56 | 60 | 68 | 64 | 63 |
| 6 | 71 | 64 | 53 | 60 | 50 | 53 |
| 7 | 79 | 71 | 50 | 57 | 84 | 77 |
| 8 | 55 | 49 | 47 | 53 | 49 | 53 |
| 9 | 64 | 57 | 47 | 53 | 52 | 55 |
| 10 | 90 | 81 | 71 | 80 | 74 | 70 |
| 11 | 84 | 75 | 61 | 69 | 54 | 56 |
| 12 | 59 | 53 | 66 | 75 | 45 | 50 |
| 13 | 49 | 44 | 38 | 43 | 19 | 32 |
| 14 | 45 | 40 | 41 | 46 | 30 | 40 |
| 15 | 58 | 52 | 54 | 61 | 77 | 72 |
| 16 | 52 | 47 | 30 | 34 | 37 | 45 |
| 17 | 60 | 54 | 42 | 48 | 77 | 72 |
| 18 | 73 | 66 | 59 | 67 | 63 | 62 |
| 19 | 79 | 71 | 62 | 70 | 56 | 58 |
| 20 | 89 | 80 | 49 | 55 | 86 | 78 |
| 21 | 74 | 66 | 50 | 57 | 71 | 68 |
| 22 | 75 | 67 | 56 | 63 | 39 | 46 |
| 23 | 60 | 54 | 63 | 71 | 41 | 47 |
| 24 | 54 | 48 | 35 | 40 | 60 | 60 |
| 25 | 50 | 45 | 60 | 68 | 72 | 68 |
| 26 | 65 | 58 | 58 | 66 | 36 | 44 |
| 27 | 89 | 80 | 69 | 78 | 68 | 66 |
| 28 | 71 | 64 | 64 | 72 | 57 | 58 |
| 29 | 82 | 74 | 63 | 71 | 87 | 79 |
| 30 | 74 | 66 | 57 | 64 | 46 | 51 |
| 31 | 56 | 50 | 37 | 42 | 49 | 53 |
| 32 | 67 | 60 | 41 | 46 | 59 | 60 |

Candidate number 15 obtained 58 raw marks in component A. His scaled score is therefore

$$X_s = \frac{12}{13 \cdot 31} \, 58 - \left[ \frac{12}{13 \cdot 31} \, 66 \cdot 88 - 60 \right]$$
$$= \frac{696}{13 \cdot 31} - \left[ \frac{802 \cdot 56}{13 \cdot 31} - 60 \right]$$
$$= 52 \cdot 29 - (60 \cdot 30 - 60)$$
$$= 52 \cdot 29 - 0 \cdot 30$$
$$= 51 \cdot 99, \text{ i.e. } 52.$$

Similarly the raw mark of 89 by candidate number 20 becomes 79·94, i.e. 80. It is possible to scale each of the raw marks in this way. This is a tedious and time consuming process. The transformation process is a linear one and therefore a graphical method may be used. The two raw marks and their equivalent scaled score are plotted and a straight line is drawn through the two points. The vertical axis is used for raw marks and the horizontal for scaled scores. The graph below relates to component A.

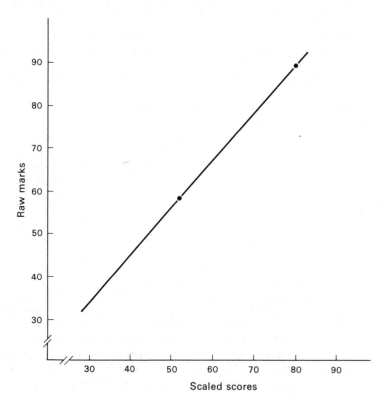

The scaled scores corresponding to the required raw marks are now read off the graph to form a table as follows:

| Raw mark | Scaled score |
|----------|--------------|
| 90 | 81 |
| 89 | 80 |
| 88 | 79 |
| 87 | 78 |
| 86 | 77 |
| 85 | 76 |
| 84 | 75 |
| etc. | etc. |

The table is then used to enter the scaled score for each candidate's raw mark. To move straight from the graph may lead to the same raw mark being given a different scaled score on a second occasion. (The mathematically inclined reader will notice that the ratio $\frac{\sigma_s}{\sigma}$ can be used to calculate the slope of the line.)

Further graphs will need to be produced to find the scaled scores for components B and C.

An inspection of the table given on page 204 will show the following:

(a) the scaled scores for component B are higher than their corresponding raw marks but that the higher marks have been raised more than the lower;

(b) the range of scaled scores for component C is smaller than the range of raw marks;

(c) the scaled scores for component A are lower than the corresponding raw marks.

These changes (with others) are the direct result of the scaling process.

It is now possible to combine the scaled scores to produce scores so that a class order of merit is possible with the knowledge that the desired weighting between components has been achieved. Alternatively grades may be given to candidates and a final grade obtained in the manner suggested in Chapter 8.

It is now possible to consider again the question posed on page 199 concerning the simple adding together of the marks from various components in an examination. If they are added there can be no guarantee that the resulting final set of marks will reflect the weightings that a teacher would wish the components to have. First a check must be made to see just what weight is attached to each component by calculating the standard deviations. If they are in the correct order and are roughly in suitable proportions then all is well; marks may be added in the knowledge that the total marks reflect the desired result. When they are not then a decision has to be made either to make adjustments or to leave the marks as they are knowing that in the final rank order some candidates will be misplaced in terms of their performances in one or more components. As was shown earlier a high mark in a set of marks where the spread is smaller than anticipated brings poor rewards.

Two warnings must be given. The transformation of a set of marks in any way does not increase their reliability; errors in marking, lack of consistency in the marker from occasion to occasion and similar vagaries of human nature are not removed by changing the mean and/or standard deviation of a set of marks. Second, when the distribution of a set of marks is very different from what was expected, changing the mean or standard deviation may mask faults in the examining procedure; adding 20 marks to each candidate (i.e. changing the mean) does not indicate that the pupils are any 'better'. The original marks could show, for example, that the syllabus had not been fully covered or that some of the questions were inappropriate or that the marking had been too severe.

This chapter started by referring to the prestige of the percentage; it is hoped that by now the reader will appreciate the strength of a scaling procedure. Percentage marks cannot be manipulated (for example, added or averaged); scaled scores can.

If, as it is hoped this chapter has shown, it is possible for an individual teacher to produce profiles of his pupils' achievements it may well be asked why it is that public examination results are not given in the form of profiles. To start with not all such examinations have official grades (page 197) and even where they do it could be that the components which go to form the overall grade may really be parallel papers for example, two History papers covering the same period. Not all examining bodies have the data processing equipment needed to enable the necessary transformation and scaling operations to be undertaken even if the formulation of the examination objectives is sufficiently advanced for them to be reflected in the examination components. The users of examination results are familiar with overall grades; their re-education would be required. Nevertheless, despite these factors, which all militate against change, it would be possible to report candidates' performances in certain subjects in the form of very simple profiles; in foreign languages the components could be 'written' and 'oral' and in the sciences they could be 'theory' and 'practical' skills.

## References

[1] Secondary School Examinations Council. The Certificate of Secondary Education. *Examinations Bulletin No. 1. Some Suggestions for Teachers and Examiners* (London, HMSO, 1963), p. 122.

[2] Secondary School Examination Council. Third report. *The General Certificate of Education and Sixth Form Studies* (London, HMSO, 1960).

# 13 Question Banking

## R. Wood

### Substantive aspects of question banking

BACKGROUND

Like fume-free cars and the Kingdom of Heaven, question banking is one of those ideas which has great appeal but which people do little about. In that respect, the position is little changed from 1968 when the pilot project on question banking was completed.[1] At that time, the Schools Council, having provided what was essentially 'seed' money, could say it was a good idea *but*, and a proposal to continue the project was turned down. Perhaps the rationalizing possibilities of question banking were overdone; certainly some CSE boards were suspicious of their autonomy being usurped and there were those who thought that question banking would have an oppressive effect on teaching. Not unnaturally, I believe that these were basic misunderstandings of the purpose of question banking and I hope in the course of this chapter to dispel these fears.

The basic idea behind question banking could hardly be simpler. A library of questions of all descriptions is put at the disposal of teachers wishing to set either terminal examinations—as in the case of mode 3—or periodic classroom tests, or, in the case of examining boards, written external examinations.

Having said that, it may be wondered why a chapter on the subject is thought necessary; one might as well explain the point of *Exchange and Mart*. The fact is that there is more to question banks than first meets the eye; in particular, they can be regarded as measuring instruments, in the broadest sense. Nevertheless, the fundamental notion is undoubtedly that of sharing a resource and this is what I shall start with.

QUESTION BANKING AND EXAMINING BOARDS

It can be taken for granted that, if they so wished, the GCE and CSE examining boards could, at any time, separately or perhaps in concert, band together to produce question banks in all the subjects they examine in common. There are, of course, differences in syllabuses and philosophies of question-setting but even so sizeable common cores of questions could be assembled immediately simply by combining past papers. That the boards do not choose to do this may say more about their wish to remain independent than about their evaluation of the merits of question banking.*

There is no reason to doubt that some of the examining boards, at least, are aware of the potential value of centralized question production and testing. Getting a multiple-choice paper before the candidate is an alarmingly expensive business and economies could be made, especially with regard to pretesting. If the experience of the London GCE board is anything to go by, one of the biggest headaches is that the number of competent multiple-choice item-writers is, in the first place, small and then dwindles markedly in quite a short time. (For further observations on the benefits of question banking to examining boards, see Wood, 'The Place and Value of Item Banking'[2]).

ARE THERE ANY LIMITATIONS ON WHAT A QUESTION BANK MAY CONTAIN?

No, this is why it is called a question bank, rather than the earlier name of item bank, which carried the implication that only multiple-choice items were permissible. It is envisaged that the whole spectrum of known question types—and those yet to be invented—will be represented in a question bank, from the most open-ended of essay questions—'History is bunk. Discuss'—through all the degrees of structuring to the straight multiple-choice item.

It is sometimes asked whether the user who selects essay questions will be provided with marking schemes. The answer is yes, if he so wishes; but the point ought to be made that in the classroom situation the interpretation which the teacher places upon the answers he gets to the questions he chooses and sets is expected to be very much his own. Presumably it is the feedback which questions provide which is of paramount importance, rather than any ordering of candidates. Even in the mode 3 terminal examining situation, one would expect the teacher to use any marking scheme supplied as a guide rather than holy writ.

Going beyond written questions, there is no reason why other kinds of tasks, such as oral questions, dictation, musical passages, project topics, practical experiments and so on, should not be stored, providing some quantitative evaluation of them can be made. Perhaps question bank is itself too restrictive a description of the enterprise; maybe 'task' or 'stimulus' bank is more appropriate—a shift in emphasis which brings the conception very close indeed to two other kinds of educational bank bruited about recently, a *resource* bank[3] and a *syllabus* bank.[4] A question or stimulus bank could be incorporated into a resource bank or serve as a natural counterpart to a syllabus bank.

QUESTION BANK AND MODE 3 EXAMINING

Teachers choose mode 3 for different reasons. Some use it to examine their brightest candidates by submitting them for a GCE-type examination

* It is recognized, of course, that some boards maintain *their own* question banks, usually consisting of multiple-choice items. Whether or not they make full use of them is another matter; worries about security tend to bulk large.

of their own devising and entering the remainder for mode 1 CSE. Question banking will presumably find a use here. Others—one hopes the majority—use mode 3 in the way originally intended—to examine unusual subjects or subjects which they teach in an unusual way. The weakness of question banking is thought by some to lie right here. If the subjects and the way they are taught are so idiosyncratic how can a bank satisfy these teachers' needs? It cannot be denied that in these circumstances a bank is liable to be found wanting but even if the questions on a topic are meagre, a question bank can still help to put kindred spirits in touch, whether the subject is Biomathematics, Flower Arranging, or whatever. Remember also that a question bank can supply *ideas* for questions sometimes crossing subject boundaries; a history question based on a Rowlandson cartoon might inspire an economics teacher to come up with something similar of his own.

There is a general issue at stake here concerning the adequacy of question banks. How fastidious will the average customer be? Certainly there are cases, such as pieces of music or set books, where nothing but questions set on these materials will do. But how about otherwise? Will

'Describe any *two* frescoes by Giotto from his series at the Arena Chapel, Padua, and say whatever has particularly struck you about the style of this artist' (University of Cambridge Local Examinations Syndicate, Ordinary level Art, Summer 1970)*

do as well as

'Describe the decorative scheme of Giotto's frescoes in the Arena Chapel, Padua, noting his choice of subjects and the use he made of perspective devices' (University of Cambridge Local Examinations Syndicate, Ordinary level Art, Summer 1971)*?

One assumes that the two might well be interchangeable. But would a question asking for a detailed description of a Nash terrace house be acceptable when the teacher might have wanted a description of the devices employed in landscape gardening? How particular will users be? We shall only know when question banks are established. Those who know exactly what they want and will take no substitutes will devise their own questions whereas those who will accept questions as a sample or token of acquaintance with a certain idea or period, and who are thus prepared to tolerate a certain amount of arbitrariness in gauging achievement will be more disposed to use question banks. Much will depend on the nature of the testing. Periodic classroom testing is bound to place more exacting demands on a bank than terminal testing, which, in the nature of things, is a sample of attainment.

Regardless of what a question bank can offer, there will always be those who insist on writing their own questions, perhaps because they feel it is an

---

* Reproduced by permission of the University of Cambridge Local Examinations Syndicate.

integral part of mode 3 examining. It seems to me, however, that the following extract from a letter written by the deputy headmaster of a large mode 3 inclined school* is evidence that even the most dedicated mode 3 teachers can use some help in setting examination papers.

This year 88% of our subject entries were mode 3 and, as you suggest, the main reason for this was the wish of Heads of Departments to devise more interesting and relevant schemes of work and also to drastically reduce the coaching aspects inherent in any mode 1 type of examination. Also in some cases, to provide a more extensive assessment for the best candidates thus reducing the chance element of some mode 1 papers for grade 1 and enabling more pupils to be advised to take CSE rather than GCE.

The freedom of mode 3 and the improved relationships in the teaching groups have been much welcomed but there has been alarm at the magnitude of the efforts which have had to go into examination (not necessarily just the final examination) setting and production especially in subjects such as science and to a slightly less extent, mathematics. Having put considerable effort into the CSE courses, teachers have naturally wished their examinations to reflect the same principles and attitudes established there. This is especially necessary when a wide ability range is being tested so that both weakest and strongest have plenty of opportunity to show what they can do. Furthermore, considerable efforts have been made to present the questions and question papers in an attractive way and one, it is hoped, which will reassure and encourage the candidates. Thus many diagrams, multiple-choice questions, examination paper cover sheets designed by the Head of Art Department, etc. have been used.

Production as well as setting has been a big problem because, like the majority of schools, our secretarial staff is not sufficient to cope with major projects such as CSE examinations.

The overall picture is disturbing—one must ask, 'Has all the effort been worthwhile? Would I not have done better to choose mode 1 and put some of this extra effort into more sophisticated lesson preparation?'

The case for mode 3 in my opinion is a strong one but it does not help to realize that one's questions must in general be inferior to properly validated and expertly produced ones. As a big mode 3 school, my verdict is that the Item Bank is a winner! Just two additional thoughts not included in your article:

(1) In mathematics we expect to set two examinations next year. One for the majority of candidates and one for weaker candidates. The latter will have easier questions but the best grade obtainable will be 3. Twice as much work for our maths staff under existing methods—but how easy with the Item Bank.

---

* First reproduced in Wood and Skurnik (pp. 106–107)[1]. Reproduced here by permission of the National Foundation for Educational Research.

(2) Could the item bank be stored in a computer which could print complete question papers? Diagrams would presumably be a problem but such a service would be most welcome in the schools and highly efficient viewed on a national level.

Yours, etc.

QUESTION BANKING, TEACHING AND TESTING

From a pedagogic point of view, the best case for question banks I know was made by Scriven.[5] From this seminal paper grew the notions of mastery learning, formative and summative evaluation and criterion-referenced testing which are increasingly tossed around these days.

The principle involved is simple—almost to the point of banality—and it is that the setting of specific learning objectives, both terminal and intermediate, coupled with terminal and intermediate testing and with directed and meaningful feedback, will enrich the learning process for most students.

Now insofar as a question bank can supply questions which are compatible with the objectives being pursued, it will serve its purpose. One can foresee situations occurring however, where, because a systematic course is being followed, the question bank will be found wanting since enough questions suitable for this particular course were never contributed. Here is a case for marrying question and syllabus banks.

The fear is sometimes expressed that testing will get on top of teaching. Harry Judge, for instance, contends that 'if you wish to have a sophisticated and continuous assessment, and a national system of examinations, then even more of the time and energy of teachers will be spent in examinations than at present. Schools will become like hospitals in which doctors have no time for anything but using their stethoscopes.'[6] No doubt Judge would regard question banks as aiding and abetting this development. As to whether his prognosis is correct, much depends on the commonsense of teachers; we must rely on them to get the balance between testing and teaching right. At the moment I would imagine we are a long way from the situation he portrays; if anything there has not been enough testing of a diagnostic kind.

Actually, little is known about the extent to which teachers use classroom tests or wish to use them or more of them. A little evidence that question banks would be welcome comes from the replies to a question taken from a questionnaire given to 100 GCE teachers at the London GCE board's last Annual Conference. To the question

A bank of questions which teachers could utilize for testing their students would be a good idea.

the teachers responded as follows:

| Strongly agree | Agree | No opinion | Disagree | Strongly disagree | No reply |
|---|---|---|---|---|---|
| 30 | 42 | 9 | 13 | 2 | 4 |

The question could be criticized on the grounds that it invites positive endorsement—it would have been better to have asked 'Would you use a question bank tomorrow?'—but I think one is still entitled to be encouraged by the response, even if the cynic in one suggests that some of those voting in favour may see question banks primarily as coaching aids.

QUESTION BANKING AND INDIVIDUALIZED TESTING

It is a fair assumption that most users of question banks will want conventional tests or examinations in which every candidate does every question or, where a choice is offered, a fixed number of questions. There is no reason, however, why someone should not pick questions which he believes are tailored to particular groups or even ultimately to individuals. A rudimentary example of individualization occurs where a teacher with two groups of students of disparate ability wishes to set them different questions with perhaps a common section which both groups can tackle (cf. the letter reproduced above).

As intuition will confirm, measurement is most efficient if students can be programmed through an examination so that they spend most of their time working on questions for which they have roughly an even chance of success. Given a sufficiently large bank of calibrated questions it is possible, in principle, to construct tests which will do the job.

The most satisfying way of implementing this kind of testing is to interface with a computer via a terminal. Questions can then be selected during test administration, making use of information about the respondent as he provides it so that testing is adapted to the individual. Lest I be accused of living in Cloud Cuckoo land, I hasten to add that this procedure—attractive though it is—is (a) expensive and (b) only really suitable to multiple-choice items and then only those of a non-pictorial nature. I have to admit that computerized adaptive testing is only suitable for certain specialist measurement purposes where high precision is required (see Wood[7]).

Various attempts have been made, however, to realize tailored testing in a humbler paper-and-pencil format.

A somewhat rough-and-ready method which is not really recommended was tried out by Wood[8] and more recently, Lord[9] has invented what he calls a *flexilevel* test which looks to have promise although it does require a somewhat elaborate and expensive response format. In the informal classroom situation a teacher might do as well by simply asking his students to attempt only those questions which are neither too hard nor too easy for them.

One does not seriously expect much call for tailored tests. But the facility ought to be there, in case someone wants it. It is best to think of a question bank as a sort of measurement kit which can be used to make up different test forms, according to the purpose in mind. The versatility of a bank in this respect will depend on the number and quality of items and the broadness of the coverage.

## Statistical aspects of question banking

The matters discussed in this section are not forbiddingly technical but those who wish to avoid it can do so without losing the thread of the chapter.

In the original item banking study the statistical aspects bulked large, for item banking was conceived of primarily as a means of ensuring comparability of standards between examinations, and much effort was spent devising statistical machinery for this purpose.

It seems to me that this application is no less relevant today, perhaps more as a moderating than a determining mechanism, but I think one can also see that, compared to five years ago, it is now quite proper to place more stress on the teaching/learning potentialities of question banking.

### ENGINEERING EXAMINATIONS

It is only realistic to suppose that teachers subscribing to the bank will not be much interested in question statistics, particularly if they are using questions for interim rather than terminal evaluation. By and large, it is the content of the questions that will be decisive.

Nevertheless, it is worth noting that given a knowledge of question statistics examinations can be *designed* so as to have certain desirable characteristics, such as a particular distribution of marks. (This application will be most relevant to examining boards, since the calculations make assumptions about the normality of the candidate population which might not obtain with a single school's entry.) For example, the flatter a mark distribution the more effectively candidates are separated and, if grading is to be applied, the less is the probability of misgrading. As Scott[10] has shown, the way to achieve a flat or uniform distribution of marks is to select questions which are of median difficulty and have an average inter-correlation of the order of 0·33. With this specification one could enter the question bank and attempt to locate a set of questions which fits the bill. If such a set can be found, then, of course, one will want to check that the content is compatible with the blueprint or content specification; one would, in fact, constrain the set of items to fit the blueprint. Note, though, that unless the bank is large, this might very well result in a negative search and some compromise would have to be made.

### COMPARABILITY AND MODERATION

The principle of combining question statistics to derive expected test statistics also governs the statistical machinery for checking comparability which was mentioned earlier. It will be recalled that the original problem was how to enable schools to set mode 3 examinations which would produce nationally comparable results.

The first stage in calibrating is to test all questions in the bank on CSE or GCE candidates shortly before they take the CSE mode 1 or GCE Ordinary level examination in the subject. Once the grades of these candidates become available, a simple calculation gives the grade value corresponding to the 50% correct rate. This figure then serves as a sort of grade-equivalent, so that on combining any number of questions, it is possible to supply a conversion scale which will enable any teacher to convert the raw scores his own candidates obtain into nationally comparable grades. Figures 1 and 2 will give some idea of how calibration works, using CSE as an example. Item characteristic curves are 'added' to give the test characteristic curve.

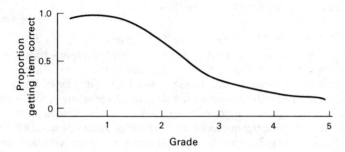

**Figure 1** Item characteristic curve and CSE grade-equivalent

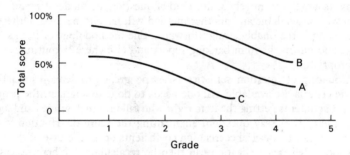

**Figure 2** Test characteristic curve and CSE grade-equivalent

It is evident that the permissible score range for a test need not cover all grades. A teacher who chose a test from the bank which was too easy for his students—and this might have been deliberate or not—would find that even those who scored full marks would not be eligible for any grade better than, say, 3, as represented by line B in Figure 2 (cf. the penultimate paragraph of the letter quoted above.) Similarly, line C represents a very difficult test for which a quite modest score could earn a grade 1. By operating a sort of tariff system, the aim is to make all grades comparable, whatever the set of questions undertaken by the candidate.

More details of how this system works can be found in the original report (Chapter 9). The example there is worked out in terms of multiple-choice items which are scored zero–one in the usual way but the theory can be generalized to the essay question, where, of course, scoring is on a graded scale. (A paper on this subject is in preparation.[11]) Similarly binary and graded questions can be combined in a straightforward manner.

In practice, teachers using bank questions for a mode 3 examination would not necessarily be obliged to convert the raw marks into grades themselves. This could be the job of the examining board who would then be using the question bank as a *moderating* instrument. Exactly the same principles apply when a teacher elects to use some bank questions and some of his own. Providing there is a reasonable balance, the bank questions can serve a moderating function.

PRE-TESTING AND UPDATING

These are two technical issues which will face the administrators of any question bank. One of the problems that was raised in the original report was that of pretesting or calibrating unusual questions based on material which might be familiar to only a few students. Canvassing schools on their syllabus coverage was suggested as one way of locating students who could properly undertake the questions and so provide authentic question statistics. Perhaps, on reflection, this is too elaborate a strategy. One may have to face the fact that some questions in the bank will not be calibrated until they come to be used in practice. In those cases where a mode 3 examination consists largely or entirely of this kind of question, no moderating information will be available and another method will have to be used. Otherwise pretesting is reasonably straightforward. The methodology of item sampling, laid out in the item banking report and elsewhere,[12] continues to be appropriate.

Updating of question statistics poses no great problems, especially if grade criteria are available. All one needs to do is to augment the proportions of students getting the item right who fall into each grade band, or, in the case of the essay question, augmenting the score distribution within each grade. The biserial correlation coefficients or, in the case of the essay question, their generalization can then be recalculated. Where necessary, question inter-correlations can be dealt with in similar fashion.

Where new data on a question become available as the result of the performance of a single group of students, and where criterion (grade) information is not available, care will have to be taken. It will perhaps be best to store statistics based on this sort of testing separately and maintain the grade-related statistics, where they are available, as the official question statistics.

## Logistics of question banks

ORGANIZATION

People are often curious about how question banks work. Without going into the nuts and bolts, an attempt will be made to communicate the essential working as it affects the user.

First, be wary of anyone who says he has a question bank. As often as not it will turn out to be a scruffy collection of questions thrown into a filing cabinet, from which choosing questions is like finding bargains in a jumble sale.

Beware also of those who talk blithely of computerized question retrieval systems. Of course a question bank is an obvious candidate for computerization[13] but there is a great gap between the thought and its realization, especially where retrieval of question content is concerned. Thus one treats with a grain of salt anything, like the *Guardian* article on resource banks already referred to,[3] which is entitled 'At the touch of a button'. The motto is 'Only computerize if there are good reasons for doing so.'

Perhaps the biggest logistical problem is arriving at a sufficiently pliable content classification system. The trick is to refine the classification only as far as the average user needs. (For ideas about storing information, see Appendix 7 of the item bank report.)

As one might expect, it is when the number of variables comprising the specification increases that a manual system loses efficiency. A computerized system in which all the question parameters, including statistics, are stored on disc, then comes into its own. Computerization also facilitates book-keeping and enables the bank administrators to keep track of what they have got. Note, however, that it will still be necessary to retrieve the actual question material from the filing cabinets or wherever it is kept. It is quite feasible to store text in a computer, costly though it might be, but pictorial material and certain mathematical and chemical symbols are beyond the reach of available technology, certainly on a routine basis.

HOW TO CHOOSE QUESTIONS

In the item bank project the items were collected together in a brochure —a sort of mail order catalogue—which was circulated to teachers. Providing the brochure is conveniently laid out and properly indexed, this may well be the best way of acquainting teachers with the contents of a bank. A teacher could then simply copy out what he wanted or alternatively fill in an order form and return it to the bank organizers who would make up the test in suitable order and reproduce it in the copies specified.

One objection to this procedure is that the capital of the bank passes out of the organizers' hands. Clearly they will wish to have feedback about the performance of questions whenever they are administered. Once the contents of a bank are released to all and sundry, it will be most difficult to keep track of who is using what questions. Another objection is that if, as one would hope, there is a reasonable turnover of questions in a bank, the problem of keeping a brochure up to date might be overwhelming.

It might, therefore, be necessary to ask bank subscribers to specify their needs in terms of content/learning objectives/question difficulty and leave it to the bank administrators to make appropriate selections. This could be done by sending out a brochure containing content and objectives rather than questions. Whatever scheme is adopted, it should always be possible for a teacher to inspect a bank on site if he so wishes.

I have said nothing about the problems of stocking and replenishing a bank. Clearly bank administrators will have to be in touch with question writers who can fulfil commissions to fill holes in a bank or satisfy new demands.

It is also assumed that question banks ought to provide ancillary facilities available on request, such as composition and reproduction of test forms, scoring of tests and examinations, reporting of results and possibly diagnostic feedback, providing some workable scheme can be found. Maintenance of cumulative records on students whose teachers use a bank regularly and systematically as an assessment aid might also be feasible.

## Other work on question banking

This section does not claim to be encyclopaedic. Far from it. The trouble is that descriptions of question banking enterprises tend to appear, not in recognized journals, but in what is known in the trade as 'fugitive' publications. Perhaps the best known projects—in America, at any rate—are the Portland, Oregon scheme, sometimes known as COMBAT[14] and Project CAM based on Massachusetts.[15]

Inevitably most work is American although one has the feeling that question banks there have not developed quite as expected. I think there is a tendency to get carried away with the technological and millenial glitter of question banking which leads people to overestimate the readiness of the teaching fraternity for a question banking service. The story is told of one set-up where teachers were invited to telephone in their requests to a central headquarters and to receive multiple copies of the examination within 48 hours. Unfortunately, the traffic on the bank was much lighter than expected so that the telephonist was chronically under-employed—a warning to us all!

As you might expect, the commercial possibilities of question banking have not escaped the entrepreneurial mind. Published books of questions, which are essentially crude question banks, come to mind immediately. One product in the United States that has come to my attention is called Mentrex (formerly Mentorex). Marketed by Cognitive Systems Incorporated of Beverley Hills, it claims to be a 'computer-based tutorial/testing system'.[16] One reviewer[17] was less than enchanted with the Mentrex material, feeling that it was 'overly accommodating to the basest motives of the students, as if participating in a conspiracy with the students to "psych out" the examiners.' This unhealthy aspect of question banking—already referred to in remarks about coaching earlier—will be deplored by the responsible teacher. There will always be people who will attempt to pervert the purpose of question banks and it is doubtful if anything can be done about them. Whether such tactics would pay off, or would even be realistic, is another matter. As is often observed, any candidate who can remember how to answer 500 questions is worth all the marks he gets!

As far as question banking in this country is concerned, there is presently nothing to rival an operation based at Middlesex Hospital Medical School.[18]

Serving in the region of sixty University departments mainly in the field of pathology, and consisting entirely of multiple-choice items, this system has been fully operational since 1968 and is patronized by teachers who seek questions for inclusion in anything from terminal examinations to classroom quizzes. Comprehensive reproduction and scoring facilities are also offered. Perhaps a weakness of this set-up is that the writer of a question has to give his permission before someone else can use his question, a restriction which would seem to be inimical to the spirit of sharing on which question banking is founded. Concern about copyright seems to be exaggerated; presumably contributors to a bank can be persuaded to relinquish their interest through suitable payment.

Question banking in the University of London may soon receive a fillip. A working party set up by the Joint Standing Committee on Multiple-choice Examinations is expected to recommend that the University establish multiple-choice item banks in a number of subjects, mostly medical, but including Chemistry and Physics. Similar schemes in Chemistry are already in operation at Dundee and Sheffield Polytechnic.[19]

Another auspicious sign is that after their unwillingness to fund the continuation of the first item banking project, the Schools Council has now commissioned the NFER to extend the earlier work, this time in the field of biology.[20] A team of 20 teachers selected from all parts of the country is collaborating with the research people. This work will be watched with interest.

### Conclusions

Question banking remains in the category of promising ideas. Two developments could change this; examining boards could join together to pool resources and teachers could begin to request, more vociferously than in the past, access to banks of questions for the purpose of classroom testing and continuous assessment. Examining boards already have question banks which they could put at the disposal of teachers. Not that there is anything to stop local groups of teachers banding together immediately to form their own question banks, using their own and other materials. Advice on setting up and maintaining banks, including the calibration of questions, ought to be available to anyone who wants to do this. The notion of extending resource banks to include questions should also be explored.

### References

[1] R. Wood and L. S. Skurnik, *Item Banking* (Slough, National Foundation for Educational Research, 1969).

[2] R. Wood, 'The Place and Value of Item Banking'. *Educational Research* (1968), 114–125.

[3] G. Sheridan, 'At the Touch of a Button'. *Guardian* (21 November 1972).

[4] Schools Council. 16–19: Growth and response. 1. Curricular bases. *Working Paper No. 45* (London, Evans/Methuen Educational 1972), p. 63.

[5] M. Scriven, 'The Methodology of Evaluation'. In *Perspectives on Curriculum Evaluation*, edited by R. W. Tyler *et al.*, AERA Monograph Series on Curriculum Evaluation (Chicago, Rand, McNally, 1967).

[6] H. Judge, with Michael Marland, 'Putting Tests on Trial'. *Guardian* (13 June 1972).

[7] R. Wood, 'Response-contingent Testing'. *Review of Education Research* (1973). To appear.

[8] R. Wood, 'The Efficacy of Tailored Testing'. *Educational Research* (1969), 219–222.

[9] F. M. Lord, 'The Self-scoring Flexilevel Test'. *Journal of Educational Measurement* (1971), 8, 147–151.

[10] W. A. Scott, 'The Distribution of Test Scores'. *Educational and Psychological Measurement*, 32 (3), 725–746.

[11] R. Wood, 'Item Analysis for Structured Questions'. (In preparation, 1973.)

[12] T. R. Knapp, 'Item Sampling'. Unpublished document. Department of Education (University of Rochester, 1971).

[13] M. G. Epstein, 'Computer Assembly of Tests from an Item Bank'. Unpublished paper presented at the annual meeting of the American Psychological Association, 1968.

[14] J. H. Beaird (Ed.), *Computer-based Test Development*. An NCME symposium presented at Minneapolis, 5 March 1969 (Monmouth, Oregon, Teaching Research, 1970).

[15] W. P. Gorth, D. W. Allen and A. Grayson, 'Computer Programs for Test Objectives and Item Banking'. *Educational and Psychological Measurement* (1971), 245–250.

[16] R. B. Libaw and J. Kirschenbaum, *Mentorex Student Study Skills for Introductory Psychology* (Beverley Hills, Cognitive Systems, 1969).

[17] A. Parducci, 'Computerised Examinations?' *Contemporary Psychology* (1970), 15, 434–6.

[18] M. D. Buckley-Sharp and F. T. C. Harris, 'The Banking of Multiple-choice Questions'. *British Journal of Medical Education* (March 1970), 45–52.

[19] *Education in Chemistry*, November 1972, p. 215.

[20] 'Banking Biology Questions'. *Educational Research News*, September, 1972. National Foundation for Educational Research.

# 14 The Preparation of School-Based Assessment

## H. G. Macintosh

The preparation and implementation of school-based or mode 3 assessment provides the only opportunity at the present time for teachers in secondary schools to marry an evaluation of their own currricula and teaching methods with the certification of their pupils in officially recognized external examinations.* To achieve a successful and lasting marriage is, however, a formidable, albeit rewarding, task and demands the best professional endeavours of those teachers who undertake it. It is unfortunate, therefore, that this opportunity has become available to teachers at a time when there are very great demands being made upon their time and when training in the practice of curriculum development and in the basic principles of educational measurement is scanty.

Although it is hoped that this chapter will give teachers some practical advice on the preparation of school-based assessment, it has also a more general purpose. This is to emphasize the importance of assessment as an integral and fundamental part of the whole teaching/learning process. The

---

* The term mode 3 was introduced with the establishment of the Certificate of Secondary Education (CSE) in 1964. Although in theory mode 3 is available in both CSE and GCE, in practice GCE boards vary greatly in their attitudes to it. There has so far been virtually no mode 3 at A-level and this chapter is therefore concerned with developments at 16+ rather than at 18+. The possibility of a reorganized pattern of sixth form curricula and assessment could, however, change this situation. In a mode 3 the syllabus and its assessment, is proposed by a single school or a group of schools who also carry out the grading of the pupils concerned, these grades being moderated by the examining board. This definition, as so often happens with educational terminology, has become blurred in use. There are, for example, many current mode 1 or external examinations in which there is a substantial mode 3 component. In this chapter, therefore, the term school-based assessment will be used. It refers here, of course, to assessment which is externally certificated. The deliberate use above of the word 'an' before evaluation is intended to underline the point that while formal assessment is a particularly useful tool for evaluation of curriculum it is by no means the only one. It does also, as Eggleston (Chapter 15) and Rogers (Chapter 9) point out, require the adoption of a different attitude to assessment than the one commonly held by those concerned primarily with attainment testing.

teacher as assessor is therefore the underlying theme of this chapter and indeed of the whole book.

The first and really key question that must be asked and answered by anyone contemplating the introduction of school-based assessment is Why do I want to do it? Unless those concerned are quite clear about their reasons, then an appropriate return for the work involved is unlikely. The motivation for successful school-based assessment ought to result either from a desire to introduce new curricula which it is intended to assess within the external secondary examination structure, or from a desire to assess existing curricula in a different way from that adopted by an examining board.

Unfortunately, at the present time the motivation for the introduction of school-based assessment is often practical and administrative rather than educational. The problems created by the existence today of two examinations at 16+, one graded, the other pass/fail, and two sets of boards with different syllabuses, one set obliged to accept mode 3 proposals in principle, the other not, can be solved at least in part, through school-based assessment. A school can, for example, submit proposals to a CSE board based upon a GCE syllabus, or it can make use simply by requesting permission, of proposals already accepted by a CSE board from another school. The assessment resulting from these actions may well achieve its purposes in the short run since these are limited, but little or nothing will be achieved in terms of worthwhile evaluation and long-term curriculum development.

If the decision has been taken for educational reasons, then the teachers concerned will face a threefold challenge.

(1) The development of the relevant curricula.
(2) The development of appropriate patterns of assessment.
(3) The meeting of the necessary administrative requirements.

In those cases where the primary concern of the teachers lies with the development of new patterns of assessment for existing curricula, then the first challenge does not have to be met. The linkage, however, between the objectives of the course, the teaching methods adopted, and the techniques of assessment used, makes it likely that any attempt to isolate assessment from curriculum development will, in the long run, be unsuccessful. For teachers the problem of curriculum development lies not with its theory but with its practice. Whilst a number of different theoretical models have been proposed for curriculum development, one need not here look beyond the familiar one which postulates the interaction of course objectives, content and teaching methods. The results of such interaction require evaluation, which in its turn may lead to modification. This cycle of evaluation/modification should remain continuous so long as the curriculum is in use. Few teachers, at the secondary level however, put theory into practice and develop curricula in any systematic fashion. The main reasons for this are twofold.

(1) An unwillingness to discuss objectives systematically.
(2) A tendency to fragment the total process and to take decisions upon objectives, content, and teaching methods as if these were independent of each other.

Both these points underline the vital importance of curriculum development being the work of a group rather than of individuals. The opportunity needs to be provided for teachers to exchange ideas with colleagues both in the same and in different disciplines. An extension of the advisory expertise available within local authorities and the provision of courses in practical curriculum development as a part of in-service training, are other essentials. All such provision will be of little avail, however, if teachers are not willing to become both more explicit and more systematic in their analysis of what they are doing and of what they would like to do. Concern is often expressed that this will result in a loss of flexibility and will take place at the expense of the creative and innovative aspects of the curriculum. This is a matter of opinion but the author considers that the equation of a systematic approach with a lack of ideas has no sound evidence to support it. Clearly, however, curriculum development depends upon a willingness to throw ideas into the arena and to invite discussion and criticism from colleagues. From this a framework, however loose or unstructured it may be, must emerge. As the Introduction suggests, this framework may be tightened by the discussion of objectives in relation to assessment and this leads teachers on to the second challenge that faces them that of providing appropriate patterns of assessment.

The effect of this tightening of the framework needs to be looked at carefully. If it serves to crystallize and clarify course objectives, then it can do nothing but good. If, on the other hand, such tightening results in the removal of certain important objectives merely because they are difficult to assess then the effect can only be harmful. As always the key lies in obtaining a balance and the nature of this balance will reflect the knowledge and practical experience possessed in the fields of curriculum development and assessment by the teachers concerned.

The teacher as an assessor is nothing new; all teachers are assessors and spend a large part of their time evaluating their pupils, themselves and their courses of study. What is new is the opportunity to participate directly in the assessment of examinations which are nationally recognized. The implications of this in respect of curriculum development, have already been touched upon and great stress was laid there upon the need to develop practical experience and upon the desirability of a group rather than an individual approach. These same points are equally relevant to assessment but perhaps even more important here is the need to break down the barriers that have grown up in the minds of many teachers between assessment as a natural classroom activity and assessment as an external artificial exercise conducted by some outside agency. This separation is entirely artificial and has caused teachers to neglect assessment as an integral part of their professional work. Its cause lies with the organization and structure of the secondary school examination system in England and Wales at least until the coming of CSE. It still remains a formidable obstacle to the implementation of real teacher control of examinations, despite the opportunities now available for school-based assessment.

It is nearly always suggested that the solution lies in a massive programme of 'pre' and 'in' service training in respect of the techniques and problems of assessment. Such training while obviously essential, needs to be looked at very carefully. What is wanted first of all is to persuade teachers of the need to ask themselves why they teach particular subjects at particular levels. After devising curricula to meet the answers they give to these questions, they should then ask themselves what they would expect pupils who had undertaken courses taught by them to be able to do after their completion which they could not do before. The answers to this second question will provide the information upon which to create patterns of assessment.

Emphasis should be given in pre-service training upon the reasons for teaching particular subjects together with the central issues involved in defining objectives and their effect upon instructional methods as well as to the general principles and techniques of assessment. This part of the training will remain essentially theoretical until those concerned have taught in schools and gained the necessary practical experience to revise and refine their views. In-service training should then be used to show how to apply principles in practice. Such training will need to be carried out at varying levels and by a wide variety of bodies. Not all teachers will wish, for example, to write objective items or to undertake item analysis or question validation and it is not necessary that they should. There will always be some who are more interested in the problems and techniques of assessment than others and whose talents lie in this direction. For these latter, more advanced courses will need to be provided. What is desirable, however, is that all teachers should be aware of the essentials in order that they can accept or reject the use of particular patterns of assessment on the basis of knowledge and not of ignorance. Many mistakes have been made and many desirable developments hindered in recent years because this level of competence has been reached by few teachers.

The reader may well be saying with some justification, at this stage, that all that this chapter has done so far is to emphasize the difficulties facing teachers and make suggestions which impose further demands upon an already hard pressed profession. Any remedies suggested, moreover, seem to lie in the future, while school-based assessment in CSE has been in existence for some ten years. Surely it is important to provide some practical answers now. This leads to the third of the three challenges, namely that of meeting the necessary administrative requirements for school-based assessment. In discussing this, suggestions of a more practical kind will be made; their implementation, however, may well require teachers to put pressure upon their examining boards and this will inevitably be easier with CSE than with GCE boards.

The constitutional responsibilities of a CSE board* in respect of school-based assessment are clear and limited; they can reject a proposal on two grounds only:

(1) that the subject is unexaminable; that is to say the board is unable to find suitably qualified Examiners/Moderators;

(2) that the subject description requested by the school is misleading.

Within this constitutional framework, boards regard themselves as having two principal functions:

(1) to maintain, as national examining bodies, comparability of standards between all their examinations whatever their mode;

(2) to help individual teachers or groups of teachers to clarify their aims and objectives, choose their patterns of assessment and set their examinations.

The practical application of these functions may, and indeed does, vary considerably from board to board and this in its turn may lead to the adoption of quite different attitudes to school-based assessment. Administrative procedures also vary and the only advice that can be given here is that from the very outset, any school wishing to introduce school-based assessment should work as closely as possible with its examining board.

Whatever help a board is able to offer teachers, does not, however, affect the components of successful school-based assessment. These are four in number.

(1) The objectives of the course proposed for assessment.

(2) The skills to be developed in the course and the content to be covered —the syllabus.

(3) The techniques of assessment to be used.

(4) The weighting of the various parts of the assessment.

Of these four, the first has been covered in the Introduction and has been a constant theme throughout this chapter, and indeed throughout the whole book, while the second has also been referred to frequently. All that one can do here is to emphasize once again that objectives must come first and to stress the necessity of stating them in detail. Such a statement must include a description of those skills which teachers consider should be mastered by their pupils and whose acquisition they wish to test. Skills cannot, of course, be acquired in a vacuum nor can a course be taught without content. Any course description, therefore, requires a statement of both content and skills.

In order to achieve the objectives of any course a wide array of teaching methods can be used. Equally a wide array of techniques for assessment can be used and here we come to the third component. Those available fall

---

* As far as GCE boards are concerned, they may apply such criteria for school-based assessment as they think suitable and are thus under no obligation whatever to accept proposals.

broadly into the following six categories—all of which have been covered in earlier chapters.

(1) Written questions.
(2) Practical assessment.
(3) Aural and oral assessment.
(4) Projects or individual studies.
(5) Course work.
(6) Continuous assessment.

The brief comments which follow raise a number of general issues. The chapters themselves go into the nature of the techniques concerned and the problems associated with their use in more detail.

(1) Written questions have been considered in three separate chapters (Nos 1, 2 and 3) entitled 'Open-Ended Questions', 'Structured Questions' and 'Short Answer Questions and Objective Items'. This separation is largely artificial and has been used to permit the fullest possible treatment of this topic. Current use of terminology in relation to written questions is loose. Words and phrases like 'objective type', 'structured questions', 'guided essay', 'open-ended' and 'free response' are all too often bandied about without any attempt at definition. It may be found useful indeed to abandon the notion of specific types of written question altogether and to look upon all such questions as ranging along a continuum from 'open to closed'. The words 'open to closed' refer to the structure or framework within which those answering the questions are placed by the wording of the questions themselves. The more restrictive the structure, the more closed the question; the less restrictive the structure the more open the question. It follows from this definition that the most extreme form of closed question is the 'true/false' objective item in which the candidate's room to manoeuvre is restricted to the selection of one of two given alternatives. At the other end there is the kind of question often referred to as the open-ended essay, such as '"History is bunk"—Discuss.' This is open-ended in the sense that those answering it are given the absolute minimum of information and instructions about the kind of answer that they are expected to supply. Between these two extremes lies an infinite variety of possible structure.

It is important to stress that a continuum of the kind envisaged here does not bear any direct relationship to hierarchies of skills of the kind proposed by Bloom and others. The degree of openness or closedness in any particular question ought not to become specifically associated with the testing of any particular kind or level of skill. All questions must, moreover, be of a precision appropriate to their purpose. It is often assumed that questions at the open end of the continuum do not require to be precisely worded. The consequences of this assumption, often fatal to candidates, have been demonstrated with regularity in our public examinations in the past. Even if a question is not intended to have any correct answer, and expects those answering it to put forward a variety of interpretations, then this expectation should be made absolutely clear in its wording.

(2) The key to the preparation of practical assessment lies in making it as natural as possible. This point has been well brought out in Whittaker's chapter (No. 6). Practical skills are far more likely to develop in a natural situation in relation to problems which are relevant both to the student and to the subject concerned. It is worth bearing in mind that by no means all experimental work is successful, that those undertaking practical work in real life nearly always have access to data and reference material and that accurate recordings of what is happening and concise accounts of what has happened are essential aspects of practical work. Such considerations, while not ruling out written practical assessment or formal practical tests, make it likely that continuous assessment of practical work will be more appropriate for school-based assessment. As always, however, the assessment must match up with the stated objectives and these will vary.

(3) The range of possible uses for oral assessment needs stressing. With the widening of the ability range entering for examinations at 16+, the point made in Examinations Bulletin No. 4 in 1964, is as valid now as it was then, namely that all assessment should employ as nearly as possible the same medium of expression as that in which the student will eventually make use of his attainment. Judged by this criterion oral assessment is still sadly under-used today.

The conduct of an oral probably places more demands upon the person conducting it than any other form of assessment. Unless carefully planned and executed, the oral can easily degenerate into an artificial exercise involving the repetition of prepared vocabulary on the one hand or an unrelated series of monosyllabic answers to misunderstood questions on the other. If well thought out and executed, making use for example of the kinds of stimuli suggested by Park in Chapter 5 then it can have profoundly important effects upon the success of the courses concerned and lead to a growing awareness of the range of vocabulary both written and spoken. In general, it is better initially for those making use of oral testing as a part of a school-based assessment, to build upon a comparatively modest platform and to expand from there rather than to be too ambitious at the outset.

There has been in recent years, again largely in Modern Languages, an increasing tendency to assess aural or listening comprehension as well as the ability to use the spoken language. This also has value elsewhere as, for example, in Music. Its use, however, as with all forms of assessment must not relate primarily to its convenience or reliability as a technique but rather to its appropriateness for assessing those skills which it is desired to test.

(4) Deere in his chapter (No. 7) deals with the general principles of the project using, by way of illustration, Creative Technology. Another major area in which the project has been widely used in recent years is History. It is doubtful, however, whether it has been as successful here as many of its advocates hoped. This is, perhaps, because too much value has been

placed upon the descriptive aspects of project work and upon bulk and neatness; qualities which reflect industry but little else. The inclusion of a project as part of a school-based assessment, like the use of any other technique, ought to be because certain skills considered important can best, or can only, be tested by this means. A clear-cut statement of the purposes of the project and the establishment of criteria for its assessment are, as always, required. The experience of teachers who have undertaken a considerable amount of project work would suggest that it is important to use projects to pose and answer questions about the selected topic rather than to describe it. It is also important that the chosen topic is carried to a greater depth than would be the case if it were treated as a normal part of the course in the classroom. For this purpose the availability of adequate resource 'material' is essential. Many of the best projects have local roots and are upon subjects about which evidence obtainable by the pupil is available. The difficulty is that the number of suitable topics is likely to be small and when a course has been running for several years, this problem can become acute. It is also worth considering whether all questions need to be finished or whether one could not instead ask students to indicate the kind of questions that they would need to pose and answer if they were tackling a particular subject, the kind of evidence they would expect to find and where they would expect to find it and the difficulties that they would expect to encounter. Such an approach might be as revealing of the students' mastery of certain skills as a finished project. There is no reason, moreover, why the answers to these questions should all be written down; pupils could perfectly well be assessed upon their chosen subjects orally.

The two remaining categories, course work and continuous assessment, are not in themselves techniques of assessment but rather ways of making use of other techniques, as for example orals, written questions and practicals. Since, however, both procedures are being increasingly used in school-based assessment they have been treated separately here. They are also the subject of a separate chapter (No. 9) by Rogers.

(5) The main problem facing teachers using course work as part of a school-based assessment is to determine the range and amount of work upon which they wish their pupils to be assessed. There is a great danger also when course work is used alongside a written test, that pupils may be assessed twice upon the same skills or even, on occasion, upon the same content. Course work ought to encourage the extended development of ideas and skills, and to permit a greater range of the pupil's work to be taken into account than would be possible in a purely formal examination. This range might not only include a variety of different media as in Art and Craft, but a variety of conditions under which the work was produced as, for example, restrictions upon time, no restrictions upon time, use of books, no use of books.

(6) The main difficulty with regard to continuous assessment, as Rogers points out, is the absence at the present time of any universally acceptable definition. One of the purposes of his chapter was to underline a need for

such a definition and thus, in his own words, to introduce more rigour into its use.

In essence continuous assessment is a continual updating of teachers' judgments about their pupils. The standard against which these judgments can best be moderated is the consensus judgment of fellow teachers teaching the same subject at the same level, and it is the examining board's responsibility to provide the conditions through which this consensus can be established in practice. The use of the words 'up-dating' implies that the teacher or teachers concerned will need to make constructive use both of past records and of current work in order to provide a continuous record of their pupils' achievement in relation to the stated objectives of the course. The balance is important. Over-emphasis upon last term's achievement is as undesirable as over-emphasis upon the score obtained in yesterday's test.

For the school that wishes to place the main weight of its mode 3 assessment upon continuous assessment, the consensus judgment of fellow teachers can only properly be given as the result of visits when work is actually in progress. Practical considerations inevitably mean that the number of visits which are possible will be fewer than the number that is ideally desirable. The potential disadvantages of this situation can only be overcome by the maintenance of detailed and appropriate records and by the most careful planning of the curriculum and pattern of assessment. Unless this is done, pupils can easily suffer as their qualities will not be recognized. The planning of continuous assessment is thus more demanding albeit more rewarding than that of assessment involving set examinations. The closest possible liaison between school and examining board is essential from the outset. Where the continuous assessment forms only a portion of the whole, then the need for and frequency of visits will diminish. This does not, however, in any way reduce the requirement for clear-cut statements of objectives, careful preparation and the maintenance of detailed records.*

One feature of proposals for school-based assessment made in recent years, notably in Science, has been an attempt to assess attitudes and this has also been undertaken in a small number of mode 1 assessments. The word 'attitude' itself requires definition. Much of what is at present called attitude assessment in relation to secondary school science, for example, does not concern attitudes as a psychologist might define the term, namely the coupling of belief with a value statement, but rather such things as the essential requirements for co-operative laboratory work and the attributes and qualities which are essential to practical work in science. Notwithstanding this problem of definition it is clear that there is an area distinct from that of knowledge, understanding and skills which many teachers of science regard as important and wish to assess and it is this which Mathews

---

* This paragraph and the previous one, reinforces virtually in the same terms, what Rogers says in his chapter. This has been done deliberately to ensure that its relevance in the context of school-based assessment is appreciated.

discusses in his chapter (No. 10). It is equally clear that such assessment can only be undertaken on a continuous basis using the student's own teacher(s). Here the teacher has two main tasks, first to compare one student's, say, persistence, with another's, and second, to measure in relation to a single student the continuous growth of something, for example, enthusiasm, which may not have had the same starting point for all. Moderation here must present difficulties but again these can be eased by clear statements of objectives, careful planning and detailed records. Present experience of assessment and moderation in this area is not, however, very great and teachers would be well advised not to make the assessment of attitudes play too great a part in the award of a final grade until they have thoroughly explored both the possibilities and difficulties involved.

The last of the four components, weighting, has not been explicitly discussed so far in this chapter. Its importance has, however, been implied throughout since the main purpose of the book has been to provide help for teachers which would permit them to construct and use balanced patterns of assessment. (This is also specifically covered in Chapter 12.) In the achievement of such a balance, the weighting of the components which make up the assessment is crucial. The weighting adopted, however it is expressed, should directly reflect the relative importance given to the objectives which the assessment is designed to measure. In a well-planned course it will also reflect the amount of work that the students are required to undertake in the various parts of the course.

It is important to make again the point that has been made in other chapters, namely that the allocation of a particular weighting to a particular part of the assessment will not of itself ensure that this is the weighting which it will actually carry in the final grading. In order to ensure that it does achieve this desired weighting the full range of marks allocated to the particular component must be used. In any assessment, therefore, it is essential that the marking procedures adopted should have the effect of spreading out those being assessed.

Throughout this chapter the emphasis has been deliberately upon the dimensions of the task facing those teachers who wish to submit school-based assessment. This has been deliberate in order to ensure that those who do undertake the work appreciate what will be necessary in order to obtain a worthwhile evaluation of their curriculum and their teaching methods. A half-hearted, ill-considered or muddled proposal will ensure that such evaluation is of little practical use. Although the task requires patience, willingness to experiment, sound knowledge of the subject matter involved, hard work and discussion these are all part of the experienced teacher's stock-in-trade. Moreover, the examining board with whom the school is involved can do a great deal to help. Although not all boards will tackle the problems in the same way all of the following should be possible.

(1) The establishment of special committees or sub-committees to consider school-based or mode 3 proposals.

(2) The opportunity for teachers submitting proposals to discuss them in person and not merely in writing with the relevant committees.

(3) The provision of a pamphlet on how to set about preparing school-based assessment.

(4) The elimination of unnecessary administrative requirements.

(5) Discussions by the Board's staff with schools and subject committees on the problems of defining objectives in different subject areas.

(6) The preparation of question banks on the lines discussed by Wood in his chapter. (No. 13.)

(7) Provision of short in-service training courses upon problems and techniques of assessment.

(8) Visits to schools undertaking school-based assessment by members of the Board's staff.

(9) Development studies between schools and examining boards in relation to methods of moderation for school-based assessment.

If schools are not receiving this kind of assistance from their examining boards then they should ask for it. If teacher controlled examinations involving school-based assessment are to continue to develop and improve then these are the services that examining boards must provide either on their own or in co-operation with each other where this can improve quality and avoid wastage. The validity of school-based assessment ought to be unquestioned and it is up to both schools and examining boards to ensure that in the future it is also reliable. If this is done then assessment can really play a constructive part in curriculum development and its old role as an obstacle to progress will disappear, hopefully for ever.

# 15 Measuring Attainment for Curriculum Evaluation

## J. F. Eggleston

> As testing and other forms of evaluation are commonly used in the schools, they contribute little to the improvement of teaching and learning, and they rarely serve to ensure that all (or almost all) learn what the school system regards as the important tasks and goals of the education process.
>
> Bloom, Hastings and Madaus[1]

My purpose in this chapter is to examine assessment procedures of different kinds in order to define problems associated with their use as instruments of evaluation. Whereas much of this book is concerned with the improvement of measures of attainment which facilitate the comparison of one student with another, pursuing what are assumed to be similar courses of instruction, the emphasis shifts here to the problem of comparing the effectiveness of different 'courses of instruction' on pupils assumed to be similar in their capacity to learn. Central to this concern is the possibility of 'course' improvement. Hopefully we can manipulate the conditions under which learning takes place so that more pupils will achieve whatever target-objectives are set. To be able to make the necessary comparisons we must collect reliable evidence of progress towards these goals and further we must be able to describe some essential features of the conditions under which learning is effected.

Although the widespread use of the term *evaluation* in the sense described here is a relatively recent phenomenon the search for more effective teaching methods has a longer history. The distinctive features of the present-day use of the term are methodological. Formerly, the acquisition of evidence of attainment was achieved in *ad hoc* and informal ways; any necessary adjustment of the conditions for learning was held to be a function of the teacher's personal characteristics or his professional skill. More recently the problems of evaluation have been brought into the domain of public discourse and the methods for evaluation have received more systematic investigation. These developments are closely related to the emergence of large-scale curriculum developments. If this new use of the term evaluation was not born in the curriculum aftermath of Sputnik I in America, it certainly grew to receive widespread attention at that time.

The idea that a more systematic collection of evidence of attainment might result in improvements in teaching methods can be traced at least to the work of Tyler, in America in the 1930s. But it was the rise of the curriculum development movement in America in the 1950s and in Britain under the aegis of The Nuffield Foundation and later The Schools Council in the 1960s which gave rise to a new species of educationalist—the evaluator.

As it is with living organisms, so it is with the teacher's role in the curriculum; when they become larger and more complicated the component parts, at first all equally capable of exercising all the functions necessary for their existence, respond to new and larger demands by a division of labour in which parts specialize in particular functions. The curriculum development movement may be perceived in this way.

All the functions of a curriculum development team, such as selecting and defining objectives, prescribing and organizing syllabus content, proposing teaching strategies, acquiring evidence of attainment by pupils using materials produced by the team, all constitute part of the professional equipment of the skilled teacher.

What I hope to show is that an examination of the problems which have been defined by specialist evaluators in the context of curriculum development may provide the 'generalist' teacher with useful insights in the exercise of his skills.

## Examinations and evaluation

The systematic collection of evidence of attainment may be undertaken for a variety of reasons. The use to which such evidence may be put varies. As it does so, the criteria for assessing the adequacy of the evidence and the appropriateness of the means used to collect it must also vary.

Until quite recently, the almost exclusive use to which such data was put was for the purpose of pupil selection, and therefore by implication prediction. Presumably, so long as the structure of the educational system is pyramidal and the demand for places in higher education and professional education exceeds supply, some kind of predictive measure will inevitably serve this instrumental function.

Tests of attainment when used for this purpose, like the more polished psychometrics of intelligence and aptitude testing, are designed in a fashion which facilitates differentiation between people. They are constructed in such a way as to spread candidates across a measure of attainment; some 'good', some 'bad', some 'middling'. (Such tests are called *Normative* because each candidate's score is related to some norm of performance.) A test serving this purpose which fails adequately to discriminate between candidates is a poor test.

## The properties and construction of normative tests

In the context of an attempt to define the problem, 'what instruments provide measures of attainment suitable for evaluation studies?' it is necessary to specify the kind of information which will be most useful and compare this with the information given by different instruments.

A mathematics test which constituted part of a 'test of Academic Aptitude' given to 1440 sixth form boys gave a frequency distribution as displayed in Figure 1. The average score on this test out of a total possible

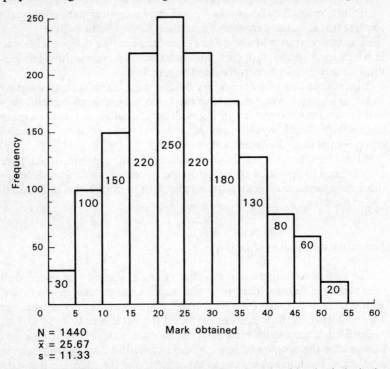

N = 1440
x̄ = 25.67
s = 11.33

**Figure 1** Distribution of scores of Sixth Form Boys in a test of Academic Aptitude (Maths)

score of 60 was 25·67. The shape of the distribution was approximately Normal or bell-shaped, relatively few boys scoring below 10 marks or above 45 marks. In fact the standard deviation of these marks is about 11 (or 18·3% of the total possible score). It follows that only about 5% of the boys' scores fell outside the range of 4–48 marks.

Now, if all we know is that John Smith achieved a mark of 40 on this test we are still ignorant of the significance of this fact. His score only acquires significance when we become acquainted with the position of his score in the defined population of which he was a member.

Figure 2 displays the same data as illustrated in Figure 1 but in the form of a cumulative frequency curve. We can read from this graph the percentage of boys who obtained scores equal to or greater than any given score. Thus for example, a score of 40 or greater than 40 was achieved by about 12% of the boys who took this test. If John Smith had scored a mark of 40 we now know that he did better than 88% of his fellow pupils. His mark has achieved some meaning but does this tell us anything significant about John Smith? Is this information which either reflects the effectiveness of his

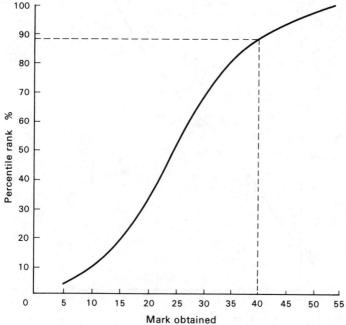

**Figure 2** Cumulative frequency graph based on data in Figure 1

former mathematics learning or on which his teachers can take any effective action?

In this case the test was designed to be a test of 'academic aptitude'. More meaning may therefore be attached to this score if the validity of the test can be demonstrated, that is to say, if it can be shown that predictions of future 'academic performance' based on this test are accurate. However, even if the test were shown to be an accurate predictor and therefore valid, what is still unknown is what components of John Smiths' intellectual achievement which were manifest during the test made his later academic success more probable.

Now it may be justifiably argued that aptitude tests are specialized tools designed exclusively for the purpose of prediction and to complain that they do not yield a comprehensive array of information on which teachers or pupils may act is inappropriate.

The same arguments, however, apply to most achievement tests currently in use.

Observe the cumulative frequency of O-level physics results displayed in Figure 3. We may now rehearse the same arguments as we used in the case

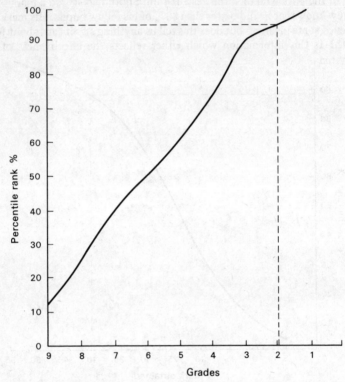

**Figure 3** Cumulative frequency graphs of the distribution of O-level grades in Physics

of the Aptitude test. John Smith now has achieved a grade one in O-level physics. Again this fact has meaning only because of its position in relation to the frequency distribution of grades, in this case a percentile rank of 95, i.e. achieved by only 5% of candidates. If it could be shown that O-level physics grades predicted later performance in sixth form courses or at University in further courses in physics, John Smith's grade I physics would achieve greater significance.

However, if we require information about what, in the context of school physics, John Smith can apparently do better than 95% of his colleagues, we have to look further. We may subject the particular examination papers he took to a detailed analysis and from this analysis infer what intellectual equipment he used, what facts he had to recall, which principles to apply, and so on.

Recent trends in examining include a diversification of the procedures used to collect evidence of attainment. So called objective tests are now in fairly widespread use. The orthodoxy of objective test construction, once the almost exclusive province of psychometricians and American educationalists is rapidly becoming accepted practice in English education. Whatever the limitations of these tests, some procedures used in the construction of objective tests of attainment are potentially useful for the purpose of collecting evidence of attainment in ways which might assist the evaluator in his task.*

An objective test of attainment usually consists of a relatively large number of items. Because the number of items is large and because each item can be designed to make a specific demand, the use of this form of test allows a more adequate sampling of the course, in terms both of its factual content and the range of intellectual skills developed by students during their exploration of the content.

The first step in the construction of an objective test of attainment is that of prescribing a table of specifications to which the item writers will work.

Consider for example the attempt made by R. Wood of the NFER in his researches for the Mathematics Item Banking Project[2] reported in *Educational Research* 1969, to arrive at an acceptable analysis of the intellectual skills associated with attainment in mathematics at CSE level. In this study, Wood suggested the following classification of 'behavioural objectives' in order to 'stimulate the thoughts of six CSE mathematics teachers on their instructional objectives'.

*A*. Knowledge and information: recall.of definitions, notations, concepts

   While it is recognized that knowledge is an integral part of the more complex categories, it differs from the others in that remembering is the major psychological demand, whereas in the other categories, remembering is only one part of a much more intricate process of relating, judging and reorganizing. Comprehension is not expected. A pupil may be said to know a theorem without understanding it, although the value of this sort of learning is dubious. Mathematical knowledge can be split into a number of sub-categories of which the three most significant are:

   (i) Knowledge of terminology and conventions. This can be rephrased simply as 'familiarity' with the language of mathematics.
   (ii) Knowledge of specific facts. This objective refers to knowledge of formulae and relationships, displayed without recourse to first principles.
   (iii) Knowledge of principles and generalizations. These are the abstractions which are of greatest value in explaining, describing and predicting, or in determining the most appropriate and

* See Chapter 3 for a more detailed discussion of this topic.

relevant action to be taken. Here, all that is required is that the student should know the principles or generalization, i.e. that he should be able to recognize or recall correct versions of them.

### B. Techniques and Manipulative Skills

A skill is defined as anything that an individual has learnt to do with ease and precision. A pupil who can demonstrate that he can carry out the following tasks is displaying *Technique* behaviour.

(a) Manipulate formulae involving dimensions.
(b) Use measuring instruments to stipulated accuracy.
(c) Make simple constructions with ruler, compasses, protractor, etc.
(d) Differentiate and integrate simple functions (not basic derivations).

### C. Comprehension

Comprehension is used to denote a quite modest ability. It is not meant to be synonymous with complete understanding or even with the fullest grasp of the implications of a message. When a pupil is confronted with a communication in oral, written or symbolic form, all that is demanded of him is that he should understand the gist of what is being communicated and that he is able to make some use of it.

Wood identifies three 'species' of behaviour.

(a) *Translation:* This he defines as an activity which requires the individual to transform a communication into another language, into other terms, or into another form of communication.
(b) *Interpretation:* Defined as 'to sift the important factors from the less important ones, or put more succinctly, to show judgment'.
(c) *Extrapolation:* This, Wood describes in the following terms—'the underlying relationship governing a sequence must be perceived before it can be either extended or completed'.

### D. Application

The effectiveness of a large part of the mathematics curriculum is dependent upon how well the students transfer learning from one situation to another. The essential feature of behaviours placed in this category is that they are evoked in novel situations. Items testing this skill must 'frustrate a solution by routine processes'. An example of this latter behaviour is that required to answer the following question.

Assuming that all the pages of a telephone directory are of equal thickness, how could you find the approximate thickness of one page? Express your method of obtaining a result in the form of an algebraic formula explaining clearly the meaning of the letters used.

### E. Inventiveness

'The assembling of elements and parts so as to form a pattern or structure not clearly visible before' represents an attempt to define this class of behaviours. Such a behavioural category differs from Application and Comprehension in its unique nature; the individual is encouraged to strive beyond previous endeavours and make discoveries which to him, although not necessarily to anyone else, are original and unique.

Given such a set of defined behaviours item writers or examiners might be asked either to write items which could be placed in one of the categories *A* to *E*, or judges might be asked to classify a previously constructed batch of terms into these categories. In this way tests may be constructed which have a demonstrable claim to content validity. The relative weighting of teaching effort made towards the achievement of a set of objectives may be matched by making an appropriate selection of test items from related categories.

At first sight the procedure outlined above would seem to be ideally suitable to the purpose of the evaluator. Any attempt to describe the effectiveness of a 'course of instruction' must benefit from a prior definition of course objectives and when these are operationally defined in behavioural terms and translated into test items, the necessary conditions seem to exist for obtaining evidence which would substantiate hypothetical propositions that certain methods of instruction lead to the achievement of particular objectives.

It will, however, become apparent, that the procedures used for the construction of objective achievement tests whittle away the initial advantage gained by the definition of objectives and their translation into test items.

Test constructors who proceed according to the conventions of normative testing use criteria for the selection of pre-tested items which result in tests with an average score (for the defined population tested) of about 50% of the total possible score, and with a spread of scores such that about 70% of candidates achieve scores between 35% and 65%, and such that 5% of candidates achieve scores of more than 80% or less than 20%. In short the function of such tests is to differentiate between candidates.

A criterion almost universally quoted when normative achievement tests are produced by the application of objective test technology is a measure of internal consistency or rational equivalence between items in the test. It is clearly desirable that when the *result* of a test is described in terms of a single score that the score demonstrably stands for one thing—a measurable entity which enjoys some claim to be an integrated whole.

The achievement of these criteria depends on the selection of test items based on their properties already known from their performance on pre-testing. It is the selective procedures necessary for the construction of an efficient normative test which cast serious doubt on the effectiveness of such tests as instruments of evaluation.

Consider the property of *facility*, defined operationally as the percentage of the pre-test population getting the item right. If an item has an *F*-value of between 20% and 80%, that is, if no fewer than 20% of candidates failed on the item or no more than 80% succeeded, the item is likely to be selected for the final version of the test. For the evaluator the inclusion of items which, from previous testing, we expect less than 80% of candidates to answer correctly, could only be the result of a misunderstanding of his function. If a course of instruction is devised in order to achieve specified objectives it is not unreasonable to expect that all pupils exposed to it will achieve the objectives.

It does not follow that the evaluator will only select easy items. What is at issue here is that he will not select items in order to spread scores across a normal distribution, he will use criteria which derive from the objective, not from facility levels. The success of a course for training airline pilots is demonstrated when more pilots achieve all the 'course objectives'.

A second criterion used for the selection of items for normative testing is that of *discrimination*. This property of a test item is a function of variability of the scores obtained by candidates in the whole test and variability in candidates' scores on the item under investigation.

Take three test items from the same test *A*, *B* and *C* data for which are illustrated in Table I below:

**Table 1**

|  | Item A | | Item B | | Item C | |
|---|---|---|---|---|---|---|
|  | above | below | above | below | above | below |
| Number of candidates answering right | 30 | 5 | 20 | 15 | 15 | 20 |
| Number of candidates answering wrong | 5 | 20 | 15 | 10 | 20 | 5 |

Of the sixty candidates who took the test, 35 scored above the mean in the test as a whole, 25 scored below the mean. The test item data are given in the Table. The performance of the two-sub-groups, one scoring above the mean and one scoring below the mean on each item, is given.

Although the *F* (facility level) is the same for each item, 35/60 obtaining a correct response, the items clearly differ in the patterns of scores illustrated in the table. These variations are due to differences in discrimination. Item A was answered correctly in 30/35 cases by candidates who scored above the mean in the whole test. Conversely, it was answered incorrectly in 20/25 cases by candidates who scored below the mean in the whole test. The item discriminated in favour of the candidates with the highest scores in the whole test. Item *B* fails adequately to discriminate in either direction and item *C* discriminates negatively, i.e. in favour of candidates who scored low marks in the test as a whole.

Only the first of these items, namely $A$, would have any chance of being included in a normative achievement test. Now, if the items $B$ and $C$ did not fail for technical reasons (for example, if they were multiple-choice items the distractors were poor), it might well be that competence in the skills required to answer these items do not correlate highly and positively with the skill most heavily represented in the test. It might nevertheless, for the purpose of evaluation, be important to know if candidates could display competence in the skill demanded by such items. Rather than remove such items the avaluator might find it necessary to include them.

The significant point in the conventional procedure for selecting test items is the use of the whole test score as a criterion for selection. This technique is justified only insofar as it is demonstrable that the test measures some unitary trait or achievement, and that this enjoys some measure of homogeneity throughout the items. Now, it may be that such a procedure is based on a contradiction. If the test items initially were selected to fit a number of supposedly discrete categories of intellectual achievement, the lumping of the scores of separate categories is suspect. The differential performance of candidates across categories is lost; two candidates may achieve the same total score but exhibit markedly different achievements. If, on the other hand, the scores in the sub-tests all correlate highly and positively, the lumping is justified but the discreteness of the categories is in doubt. If the sub-test scores correlate lowly, not at all or negatively, lumping is not justified but the discreteness of the categories may be validated.

The evaluators' concern is that of demonstrating the relative effectiveness of 'instructional methods' in achieving defined objectives. An operationally defined objective may be incorporated in a test item which, in normative test procedures might be eliminated as too easy (if 90% of candidates got it right) or as failing to discriminate if it did not correlate positively and highly with other test items. Popham and Husek[3] point out that the 'helpmates' in normative testing, i.e. measures of facility and discrimination are not only irrelevant but are 'actually injurious' in the construction of those tests which are most profitable to the exercise of evaluation, when the effectiveness of a course of instruction is being measured in absolute or relative terms.

The same argument applies to that property of a set of test items described as their internal consistency or rational equivalence. This is measured either by dividing the $N$ items in the test into two random sets of $N/2$ and comparing candidates' scores in each half or by such measures as the Kuder–Richardson formula 20. In normative tests, high values of inter-item correlation are regarded as desirable. The reverse may be true of 'good' evaluative tests.

This may be illustrated by reference to a physics attainment test, set in the context of a CSE physics course in which the scores on four sub-tests were compared. The intercorrelations are given in Table 2.

Each sub-test contained items classified by judges as demanding one of four 'skills', Inferring; Organizing data; Application (of facts and

**Table 2** *

| Intellectual skill | Organizing data | Application | Observation |
|---|---|---|---|
| Inference | 0·24 | 0·34 | 0·17 |
| Organizing data | | 0·30 | 0·14 |
| Application | | | 0·25 |

principles to problem solving) and Observing. The scores on items *within* each sub-test correlated highly. The correlation *between* the sub-test totals ($N = 218$ candidates) varied from $+0·34$, between Application and Inferring, to $+0·14$ between Observing and Organizing data. If we imagine that the items comprising these sub-tests had been lumped together to construct a single test of attainment in physics; and further, that the number of Application items had outnumbered the other types, normative test procedures would in all probability have eliminated some at least of the Observation items. If, as might well be the case, the evaluation of a physics course required some measure of 'observational skill in the context of CSE physics' the normative test would not achieve this purpose.

Such considerations have led to the definition of the requirements of the evaluator described as 'criterion referenced' tests. These have been described picturesquely by Popham and Husek[3] as follows:

Criterion referenced measures are those which are used to ascertain an individual's status with respect to some criterion, i.e. performance standard. . . . The meaningfulness of an individual's score is not dependent on comparison with other testees. We want to know what an individual can do, not how he stands in comparison with others. For example, the dog owner who wants to keep his dog in the back yard may give his dog a fence jumping test. The owner wants to find out how high the dog can jump so that he can build a fence high enough to keep the dog in the yard. How the dog compares with other dogs is irrelevant.

A more formal definition of criterion referenced tests is that given by R. Glaser and A. J. Nitko[4]

A criterion referenced test is one that is deliberately constructed to yield measurements that are directly interpretable in terms of specified performance standards.

These authors indicate that by 'performance standards' they mean those standards which are specified by defining the class, or domain of tasks that should be performed by the individual.

To achieve what criterion referenced tests set out to achieve it is first necessary to define and delimit 'The classes or domains' to which these authors refer. This is a major problem which has been partly resolved by

* This table is taken from *Studies in Assessment* by J. F. Eggleston and J. F. Kerr, (English Universities Press, 1969) and is produced by permission of the Authors and publishers.

attempts to describe and systematize educational objectives in terms of behavioural outcomes, culminating in the work of the Bloom 'school', but is far from completely solved. The ideal of non-overlapping subsets of test-items, each constituting a class of test items uniquely related to particular behavioural outcomes, can never be completely achieved because of the inter-relatedness of knowledge and intellectual skills and of one intellectual skill with another. Attempts to approach this ideal can, however, be subject to empirical enquiry.

Given that objectives have been defined in terms of behavioural outcomes, or in more earthy terms, what we expect pupils to be able to do or to do better as a result of learning, the first essential step has been taken in the process of evaluation. Each of these objectives now represents, potentially, a class of test items (or questions or demands) which item writers may, with varying degrees of success, realize. From the items they produce, a further selection may be made to construct a *criterion referenced test*.

Thus initially, the difference between the table of specifications for a criterion referenced test and that for a typical normative achievement test, is in the number of behavioural outcomes involved.

|  | Normative Test Specification | | | | | Criterion Referenced Test Specification | |
|---|---|---|---|---|---|---|---|
|  | Behavioural Outcomes | | | | | Behavioural Outcome | |
| Content | A | B | C | D | E etc. | Content | A only |
| Topic I | | | | | | Topic I only | |
| II | | | | | | | |
| III | | | | | | | |
| etc. | | | | | | | |

A second difference, which relates to the function of criterion referenced tests as instruments of evaluation, which are likely to be applied at the end of each course unit, is that the content 'dimension' of the Table of specifications will be restricted to one topic. Thus we may produce a criterion referenced test for biology students consisting of 'application items on the topic photosythensis', or for history students, one consisting of 'analysis items on social change in Britain between 1850 and 1900'.

The purpose of such tests is always to inform teachers which of their pupils have achieved the objective, in order either that they may judge the effectiveness of teaching methods they have employed, or that appropriate remedial action may be taken on those pupils who failed to achieve the objective.

A major technical problem which faces the test constructor is that ( selecting items for the criterion referenced test. Consider the specificatio cited above—'application items on the topic photosynthesis'. The numbe of items which, limited by the imagination of the item writers, can poter tially be written for this class is considerable, so a selection of items must b made. The class (or domain) of items must be sampled. How large a samp of items is required? What kind of sampling procedure will yield the te which most accurately reflects achievement of the objective?

In order to answer these questions we need to know how the items witl in the class vary, qualitatively and quantitatively. All 'application items o the topic photosynthesis' will not be equally difficult; they will vary in th inclusion of subordinate objectives such as 'comprehension' or 'knowledg of facts'. They may also vary in the degree to which the demand made b the item is consistent with the definition of 'application'.

At this point, on this particular path towards the development of criterion referenced test, it may seem reasonable to proceed in a fashio analogous to normative test construction. We may construct applicatio items on this limited content, and after pre-testing on a group of pupils wh have completed a course unit on photosynthesis, perform a convention. item analysis in terms of facility and discrimination. Shortcomings of th procedure soon become apparent, however. If the course unit has bee successful it may be that any item the test construction might devise (i which the 'facts and principles of photosynthesis' are applied to problem will be answered correctly by all or almost all students. The inverse ( facility is difficulty. The empirical demonstration of difficulty is so easy tha we may not search with sufficient diligence for its qualitative rather tha quantitative significance. A factual recall item will have a facility level ir versely proportional to the obscurity of the fact to be recalled. An ite demanding some 'higher intellectual skill' *may* be demonstrably difficu because some students fail to acquire the skill, but the skill is unlikely t exist in an 'all or nothing' state. If we arranged, say, ten 'application' item in an order of increasing difficulty, how would those items low in the orde differ from those high in the order? Presumably an 'easy' application ite will be one in which one fact or one principle must be selectively recalled i order to provide a 'solution' to the problem. The problem in this simp case will be one in which the 'elements' are given in simple terms. Difficu 'application' items will probably involve more facts and principles opera ing in conjunction rather than singly and the problem may contain mo 'elements' which might relate in various ways.

Any item which is designed primarily as a task demanding 'applicatio however, may be contaminated. That is to say, skills other than 'appl cation' will be required for its correct solution. As the items become mo difficult and hence more complex, the likelihood of serious contaminatio increases. This possibility has serious implications for the construction of criterion referenced test. It may be that a substantial part of the variation ( totals achieved by students in a test of 'application' is due to contam

tion. In a typical normative test where procedures are geared to maxi-
zing the variance of test total scores, such an effect would not be serious.
any event, normative achievement tests work to such a 'global' speci-
ation—the contaminants are probably among the behaviours listed
it.

But in a criterion referenced test this effect is exacerbated by the fact that
ch tests, designed to inform teachers what a course unit has achieved,
ls to exclude those items which all or most students answer correctly.
ence the variability of total scores is limited. Of this, now limited, vari-
ce an unknown fraction may be due to contamination. Measures of
ternal consistency' and 'rational equivalence' essential for establishing
e reliability of normative tests which typically give high correlation, will
e much lower values with criterion referenced tests and may be in-
propriate.

There is as yet no generally accepted methodology for the construction
criterion referenced tests but the goal of producing, in Glaser and
tko's terms, measures which 'are correctly interpretable in terms of
ecified performance standards' is being pursued. This chapter will con-
de with a brief examination of one or two possible ways in which pro-
ss towards this goal might be achieved.

The arguments advanced above which led to the conclusion that analyti-
l procedures used to select items for a normative test were inappropriate
criterion referenced tests, rest on two basic assumptions:

(a) that items shown empirically to be easy would be retained on a
terion referenced test providing they inform teachers about the achieve-
ents of their pupils;

(b) the variability of total scores achieved by students will be relatively
all and therefore (if for no other reason such as contamination) they will
nstitute an inadequate criterion for item discrimination.

In practice, during the development of a test, it is, however, unlikely that
e objective translated operationally into test items will have been achieved
all pupils exposed to a course unit. Variation of score totals on items all
ated to the same objective will in all probability be manifest. If it could
shown that such variation as exists is due primarily to differential
hievement of the objective and for no other reason, then there seems no
ason why conventional procedures might not be used to establish rational
uivalence among the items on a list. Such a list could constitute an arbi-
ry 'base-line' test, i.e. an arbitrary performance standard interpretable
terms of the objective measured, against which the performance of more
less successful achievers of the objective might be compared. By the
me token more or less successful versions of the course-unit leading to the
hievement of the objective could be compared.

In certain circumstances it might be necessary to abandon the stringent
terion that rational equivalence between items must be empirically de-
onstrable or at least to soften the application of this criterion by rejecting

only those items which discriminate negatively with the criterion score. However, providing the achievement of the objective is not an 'all or nothing' state it should always be possible to develop a test on a sample of pupils whose responses will vary with respect to the criterion. Given a test consisting of say, *application* items in which variations of pupil responses could be virtually guaranteed it would be possible to embed in the test application items related to a specific content. Conventional item analysis would facilitate the selection of a sub-set of the latter items which at least correlated positively with the total scores on the test.

An alternative procedure might be to prepare *application* test items related to a specific content and use the same items on a group of students *before* and *after* 'instruction'. Candidates' scores in pre-instruction and post-instruction tests are now treated as independent scores and a conventional item analysis is performed. If we assume that the instruction has been even partially effective the pupils with the highest scores in the post-instruction test will be among those who have achieved the objective. The scores on items which contributed to the measure of achievement of the objective will:

(a) have higher facility values in post-instruction test;
(b) correlate positively with score totals.

The class of objective used in this discussion, namely, 'application' is, however, too unspecific in its focus for some authors on the subject of evaluation. Such a class (or domain) of items may be analysed into many discrete units limited either to sub-sets of application skills or to items of content within the topic photosynthesis, or both. At one end of a continuum there are broad generalized aims—at the other the information yielded by a single item; a quantum of skill exercised on a particle of content. Somewhere between there is a level at which information is sufficiently detailed to describe achievement effectively. The problem is that of knowing where to enter the continuum in order to facilitate the construction of a reasonably homogeneous set of tasks across which transfer of skills is demonstrably possible. Alternative approaches to this problem have resulted in attempts to conceptualize achievement by using models which differ in some respects from the taxonomic model of Bloom.

Such an approach is that of Bradfield and Moredock[5] who attempted to analyse levels of performance in 'understanding'.

*Level I*—Imitating, duplicating, repeating.
*Level II*—Recognizing, identifying, remembering.
*Level III*—Comparing, relating, discriminating, reformulating, illustrating.
*Level IV*—Explaining, justifying, predicting, estimating, interpreting, making critical judgments, drawing inferences.
*Level V*—Creating, discovering, reorganizing, formulating new hypotheses, new questions and problems.

These five levels might provide a basis for criterion test construction which would yield results 'interpretable in terms of specified performance standards'.

Bradfield and Moredock's scheme has the same hierarchical property as Bloom's Taxonomy of Educational Objectives (Cognitive Domain), but here the relationship to learning sequence is perhaps more strongly implied.

The conceptualization of learning processes as the sequential achievement of 'performances' in tasks ordered in the form of a *learning hierarchy* has been advanced within the last decade by such authors as Gagné.[6] 'Beginning with a statement of some "terminal" objective of instruction, the attempt is made to analyse this terminal performance into component tasks in a structure such that the lower level tasks generate positive transfer to higher level ones.' Thus, for example, the physics teacher producing a course-unit on Ohm's law would analyse Ohm's law into a sequence of component facts and operations such that at each level in the analysis the operations could be logically derived from those at a lower level. The sequence of tasks, initially the product of a *logical analysis*, is subjected to empirical test by measuring performance at each level.

The task of evaluation will be advanced when we are able to produce valid measures of achievement. At present the trend is in the direction of criterion referenced tests. This development has shown that the models for achievement used by the behavioural taxonomists, while offering a partial solution to the problem, may ultimately give way to more sophisticated 'structural' models of achievement.

(My thanks are due to Dr L. D. Mackay, Monash University, for his valuable comment on the manuscript.)

## References

[1] B. S. Bloom, J. T. Hastings and G. F. Madaus, *Handbook on Formative and Summative Evaluation of Student Learning* (New York, McGraw-Hill, 1971).
[2] R. Wood, 'Objectives in the Teaching of Mathematics', *Educational Research* (1969.)
[3] W. J. Popham and T. R. Husek, *Journal of Educational Measurements*, 6 (1969) No. 1.
[4] R. Glaser and H. J. Nitko, *Educational Measurement*, edited by R. L. Thorndike (second edition) (American Council on Education, 1971).
[5] Bradfield and Moredock, *Measurement and Evaluation in Education* (London, Macmillan, 1957).
[6] R. M. Gagné *et al. Psychological Monographs*, 76, (1962) 1.

# 16 The Value for the Teacher of Research into Assessment

## D. L. Nuttall

### Educational research and the teacher

Research and development work accounts for huge sums of money every year in industry, commerce, the Armed Forces and the pure scientific and medical fields, yet the amount spent each year on educational research and development (R & D) is only of the order of £3½ million, about one-sixth of one per cent of the annual national expenditure on education. Nor is the situation very different in other industrialized countries; although Britain is near the bottom of the league in terms of the percentage of its educational expenditure devoted to R & D, the percentages in other countries are not much higher except in Sweden and the U.S.A.[1]

Why does educational R & D attract comparatively so little money? The reasons are manifold, some of the faults lying at the door of the researchers and some at the door of the teachers. But perhaps the greatest drawback of educational research is its youth. This has two effects: first, it means that the techniques and tools of educational research, like those of research in all the social sciences, are primitive—if we liken the development of our understanding of the process of education to the development of our understanding of the physical world, some would say that we do not yet have the understanding of Galileo and his scientific contemporaries. Second, a normal and healthy but often intensely aggravating stage of youth is the stage of questioning all authority and accepted practice. This stage is one that no researcher ever wishes to leave, since in the words of Dr (now Professor) Wall, a former Director of the National Foundation for Educational Research (NFER):

Research is, by its nature, agnostic; inevitably it challenges faith. Here, then, is the core of the communication difficulty and the source of heat in discussions of the value of educational research to the practitioner in education (quoted in W. Van der Eyken, *Educational Research and the Teacher*, p. 2).[2]

Relations between teachers and educational researchers are often strained because of the researchers' desire to challenge the teachers' faith. All too often, teachers say, research tells them what they already know: but researchers would answer that five hundred years ago everybody 'knew' that the earth was flat. Other teachers see research as providing panaceas, seeking out the one best method to teach children how to read, the one best method to sort children into teaching groups and so on, and are inevitably disappointed by the results of research on these topics which are always stated in guarded terms and which are often conflicting.

But the researchers are far from blameless: the communication gap between teachers and researchers is often made more difficult to bridge by the researchers' unwillingness to discard their jargon and, as the teachers would say, by the researchers' reluctance or inability to write plain English. Research bodies are well aware of the communication gap and are attempting to bridge it by devoting a higher proportion of their funds to the dissemination of research results and of materials from development projects.

The most common criticism of educational research is that it is too often concerned with matters of fringe interest and that it rarely concentrates on topics of immediate relevance to the classroom teacher. In a survey of teachers' attitudes towards and priorities in research, Cane and Schroeder[3] found that teachers were generally in favour of research but favoured topics of direct relevance to the classroom, such as investigations into methods of teaching wide ability-range classes and into the diagnosis of children's particular difficulties rather than topics such as co-education and an analysis of the duties undertaken by teachers which have attracted more research attention (e.g. on co-education, see Dale[4]; on the job analysis of teaching, see Hilsum and Cane[5]).

This criticism, that research is out of touch with classroom needs, is valid but it must be remembered that the limited resources devoted to educational R & D impose great constraints on the work that can be done. Much of the work that was done in the last decade concentrated on broad issues relating to the policies of central and local government: two examples are the research carried out for the Plowden Report[6] and the research into the organization of comprehensive schools.[7,8] Other research, for example on streaming,[9] was more relevant to the interests of the individual teacher but was not aimed at giving him (or her) guidance as to the practice that should be adopted in his own classroom. Yet there are examples of research of direct relevance to the practitioner in the classroom: research into methods of teaching reading,[10] an evaluation of teaching French in the primary school[11] and research into the teaching of mathematics.[12]

Some of the benefits of these researches are indirect, increasing our knowledge of the educational process that will lead to better research in the future. One example, particularly important in the context of streaming research, is our growing understanding of the ways in which a teacher's attitudes to the educational system and the expectations he has of a child affect the attainment of the individual child (see also Pidgeon, *Expectation and Pupil Performance*).[13] Time and time again, research findings point to the crucial roles of the teacher and the child's parents and to the relative unimportance of the materials that the child works with.

Educational research and development should, and largely do, move hand in hand. Research on its own cannot chart the map for the future; its function is to evaluate the existing system and innovations in the curriculum and organization of schools that are introduced into the system. It inevitably tends to be retrospective in nature, telling us whether or not our act of faith, for example, in pioneering a new curriculum—the development stage —was justified. The words of Dr Wall are again relevant:

> At the same time, the best teachers know that, whatever research or development may produce in the way of facts, in a sense these are only second to the main value that research has for the practising teacher. This is that the asking of questions forces us to do better, and we must recognize that the asking of appropriate questions is probably the beginning of wisdom, not the end (quoted in Van der Eyken, *op. cit.*[2])

## A brief review of past and present examinations research

Turning to research in the field of examinations, we find a similar state of affairs as exists in the field of educational research in general: such research as has been carried out relates mainly to the broad issues of the validity, reliability and comparability of standards of examinations with little work which had a direct impact for the teacher in the classroom. But in the case of research into examinations there is another reason that the work had little relevance to the teacher in the classroom, namely that until relatively recently the teacher was not directly involved in the process of examining and assessing the performance of his own pupils in the context of public examinations. It is therefore not surprising that little research into suitable assessment techniques for the teacher to employ in the classroom has been carried out.

Earlier chapters in this book bear testimony to the research carried out in testing techniques such as objective testing and essay marking, but much research still remains to be done. The best-known study of marker reliability in Britain was conducted nearly forty years ago by Hartog and Rhodes,[14] who found considerable lack of agreement between markers in the marks awarded to the same script, and, indeed, between the marks awarded to the same script by the same marker on two different occasions. This research led to tighter controls on marking schemes and markers by examining boards, and to a greater degree of training for markers, involving standardization meetings and the re-marking of samples of scripts by the Chief Examiner. (For a description of current practice in marker standardization, see Christopher, *JMB/GCE: The Work of the Joint Matriculation Board.*[15])

In the years following the establishment of the GCE O-level and A-level examinations in the early 1950s, the examining boards conducted a certain amount of research, particularly into the comparability of standards at the

Pass/Fail borderline, but little research was published. The Joint Matriculation Board (JMB) was a notable exception, its series of Occasional Publications dating back to 1954 with 21 being published before the first CSE examinations were held. But it was the establishment of the CSE that heralded the new era of research and development in examinations. Rigorous analyses of trial examinations in a wide range of subjects were published in the Schools Council's series of Examinations Bulletins; and, in 1964, the Schools Council established the Examinations and Tests Research Unit at the NFER.

The Unit's first task was to enquire into the comparability of grade standards between the 14 CSE boards and, with reference to CSE Grade One, between the CSE boards and the eight GCE boards at O-level. In the four annual studies over the years 1965 to 1968, there was no evidence to suggest any marked deviations in standard on the part of any board (see Nuttall, *The 1968 CSE Monitoring Experiment*[16]). This research did not help the individual teacher with any of his problems of assessment, but it was important in that it validated many of the claims made for the teacher-controlled CSE and re-assured employers and other bodies using grade results, and indeed the teaching profession itself, over the matter of standards in a completely new examination.

More recently, the work of the Unit has concentrated on the detailed analysis of examination scripts. The item analysis of objective tests and the estimation of the reliability of such tests has long been a routine procedure in their development, in Britain as elsewhere. But the techniques were not immediately applicable to examinations where questions are not marked simply right or wrong, or where, more problematically, a choice of questions is offered. New techniques were therefore developed and hundreds of different examinations analysed using them.[17] This work was carried out in conjunction with examining boards, their research staff and others outside the boards. The techniques and results are again not of immediate practical benefit in classroom assessment techniques, but they have been useful to the examining boards in reviewing their own procedures to the ultimate benefit of the examination candidate. This research has also highlighted some of the measurement problems created by the practice of offering a choice of questions (see Appendix B of Examinations Bulletin 23, Schools Council[18]), and research conducted by the North Regional Examinations Board[19] has drawn attention to the problem that question choice creates for the candidate: many candidates, particularly the less able, showed themselves incapable of showing themselves at their best, which is one of the main virtues claimed for the practice of offering a choice of question.

During the later 1960s and early 1970s, most GCE boards and several CSE boards established their own research units and the investigations that they have performed have led to improvements in procedure and to evaluations of important experiments in the field of examinations. One example is the continuing evaluation of the JMB's experimental scheme of school assessment in English language at O-level; the third report by Christopher,

Rooke and Hewitt was published in 1970.[20] This scheme has been invest
gated from another standpoint, that of comparability of standards wi
other English language alternatives and with other subjects, by Forrest a
Smith.[21] Comparability between boards continues to be investigat
through cross-moderation exercises (e.g. South–Western Examinatio
Board[22]).

A new impetus to examinations research came with the publication of t
Schools Council's proposals for a common system of examining at 16-pl
in Examinations Bulletin 23.[8] Much of the work is more properly term
'development' since the GCE and CSE boards have formed themselv
into consortia and set up working parties to devise new syllabuses a
schemes of assessment to cater for the ability range currently covered joint
by GCE O-level and CSE. The research aspect will come into its own in t
evaluation of these feasibility and development studies, but within the
studies a number of small research studies into different forms of questi
paper have already been carried out. Meanwhile, the Examinations a
Tests Research Unit at the NFER is conducting research into vario
aspects of comparability to coincide with the effect of raising the schoo
leaving age on examination entry patterns, and into problems of pre-testi
questions with special reference to question banking, under the sponsorsh
of the Schools Council. The Schools Council has set up its own Centr
Examinations Research and Development Unit (CERDU), primarily
monitor feasibility and development studies, but CERDU is also conduc
ing research into the use of objective tests in current examinations at 1
plus, and into the use of and moderation of teacher assessment.

This brief review of past and present examinations research is sufficie
to indicate that research activity has never been greater than it is at prese
The review has inevitably been selective, even in the area of examinatio
at 16-plus, and a fuller picture may be gained from Pilliner's review
which includes a discussion of research into 11-plus examinations a
university examinations. But it is also sufficient to show that most of t
research has been aimed at producing evidence to satisfy society at large
the efficiency of the examining system, rather than to assist the individu
teacher in making his assessment more valid and more reliable. This is n
to denigrate the research that has been done—the need for such resear
will continue to exist, at least while examination certificates remain
widely used for selection purposes by employers, professional bodies a
institutes for Further and Higher Education—but there is an obvious ne
for more research which will assist the individual teacher in the assessme
of pupils' attainment, particularly since all the signs are that the teacher w
play an increasing part in the examining process. Fortunately, a number
research studies have been carried out, whose results are of immedia
relevance to the teacher as assessor; many useful results have also come
spin-off from the large-scale studies discussed above and some examples
both types of results are given in the next section. But perhaps the greate
need—a need which the Schools Council recognized in Examinatio

ulletin 23[18] and which this book helps to serve—is for the training of more achers in techniques of assessment. These techniques have evolved, and e still evolving, in partnership with research, and a programme of training uld ensure that teachers were able to take advantage of new research findgs and to start to bridge the communication gap from their side. In the ords of one teacher at the conference reported by Van der Eyken:

If somehow or other teachers could be more closely informed or made aware of what is going on in educational research, if they could be made partners in projects carried out by research workers, both parties could pull together and evolve out of this something of a self-educating and also a united profession.[2]

### ome research results of immediate relevance to the teacher

One of the best examples of research work in the field of examinations at was designed to be of immediate practical benefit to the teacher is the pic of question banking. This has already been described by Wood in an rlier chapter (No. 13) and consequently only a few points are noted here. he first point is that question banking is a technique that can be applied different levels. A question bank can be established in a school or group `schools, where it might be little more than a library of questions built up ver a period of time; an examination board could establish a bank from hich to construct its mode 1 papers to ensure comparability of standards ver a period of years and, indeed, a number of boards are setting up banks ` objective questions. In due course, when these banks contain a large umber of questions, it may become possible for teachers employing mode to have access to them. Finally, it might be possible to establish national uestion banks on the lines discussed by Wood and Skurnik[24] and in chools Council Examinations Bulletin 22.[25] Such banks could be used to rovide information to teachers (or boards) drawing questions from them out national standards of attainment without in any way infringing upon e liberty of the teacher to construct his own examinations. At all levels, uestion banking is best seen as a technique which encourages the best use `limited resources, notably that of skilled manpower.

The second point concerns the problems of pre-testing questions for clusion in a bank. These problems, which are currently being investited at the NFER, are essentially two-fold: first, how can new questions, hich must be continuously introduced into the bank as new curricula and aching methods evolve, be pre-tested with the minimum burden on hools; and second, can essay-type questions and other assessment deces which are not capable of being scored objectively be banked and, if ey can, what is the minimum information necessary for each question? or example, an essay question is likely to be of value in a bank only if it is nked and marked with a highly structured marking scheme. If no markg scheme were provided, two different markers might well award very fferent marks to the same script simply on account of their differing emphases on various educational objectives; the resulting question statistics would also be different and hence of no value in guiding a third teacher on the difficulty and standard of the question.

The third point concerns the ways in which a question might be classified in the bank. In the feasibility study conducted by Wood and Skurnik,[24] a question was classified according to both the topic and the educational objective it was deemed to be testing. This method of classification allowed a teacher who had a detailed specification of his course (see the Introduction to this book) to construct a valid and reliable examination paper.

The specification of educational objectives is another area where research is of practical value to the teacher, not just in the construction of examination papers but in thinking about teaching as well. Wiseman once said: 'No teacher who attempts such an analysis (i.e. the specification of educational objectives) is ever quite the same again',[26] and many members of the Subject Panels of examining boards would endorse this view. The Introduction gives two examples of general purpose taxonomies of educational objectives, but there are many other taxonomies which have been developed for individual subjects (e.g. Wood on mathematics[27]; Lewis on science[28]). The research on taxonomies has been largely philosophical rather than practical and there is an urgent need for research to investigate techniques of question setting and marking that will give more insight into the assessment of higher abilities, such as analysis, synthesis and evaluation in Bloom's taxonomy. Bloom, Hastings and Madaus[29] have many helpful suggestions for the assessment of attainment in a number of subjects and demonstrate Bloom's taxonomy in action.

Nowhere is careful thinking about educational objectives more needed than in teacher assessment. Some boards give explicit guidance to teachers as to the intellectual qualities they should look for in assessing course work or practical skills, while others leave the nature of the assessment almost entirely to the discretion of the teacher. In the latter case, the validity of the assessment is open to criticism, and the teacher would be in a much better position to make the assessment and to communicate with moderators if the objectives were spelled out. The whole field of teacher assessment could benefit from further research into the validity of the various methods employed and, in more depth, into the judgment processes involved. It would also be valuable to compare the two major types of approach, that is, a separate assessment by the teacher of each educational objective vs. a global assessment of the candidate's work (based, nevertheless, on a consideration of each objective). Such research could further assist teachers in the making of their assessments, and could also shed light on the value of reporting attainment in terms of profiles across a variety of dimensions rather than in terms of a single grade. (For further discussion of 'Profiles' see Chapters 8 and 12.)

On a related theme, that of allocating grades, a number of CSE boards are attempting to make explicit the behaviours which the candidate must exhibit to qualify for the award of a certain grade. In terms of Bloom's categories, for example, a board might specify that a candidate must demonstrate his knowledge of most topics in the syllabus to qualify for a grade 4, but that to qualify for a grade 1 a candidate must show evidence of comprehension and application. In an attempt to assist in this work, the NFER mounted a study under the sponsorship of the Schools Council to see if it was possible to describe performance at different grade levels in terms of the educational objectives and topics covered by different types of question.[30] The analysis was done by calculating the facility values of questions separately for candidates at each grade level for 1969 CSE mathematics examinations. It might have been found, for example, that 90% or more of candidates in grade 4 could correctly answer questions involving only the basic arithmetical operations, while less than 50% of candidates in grade 5 or below could answer these questions correctly. Such questions would therefore have been useful in determining the boundary between grades 4 and 5. Similarly, it might have been found that questions involving trigonometry clearly discriminated between candidates in grades 1 and 2.

In practice, no such clear-cut results emerged. Although some questions showed very good discrimination between candidates in adjacent grades, no pattern emerged either in terms of their content or in terms of the educational objectives they tested. It was felt that these results, which were disappointing in that they did not provide any useful guidance for grading procedures, reflected the fact that most examinations were not constructed with these sort of criteria in mind. Grading is most commonly done by way of a rank order based on total marks. A mark of 50%, say, might qualify for a grade 3 and little account would be taken of how the candidate attained that mark: he might, for example, have shown roughly average performance in all the areas of the syllabus, or weak performance in some areas compensated for by good performance in the remaining areas. In other words, he could have attained a mark of 50% in any number of ways. The results of this research do not, however, lead to the conclusion that it is not possible to specify criteria for the award of different grades, but simply that the examining techniques most commonly used do not lend themselves easily to such an approach.

Another topic recently investigated at the NFER has important implications for the teacher making his own assessments.[30] The study investigated the weighting given to each component of the examination and, in particular, the relationship between the desired weightings and the weightings achieved in practice. It was found that it was relatively rare for the achieved weightings to match the desired weightings, although the discrepancies were not usually very large. These results arose because of a common misunderstanding about weighting: the total mark on a paper marked out of 100 does not necessarily contribute twice as much to the grand total as the total mark on a paper marked out of 50. It is not the ratio of the maximum marks that is important but the ratio of the spread of marks (as described by the standard deviation) on the two papers. The correlations between the component marks and the grand total marks are also important, particularly when they vary considerably, a situation which is quite common when the examination consists of written papers and assessments made by teachers. The statistical procedures needed to adjust the marks in such a way as to ensure that desired weightings are exactly achieved are simple in theory but time-consuming to carry out (details are given in Fowles, *The CSE: Two Research Studies*[30]). The main message of this research for the teacher is alert him to the problems of weighting and to encourage him to think more carefully about the weightings he attaches to each component in his own assessments.

Research on marking techniques has been conducted on a large scale over a considerable period of time, and the results offer many useful guidelines to the teacher doing his own assessments. Pilliner[23] demonstrates in his review of research in this area that impression marking is nearly as reliable an analytical marking and obviously much quicker. Multiple impression marking, using a team of three or four markers, often takes only a little more time than one analytical marking but is more reliable and no less valid (see also Britton, Martin and Rosen, *Multiple Marking of English Compositions*[31]). Greater use of multiple marking techniques (see Chapter 1) in the school situation would have other benefits, encouraging discussion about educational objectives and course content among colleagues and inculcating knowledge of the standards to be expected. Other research shows marking to be more reliable and less subject to 'halo effect' if all answers to Question 1 are marked first, then all answers to Question 2 and so on, rather than if each complete script is marked in turn. Teachers should also be aware of the dangers of being over-influenced by neat handwriting when marking.[32]

It would be pleasant to be able to say that the five areas (question banking, objectives, criteria for grades, weighting and marking techniques) chosen for discussion in this section were chosen at random from a long list of possible topics. But unfortunately this is not the case: there are few other topics that would qualify for inclusion. There are grounds for hope that the situation will slowly be remedied as the teacher expands his role as assessor: as is usually and rightly the case, where the teacher leads, the researcher will follow.

## Conclusions

The burden of this chapter has been that teachers and researchers alike could benefit from working more closely together and from understanding each other's position more fully. Research into examinations is no exception and there are examples of research work where the results are potentially of immediate benefit to the teacher and where the researchers have gained from their close collaboration with teachers. There are many other areas (witness the Problems section of this book) where more research is urgently needed to assist teachers and examining boards in their continuing search to make examinations as fair to the individual candidates as they can possibly be.

The need for large-scale technical research is likely to continue to exist and such research will probably attract a large share of the resources available for investigations into examinations. This research can be of value to the teacher and to the teaching profession, as well as to the policy-makers, in its ability to stimulate thought or, to borrow a word from Taylor to *sensitize* educational thinking.[33] In any discussion of research priorities and their possible value, it is fitting to conclude with the words of Pilliner[23] (p. 183):

> In the area of examinations, as in other areas, it is easier to answer—or to seek answers to—the question 'HOW?' than the question 'WHY?'

# References

[1] V. Ward, *Resources for Educational Research and Development* (Slough, NFER, in preparation).

[2] W. Van der Eyken (Ed.), *Educational Research and the Teacher* (Slough, NFER, 1966).

[3] B. S. Cane and C. Schroeder, *The Teacher and Research* (Slough, NFER, 1970).

[4] R. R. Dale, 'Co-education'. In *Educational Research in Britain*, edited by H. J. Butcher (London, University of London Press, 1968).

[5] S. Hilsum and B. S. Cane, *The Teacher's Day* (Slough, NFER, 1971).

[6] Central Advisory Council for Education (England), *Children and Their Primary Schools*. The Plowden Report (London, HMSO, 1967).

[7] T. G. Monks (Ed.), *Comprehensive Education in Action* (Slough, NFER, 1970).

[8] J. M. Ross, W. J. Bunton, P. Evison and T. Robertson, *A Critical Appraisal of Comprehensive Education* (Slough, NFER, 1972).

[9] J. C. Barker Lunn, *Streaming in the Primary School* (Slough, NFER, 1970).

[10] J. F. Reid, 'Reading'. In *Educational Research in Britain*, edited by H. J. Butcher (London, University of London Press, 1968).

[11] C. Burstall, *French in the Primary School: Attitude and Achievement* (Slough, NFER, 1970).

[12] F. Land, 'The Teaching of Mathematics'. *Educational Research in Britain 2*, edited by H. J. Butcher and H. B. Pont (London, University of London Press, 1970).

[13] D. A. Pidgeon, *Expectation and Pupil Performance* (Slough, NFER, 1970).

[14] P. Hartog and E. C. Rhodes, *The Marks of Examiners* (London, Macmillan, 1935).

[15] R. Christopher, *JMB/GCE: The Work of the Joint Matriculation Board*. JMB Occasional Publication 29 (Manchester, JMB, 1969).

[16] D. L. Nuttall, *The 1968 CSE Monitoring Experiment*. Schools Council Working Paper 34 (London, Evans/Methuen Educational, 1971).

[17] D. L. Nuttall and A. S. Willmott, *British Examinations: Techniques of Analysis* (Slough, NFER, 1972).

[18] Schools Council, *A Common System of Examining at 16 +*. Schools Council Examinations Bulletin 23 (London, Evans/Methuen Educational, 1971).

[19] North Regional Examinations Board, *Instructions to Candidates: A Study of Question Papers in Mode 1* (Newcastle-upon-Tyne, NREB, 1971).

20 R. Christopher, H. M. Rooke and E. A. Hewitt, *An Experimental Scheme of School Assessment in Ordinary Level English Language.* JMB Occasional Publication 31 (Manchester, JMB, 1970).

21 G. M. Forrest and G. A. Smith, *Standards in Subjects at the Ordinary Level of the GCE, June 1971.* JMB Occasional Publication 34 (Manchester, JMB, 1972).

22 South-Western Examinations Board, *Bristol Experiment* (Bristol, SWEB, 1968).

23 A. E. G. Pilliner, 'Examinations'. In *Educational Research in Britain*, edited by H. J. Butcher (London, University of London Press, 1968).

24 R. Wood and L. S. Skurnik, *Item Banking* (Slough, NFER, 1969).

25 Schools Council, *Question Banks: their use in School Examinations.* Schools Council Examinations Bulletin 22 (London, Evans/Methuen Educational, 1971).

26 S. Wiseman (Ed.), *Examinations and English Education* (Manchester, Manchester University Press, 1961), p. 147.

27 R. Wood, 'Objectives in the Teaching of Mathematics', *Educational Research*, 10 (1968), 83–98.

28 D. G. Lewis, 'Objectives in the Teaching of Science', *Educational Research*, 7 (1965) 186–199.

29 B. S. Bloom, J. T. Hastings and G. F. Madaus, *Handbook on Formative and Summative Evaluation of Student Learning* (London, McGraw-Hill, 1971).

30 D. E. Fowles, *The CSE: Two Research Studies.* Schools Council Examinations Bulletin 28 (London, Evans/Methuen Educational, in press).

31 J. N. Britton, N. C. Martin and H. Rosen, *Multiple Marking of English Compositions.* Schools Council Examinations Bulletin 12 (London, HMSO, 1966).

32 D. Briggs, 'The Influence of Handwriting on Assessment', *Educational Research*, 13 (1970) 50–55.

33 W. Taylor, 'Retrospect and Prospect in Educational Research', *Educational Research*, 15 (1972) 3–9.

# Some Suggestions for Further Reading

These suggestions are set down in two major sections. The first is concerned with general reading about assessment, while the second makes suggestions for reading upon the topics covered in the chapters of the book. These in their turn can be supplemented by references given at the end of the chapters. Inevitably there is overlap and on occasions a book could equally well have been put in another section. Not all the suggested reading is concerned with assessment. It is important that those who seek to improve the quality of assessment are aware of current thinking in regard to the nature and processes of learning. Concentration upon assessment in this book should not also cause the reader to forget that the topic is but a part of the total educational process. Like all reading lists this one is far from exhaustive and will, moreover, be out of date the moment it is printed. Readers should, therefore, try and ensure that they themselves keep it up to date. Books considered particularly useful for those who are beginning the study of the subject concerned are indicated with an asterisk.

## Section I  General

Anastasi, A. (Ed.) (1966) *Testing Problems in Perspective* (Washington, D.C., American Council on Education)

Bantock, G. H. (1963) *Education in an Industrial Society* (London, Faber)

Beard, R. M. (1969) *Outline of Piaget's Developmental Psychology* (London, Routledge & Kegan Paul)

Bloom, B. S. (Ed.) (1965) *Taxonomy of Educational Objectives*. Handbook I. *The Cognitive Domain* (London, Longmans)

Bruce, G. (1969) *School Examinations* (Oxford, Pergamon)

*Bruner, J. S. (1960) *The Process of Education* (New York, Random House)

Bruner, J. S. (1966) *Towards a Theory of Instruction* (Cambridge, Mass: Harvard University Press)

Bruner, J. S. (1971) *The Relevance of Education* (London, Allen & Unwin)

Bruner, J. S., Goodnow, J. J. and Austin, G. A. (1956) *A Study of Thinking* (New York, John Wiley)

Butcher, H. J. (1968) *Human Intelligence* (London, Methuen)

*Christopher, R. (1969) *JMB/GCE The Work of the Joint Matriculation Board*. Occasional Publication No. 29 (Manchester, Joint Matriculation Board)

De Cecco, J. P. (1968) *The Psychology of Learning and Instruction* (New York, Prentice Hall)

*Ebel, R. L. (1972) *Essentials of Educational Measurement* (New York, Prentice Hall)

*Educational Testing Service *Tests and Measurement Kit* (Princeton, N.J., E.T.S.)

*Eggleston, J. F. and Kerr, J. F. (1969) *Studies in Assessment* (London, English Universities Press)

Foster, J. (1971) *Recording Individual Progress* (London, Macmillan)

Gagné, R. M. (1965) *The Conditions of Learning* (New York, Holt, Rinehart & Winston)

Gronlund, N. E. (1971) *Measurement and Evaluation in Teaching* (London, Macmillan)

Gronlund, N. E. (1968) *Constructing Achievement Tests* (New York, Prentice Hall)

Gross, R. and B. (Ed.) (1969) *Radical School Reform* (London, Gollancz)

Guildford, J. P. (1967) *The Nature of Human Intelligence* (New York, McGraw-Hill)

Hartog, P. and Rhodes, E. C. (1935) *An Examination of Examinations* (New York, Macmillan)

*Hedges, W. D. (1966) *Testing and Evaluation for the Sciences* (Belmont, Calif., Wadsworth)

Hoyle, E. (1969) *The Role of the Teacher* (London, Routledge & Kegan Paul)

*Hudson, B. (Ed.) (1973) *Techniques of Assessment* (London, Methuen Educational)

Hudson, L. (1966) *Contrary Imaginations* (London, Methuen)

Hudson, L. (1968) *Frames of Reference* (London, Methuen)

Ingenhamp, K. (Ed.) (1968) *Developments in Educational Testing, Volumes 1 and 2*. (London, University of London Press)

Keating, L. (1969) *The School Report* (Havant, Kenneth Mason)

Lauwerys, J. A. and Scanlon, D. G. (Eds) (1969) *World Year Book of Education 1969 Examinations* (London, Evans)

Marshall, J. C. and Hales, L. W. (1972) *Essentials of Testing* (London, Addison-Wesley)

Matthews, J. C. (1972) *Examinations and Assessment. Chemistry. Nuffield Advanced Science* (Harmondsworth, Penguin)

*Matthews, J. C. (1972) *Teachers Guide to Assessment in Modern Chemistry* (London, Hutchinson)

Mead, M. (1970) *Culture and Commitment* (London, The Bodley Head)

Mehrens, W. A. and Ebel, R. L. (1960) *Principles of Educational and Psychological Measurement* (Chicago, Rand McNally)

*Montgomery, R. J. (1965) *Examinations* (London, Longmans)

Musgrave, P. W. (1970) *Sociology, History and Education* (London, Methuen)

Nedelsky, L. (1965) *Science Teaching and Testing* (New York, Harcourt, Brace & World)

Peterson, A. D. C. (1972) *The International Baccalaureate* (London, Harraps)

Pidgeon, D. A. (1970) *Expectations and Pupil Performance* (Slough, National Foundation for Educational Research)

*Pidgeon, D. and Yates, A. (1969) *An Introduction to Educational Measurement* (London, Routledge & Kegan Paul)

Reid, W. A. (1972) *Schools Council Research Studies The Universities and the Sixth Form Curriculum* (London, Macmillan)

Richmond, W. K. (1970) *The Concept of Educational Technology* (London, Weidenfeld & Nicolson)

*Rimmers, H. H., Gage, N. L. and Rummel, J. F. (1966) *A Practical Introduction to Measurement and Education* (New York, Harper International)

*Sanders, N. M. (1966) *Classroom Questions What Kinds?* (New York, Harper & Row)

Schofield, H. (1972) *Assessment and Testing. An Introduction* (London, Allen & Unwin)

*Schools Council Integrated Science Project (1973) *Teachers Handbook* (London, Longman Group/Penguin Education)

Secondary School Examinations Council (1963) *The Certificate of Secondary Education: Examinations Bulletin No. 1. Some suggestions for teachers and examiners* (London, HMSO)

*Secondary School Examinations Council (1964) *Examinations Bulletin No. 3. An Introduction to some Techniques of Examining* (London, HMSO)

Schloer, L. A. (1970) *Test Construction: a Programmed Guide* (Rockleigh, N.J., Allyn & Bacon)

Smith, R. I. (Ed.) (1968) *Men and Societies* (London, Heinemann)

Stanley, J. C. (1964) *Measurement in To-day's Schools* (New York, Prentice Hall)

Sumner, R. and Warburton, F. W. (1972) *Achievement in Secondary Schools* (Slough, National Foundation for Educational Research)

Taylor, L. C. (1971) *Resources for Learning* (Harmondsworth, Penguin)

Taylor, P. H. (1970) How Teachers Plan their Courses (Slough, National Foundation for Educational Research)

Thorndike, R. L. (Ed.) (1972) *Educational Measurement* (second edition) (Washington, D.C., American Council on Education)

Thwaites, B. (1972) *The School Mathematics Project—The First Ten Years* (Cambridge, Cambridge University Press)

Tyler, R. N. (1971) *Basic Principles of Curriculum and Instruction* (Chicago, University of Chicago Press)

Vaizey, J. (1962) *Education for Tomorrow* (Harmondsworth, Penguin)

Vernon, P. E. (1956) *The Measurement of Abilities* (London, University of London Press)

Vernon, P. E. (1964) *Personality Assessment* (London, Methuen)

Vernon, P. E. (1960) *Intelligence and Attainment Tests* (London, University of London Press)

Whalley, G. E. (1969) *The Certificate of Secondary Education* (Leeds, University of Leeds Press)

Whitehead, A. N. (1932) *The Aims of Education* (London, Benn)

Whitla, D. K. (Ed.) (1968) *Handbook of Measurement and Assessment in Behavioural Sciences* (London, Addison-Wesley)

*Wiseman, S. (Ed.) (1961) *Examinations and English Education* (Manchester, University of Manchester Press)

Wood, D. Adkins (1961) *Test Construction* (Columbus, Ohio, Charles E. Merrill)

The following journals quite often contain articles on aspects of assessment and it is worthwhile consulting their indexes which are normally issued annually. Again, the list is in no sense exhaustive.

*Educational Research* National Foundation for Educational Research

*British Journal of Educational Psychology* Scottish Academic Press Ltd

*Forum* P.S.W. (Educational Publications) Ltd
*The Journal of Curriculum Studies* Collins
*Ideas* University of London Goldsmiths' College
*Research in Education* Manchester University Press
*Secondary Education* National Union of Teachers
*Trends in Education* Department of Education and Science
*Universities Quarterly* Turnstile Press Ltd

The professional subject associations, for example the Association for Science Education and the Historical Association also cover assessment problems from time to time in their publications. These are particularly useful for keeping up to date with developments in a teacher's own particular subject specialism.

## Section II  Chapters

1. OPEN-ENDED QUESTIONS

Gosling, G. W. H. (1966) *Marking English Compositions* (Hawthorn, Australian Council for Educational Research)

*Hewitt, E. A. (1967) *The Reliability of GCE O Level Examinations in English Language.* Occasional Publication No. 27 (Manchester, Joint Matriculation Board)

Morrison, R. B. (1968) *English Language O Level Marking Experiment* June 1967 (Aldershot, Associated Examining Board)

Morrison, R. B. (1969) *English Language O Level Marking Experiment* June 1968 (Aldershot, Associated Examining Board)

Morrison, R. B. (1970) *English Language O Level Marking Experiment* 1968–1969 (Aldershot, Associated Examining Board)

*Schools Council (1966) *Examinations Bulletin No. 12. CSE Multiple Marking of English Compositions* (London, HMSO)

Schools Council (1967) *Examinations Bulletin No. 16. CSE Written English* (London, HMSO)

2. STRUCTURED QUESTIONS

Gazard, A. D. and Wilkins, E. J. (1972) *Structured Questions in Chemistry* (New York, McGraw-Hill)

3. SHORT ANSWER QUESTIONS AND OBJECTIVE ITEMS

Brown, J. (1966) *Objective Tests. Their Construction and Analysis* (London, Longmans)

*Campbell, C. V. T. and Milne, W. J. (1972) *The Principles of Objective Testing in Chemistry* (London, Heinemann)

*Frazer, W. G. and Gillam, J. N. (1972) *The Principles of Objective Testing in Mathematics* (London, Heinemann)

*Houston, J. G. (1970) *The Principles of Objective Testing in Physics* (London, Heinemann)

Hubbard, J. B. and Clemans, W. V. (1961) *Multiple Choice Questions on Medicine* (Philadelphia, Lea & Febiger)

*Macintosh, H. G. and Morrison, R. B. (1969) *Objective Testing* (London, University of London Press)

*Macintosh, H. G. (1969) *The Construction and Analysis of an Objective Test in Ordinary Level History* (Aldershot, Associated Examining Board)

*Macintosh, H. G. (Ed.) (1971–73) *Handbooks on Objective Testing*. 18 Handbooks covering major subjects for O Level/CSE (London, Methuen Educational)

Roddie, I. C. and Wallace, W. F. (1971) *Multiple Choice Questions on Human Psychology* (London, Lloyd Luke Ltd)

*Schools Council (1966) *Examination Bulletin No. 8. CSE Experimental Examinations Science* (London, HMSO)

*Schools Council (1969) *Examination Bulletin No. 19. CSE Practical Work in Science* (London, Evans/Methuen Educational)

*Schools Council (1970) *Curriculum Bulletin No. 3. Changes in School Science Teaching* (London, Evans/Methuen Educational)

Scott, D. N. (1966) 'Practical Examinations' *Physics Education*, 1, 52

*Thomas, G. H. (1971) *Item Writing* (Union of Educational Institutions)

*Vernon, P. E. (1964) *Secondary School Examinations Council Examinations Bulletin No. 4. CSE An Introduction to Objective Type Examinations* (London, HMSO)

Wilson, N. (1970) *Objective Tests and Mathematical Learning* (Hawthorn Australian Council for Educational Research)

### 4. ITEM ANALYSIS AND QUESTION VALIDATION

Connaughton, I. M. and Skurnik, L. S. (1969) 'The Comparative Effectiveness of Several Short Cut Item Analysis Procedures' (*British Journal of Educational Psychology*, 39, 225–32)

Nuttall, D. L. and Skurnik, L. S. (1969) *Examination and Item Analysis Manual* (Slough, National Foundation for Educational Research)

Nuttall, D. L. and Willmott, A. S. (1972) *British Examinations—Techniques of Analysis* (Slough, National Foundation for Educational Research)

### 5. AURAL AND ORAL ASSESSMENT

*Centre for Information on Language Teaching (1970) *Reports and Papers No. 4.* 'Examining Modern Languages' (London, C.I.L.T.)

*Hitchman, P. J. (1966) *Examining Oral English in Schools* (London, Methuen)

Otter, H. S. (1968) *A Functional Language Examination.* 'The Modern Languages Association Examinations Project' (London, Oxford University Press)

### 6. THE ASSESSMENT OF PRACTICAL WORK

*Black, P. J. Eggleston, J. F. and Matthews, J. C. (1970) *Examining in Advanced Level Science Subjects of the GCE*. Occasional Publication No. 30 (Manchester, Joint Matriculation Board)

Dave, R. H. and Patwardan, Y. B. (1970) 'Improving practical examinations in science subjects'. In *Examinations at Secondary Level* (London, Commonwealth Secretariat)

Head, J. J. *An Objectively Marked Practical Examination* (*School Science Review* 164)

Joint Matriculation Board (1973) *Experimental Scheme for the Internal Assessment of Practical Skills in Chemistry (Advanced)*. 'Notes for the guidance of teachers, Chem 3' (Manchester, Joint Matriculation Board)

Knrylak, H. (1954–5) 'The Measurement of Laboratory Achievement' (*American Journal of Psychology* 22, 442–454 and 23, 82)

Modern Languages Association Co-operative Foreign Language Tests *Material Available from Co-operative Test Division*, (Princeton, N.J., Educational Testing Service)

Pimsleur Proficiency Tests *Tests in French, Spanish and German* (New York, Harcourt, Brace & World)

*Schools Council (1966) *Examinations Bulletin No. 11 CSE Oral English* (London, HMSO)

*Schools Council (1971) *Examinations Bulletin No. 21 CSE. An Experiment in the Oral Examining of Chemistry* (London, Evans/Methuen Educational)

Schools Council Modern Languages Project *Materials in French, German, Russian and Spanish* (University of York, Materials Development Unit)

Schools Council (1970) *Working Paper No. 28. New Patterns in Sixth Form Language Studies* (London, Evans/Methuen Educational)

Valette, R. M. (1960) *Modern Language Testing* (New York, Harcourt Brace & World)

## 7. THE ASSESSMENT OF PROJECT WORK

*Cambridge Local Examinations Syndicate (1971) *Nuffield Science Teaching Project. 'A Level Physical Science. Documents on Project Assessment'* (Cambridge Syndicate)

Ferguson, S. (1967) *Projects in History* (London, Batsford)

Schools Council (1968) *Examinations Bulletin No. 18. CSE The Place of the Personal Topic—History* (London, HMSO)

## 8. THE APPLICATION OF STATISTICS TO ASSESSMENT

*Connolly, T. G. and Sluckin, W. (1958) *Statistics for the Social Sciences* (London, Cleaver Hume Press)

Garrett, H. E. (1958) *Statistics in Psychology and Education* (London, Longmans)

Fisher, G. H. (1965) *The New Form Statistical Tables* (London, University of London Press)

*Kendall, M. G. and Buckland, W. R. (1960) *Dictionary of Statistical Terms* (Edinburgh, Oliver & Boyd)

Lewis, B. G. (1967) *Statistical Methods in Education* (London, University of London Press)

*McIntosh, D. M. (1967) *Statistics for the Teacher* (Oxford, Pergamon)

Sumner, W. L. (1959) *Statistics in Schools* (Oxford, Blackwell)

## 9. COURSE WORK AND CONTINUOUS ASSESSMENT

*Christopher, R., Rooke, H. M. and Hewitt, E. A. (1970) *An Experimental Scheme of School Assessment in Ordinary Level English Language. Third Report*. Occasional Publication No. 31 (Manchester, Joint Matriculation Board)

Hewitt, E. A. and Gordon, (1965) *An Experiment in Assessing*. Occasional Publication No. 22 (Manchester, Joint Matriculation Board)

*Petch, J. A. (1967) *English Language—An Experiment in Assessing* (second interim report). Occasional Publication No. 26 (Manchester, Joint Matriculation Board)

## 10. THE ASSESSMENT OF ATTITUDES

Bloom, B. S. (Ed.) (1964) *Taxonomy of Educational Objectives. Handbook II. The Affective Domain* (London, Longmans)

The assessment of attitudes has formed part of a number of recent curriculum projects in Science with particular reference to practical work. The Teachers' Handbook for the Schools Council Integrated Science Project which is referred to in the General Section gives a good indication of what is being attempted.

## 11. MODERATION

*Mather, D. N., France, N. and Sare, G. T. (1965) *The CSE—A Handbook for Moderators* (London, Collins)
*Schools Council (1965) *Examinations Bulletin No. 5. School Based Examinations. Examining, Assessing and Moderating by Teachers* (London, HMSO)

The Publications of the GCE and CSE Examining Boards contain much useful information about different approaches to moderation.

## 12. THE PRESENTATION OF RESULTS

McIntosh, D. M., Walker, D. A. and Mackay, D. (1962) *The Scaling of Teachers Marks and Estimates* (Edinburgh, Oliver & Boyd)

## 13. QUESTION BANKING

*Schools Council (1971) *Examinations Bulletin No. 22.* 'Question Banks, Their Use in School Examinations' (London, Evans/Methuen Educational)
Wood, R. and Skurnik, L. S. (1969) *Item Banking* (Slough National Foundation for Educational Research)

## 14. THE PREPARATION OF SCHOOL BASED ASSESSMENT

Booth, M. R. (1969) *History Betrayed* (London, Longmans)
Eggleston, J. F. (1965) *A Critical Review of Assessment Procedures in Secondary School Science* (Leicester, University of Leicester Press)
The Humanities Project (1970)—*An Introduction* (London, Heinemann Educational Books)
Kibler, R. J., Barker, L. L. and Miles, D. T. (1970) *Behavioural Objectives and Instruction* (Rockleigh, N.J., Allyn & Bacon)
Lindvall, C. M. (Ed.) (1964) *Defining Educational Objectives* (Pittsburgh, University of Pittsburgh Press)
*Macintosh, H. G. (1972) *The Teacher as Assessor. Secondary Education* Vol. 3 No. 1. (National Union of Teachers)
McAshan, M. M. (1971) *Writing Behavioural Objectives. A New Approach* (New York, Harper & Row)
*Mager, R. F. (1962) *Preparing Instructional Objectives* (Palo Atto, Fearon)
*Misselbrook, H. (Ed.) (1972) *Nuffield Secondary Science Examining at CSE Level* (London, Longman Group)
Popham, W. J., Eisner, E. W., Sullivan, H. J. and Tyler, L. L. (1969) *Instructional Objectives* (Chicago, Rand McNally for AERA)

Secondary Schools Examinations Council (1963) *Examinations Bulletin No. 1 Some Suggestions for Teachers and Examiners* (London, HMSO)

*Schools Council (1967) *Examinations Bulletin No. 15. CSE, Teachers Experience of School Based Examining (English & Physics)* (London, HMSO)

Stones, E. and Anderson, D. (1972) *Educational Objectives and the Teaching of Educational Psychology* (London, Methuen)

Much practical information about school based assessment is to be found in the publications of the GCE and CSE examining boards, particularly the latter. A typical example of such a publication is

Southern Regional Examinations Board for the Certificate of Secondary Education (1972) Mode 3 SREB Southampton

## 15. MEASURING ATTAINMENT FOR CURRICULUM EVALUATION

Adams, G. S. (1964) *Measurement and Evaluation* (New York, Holt, Rinehart & Winston)

Ahmann, S. & Glock, M. D. (1963) *Evaluating Pupil Growth* (Rockleigh, N.J., Allyn & Bacon).

Bloom, B. S., Hastings, J. T. and Madaus, G. F. (1971) *Handbook on Formative and Summative Evaluation* (New York, McGraw-Hill)

*Coltham, J. B. and Fines, J. (1971) *Educational Objectives for the Study of History* (Historical Association Pamphlet TH 35)

*Dunn, S. S. (1967) *Measurement and Evaluation in the Secondary School* (Hawthorn Australian Council for Educational Research)

Grobman, A. B. (1969) *The Changing Classroom: The Role of the Biological Sciences Curriculum Study* (New York, Doubleday)

Hockey, S. W. and Neale, P. D. (1968) *The Schools Council Science Evaluation Project Education in Science No. 27* (The Association for Science Education)

Hooper, R. (Ed.) (1971) *The Curriculum: Content, Design and Development* (Edinburgh, Oliver & Boyd)

Lindvall, C. M. (1961) *Testing and Evaluation—An Introduction* (New York, Harcourt, Brace & World)

Nicholls, H. and A. (1973) *Developing a Curriculum* (London, Allen & Unwin)

Ramsey, G. A. (1972) 'Curriculum Development in Secondary School Science' *Quarterly Review of Australian Education*, 5(1) and 5(2)

*Richmond, W. K. (1971) *The School Curriculum* (London, Methuen)

Saivin, E. I. (1969) (Australian Council for Educational Research) *Evaluation and the Work of the Teacher* (Belmont, Calif., Wadsworth)

Taba, H. (1962) *Curriculum Development: Theory and Practice* (New York, Harcourt, Brace & World)

Tyler, R., Gagné, R. M. and Scriven M. (1969) *Perspectives of Curriculum Evaluation* (Chicago, Rand McNally for AERA)

Wheeler, D. K. (1967) *Curriculum Process* (London, University of London Press)

Whitfield, R. C. (Ed.) (1971) *Disciplines of the Curriculum* (New York, McGraw-Hill)

Wittock, M. G. and Wiley, B. E. (Eds) (1970) *The Evaluation of Instruction* (New York, Holt Rinehart and Winston)

*Wiseman, S. and Pidgeon, D. (1970) *Curriculum Evaluation* (Slough National Foundation for Educational Research)

*Wood, R. (1968) 'Objectives in the Teaching of Mathematics' *Educational Research*, 9(3) 219–222

16. THE VALUE FOR THE TEACHER OF RESEARCH INTO ASSESSMENT

Butcher, H. J. (Ed.) (1968) *Educational Research in Britain 1* (London, University of London Press)

Butcher, H. J. and Pont, H. B. (Eds) (1970) *Educational Research in Britain 2* . (London, University of London Press)

*Evans, K. M. (1968) *Planning Small Scale Research* (Slough National Foundation for Educational Research)

Lovell, K. and Lawson, K. S. (1970) *Understanding Research in Education* (London, University of London Press)

Nisbet, J. D. and Entwistle, N. J. (1970) *Educational Research Methods* (London, University of London Press)

*Schools Council (1970) *Examinations Bulletin No. 20. CSE. A Group Study Approach to Research and Development* (London, Evans/Methuen Educational)

# Index